CRIMINAL PROCEDURE

2016 Case and Statutory Supplement

CRIMINAL PROCEDURE

2016 Case and Statutory Supplement

Erwin Chemerinsky

Dean and Distinguished Professor of Law
Raymond Pryke Professor of First Amendment Law
University of California, Irvine School of Law

Laurie L. Levenson

Professor of Law and
David W. Burcham Chair in Ethical Advocacy
Loyola Law School

Wolters Kluwer

About Wolters Kluwer Legal & Regulatory US

Wolters Kluwer Legal & Regulatory US delivers expert content and solutions in the areas of law, corporate compliance, health compliance, reimbursement, and legal education. Its practical solutions help customers successfully navigate the demands of a changing environment to drive their daily activities, enhance decision quality and inspire confident outcomes.

Serving customers worldwide, its legal and regulatory portfolio includes products under the Aspen Publishers, CCH Incorporated, Kluwer Law International, ftwilliam.com and MediRegs names. They are regarded as exceptional and trusted resources for general legal and practice-specific knowledge, compliance and risk management, dynamic workflow solutions, and expert commentary.

CONTENTS

Contents

PREFACE

The second edition of the casebook was published in 2013 and includes cases decided by June 28, 2012. This Supplement is needed for two reasons. First, it covers cases decided in the 2012-2013, 2013-2014, 2014-2015, and 2015-2016 Terms. Second, it is a statutory supplement providing statutory material related to each of the chapters.

We plan to do a supplement each year. Each will include the cases decided since the casebook was published and the most recent version of this statutory material. We welcome comments and suggestions from the professors and students using our book.

Erwin Chemerinsky
Laurie Levenson

August 2016

ERRATA

The following is a list of errors we have noticed in the second edition of the casebook since it was published in 2013:

p. 84: Add "not" to following sentence:

Interestingly, in United States v. Karo, 468 U.S. 705 (1984), the Court found that the placement of a beeper in a container was **not** a search.

p. 112: Change "10 days" to "14 days":

For instance, Rule 41 of the Federal Rules of Criminal Procedure provides that the warrant shall command the officer to "execute the warrant within a specified time not longer than **14** days."

p. 619: Add "dissenting":

Justice STEVENS, with whom Justice SOUTER and Justice GINSBURG join, and with whom Justice BREYER joins, **dissenting**.

Chapter 2

SEARCHES AND SEIZURES

B. What Is a Search?

6. Use of Dogs to Sniff for Contraband (casebook p. 91)

In *Illinois v. Caballes* (casebook p. 91), the Supreme Court held that it does not violate the Fourth Amendment for police to have a dog sniff for drugs during a routine traffic stop. But in *United States v. Rodriguez*, the Court imposed an important limit: police cannot extend the duration of a stop beyond what is needed to carry out the traffic stop in order to facilitate a dog sniff.

Rodriguez v. United States
135 S. Ct. 1609 (2015)

Justice GINSBURG delivered the opinion of the Court.

In *Illinois v. Caballes* (2005), this Court held that a dog sniff conducted during a lawful traffic stop does not violate the Fourth Amendment's proscription of unreasonable seizures. This case presents the question whether the Fourth Amendment tolerates a dog sniff conducted after completion of a traffic stop. We hold that a police stop exceeding the time needed to handle the matter for which the stop was made violates the Constitution's shield against unreasonable seizures. A seizure justified only by a police-observed traffic violation, therefore, "become[s] unlawful if it is prolonged beyond the time reasonably required to complete th[e] mission" of issuing a ticket for the violation. The Court so recognized in *Caballes*, and we adhere to the line drawn in that decision.

I

Just after midnight on March 27, 2012, police officer Morgan Struble observed a Mercury Mountaineer veer slowly onto the shoulder of Nebraska State Highway 275 for one or two seconds and then jerk back onto the road. Nebraska law prohibits driving on highway shoulders, and on that basis, Struble pulled the Mountaineer over at 12:06 a.m. Struble is a K–9 officer with the Valley Police Department in Nebraska, and his dog Floyd was in his patrol car that night. Two men were in the Mountaineer: the driver, Dennys Rodriguez, and a front-seat passenger, Scott Pollman.

Struble approached the Mountaineer on the passenger's side. After Rodriguez identified himself, Struble asked him why he had driven onto the shoulder. Rodriguez replied that he had swerved to avoid a pothole. Struble then gathered Rodriguez's license, registration, and proof of insurance, and asked Rodriguez to accompany him to the patrol car. Rodriguez asked if he was required to do so, and Struble answered that he was not. Rodriguez decided to wait in his own vehicle.

After running a records check on Rodriguez, Struble returned to the Mountaineer. Struble asked passenger Pollman for his driver's license and began to question him about where the two men were coming from and where they were going. Pollman replied that they had traveled to Omaha, Nebraska, to look at a Ford Mustang that was for sale and that they were returning to Norfolk, Nebraska. Struble returned again to his patrol car, where he completed a records check on Pollman, and called for a second officer. Struble then began writing a warning ticket for Rodriguez for driving on the shoulder of the road.

Struble returned to Rodriguez's vehicle a third time to issue the written warning. By 12:27 or 12:28 a.m., Struble had finished explaining the warning to Rodriguez, and had given back to Rodriguez and Pollman the documents obtained from them. As Struble later testified, at that point, Rodriguez and Pollman "had all their documents back and a copy of the written warning. I got all the reason[s] for the stop out of the way[,] . . . took care of all the business."

Nevertheless, Struble did not consider Rodriguez "free to leave." Although justification for the traffic stop was "out of the way," Struble asked for permission to walk his dog around Rodriguez's vehicle. Rodriguez said no. Struble then instructed Rodriguez to turn off the ignition, exit the vehicle, and stand in front of the patrol car to wait for the second officer. Rodriguez complied. At 12:33 a.m., a deputy sheriff arrived. Struble retrieved his dog and led him twice around the Mountaineer. The dog alerted to the presence of drugs halfway through Struble's second pass. All told, seven or eight minutes had elapsed from the time Struble issued the written warning until the dog indicated the presence of drugs. A search of the vehicle revealed a large bag of methamphetamine.

II

A seizure for a traffic violation justifies a police investigation of that violation. "[A] relatively brief encounter," a routine traffic stop is "more analogous to a so-called 'Terry stop' . . . than to a formal arrest." Like a Terry stop, the tolerable duration of police inquiries in the traffic-stop context is determined by the seizure's "mission"—to address the traffic violation that warranted the stop, and attend to related safety concerns. Because addressing the infraction is the purpose of the stop, it may "last no longer than is necessary to effectuate th[at] purpose." Authority for the seizure thus ends when tasks tied to the traffic infraction are—or reasonably should have been—completed.

2. Searches and Seizures

In *Caballes*, however, we cautioned that a traffic stop "can become unlawful if it is prolonged beyond the time reasonably required to complete th[e] mission" of issuing a warning ticket. An officer, in other words, may conduct certain unrelated checks during an otherwise lawful traffic stop. But he may not do so in a way that prolongs the stop, absent the reasonable suspicion ordinarily demanded to justify detaining an individual.

Beyond determining whether to issue a traffic ticket, an officer's mission includes "ordinary inquiries incident to [the traffic] stop." Typically such inquiries involve checking the driver's license, determining whether there are outstanding warrants against the driver, and inspecting the automobile's registration and proof of insurance. These checks serve the same objective as enforcement of the traffic code: ensuring that vehicles on the road are operated safely and responsibly.

A dog sniff, by contrast, is a measure aimed at "detect[ing] evidence of ordinary criminal wrongdoing." Lacking the same close connection to roadway safety as the ordinary inquiries, a dog sniff is not fairly characterized as part of the officer's traffic mission.

Justice THOMAS, with whom Justice ALITO joins, and with whom Justice KENNEDY joins as to all but Part III, dissenting.

Ten years ago, we explained that "conducting a dog sniff [does] not change the character of a traffic stop that is lawful at its inception and otherwise executed in a reasonable manner." The only question here is whether an officer executed a stop in a reasonable manner when he waited to conduct a dog sniff until after he had given the driver a written warning and a backup unit had arrived, bringing the overall duration of the stop to 29 minutes. Because the stop was reasonably executed, no Fourth Amendment violation occurred. The Court's holding to the contrary cannot be reconciled with our decision in *Caballes* or a number of common police practices. It was also unnecessary, as the officer possessed reasonable suspicion to continue to hold the driver to conduct the dog sniff. I respectfully dissent.

I

Because Rodriguez does not dispute that Officer Struble had probable cause to stop him, the only question is whether the stop was otherwise executed in a reasonable manner. I easily conclude that it was. Approximately 29 minutes passed from the time Officer Struble stopped Rodriguez until his narcotics-detection dog alerted to the presence of drugs. That amount of time is hardly out of the ordinary for a traffic stop by a single officer of a vehicle containing multiple occupants even when no dog sniff is involved. During that time, Officer Struble conducted the ordinary activities of a traffic stop—he approached the vehicle, questioned Rodriguez about the observed violation, asked Pollman about their travel plans, ran serial warrant checks on Rodriguez and Pollman, and issued a written warning to Rodriguez. And when he decided to conduct a dog sniff, he took the precaution of calling for backup out of concern for his safety.

As *Caballes* makes clear, the fact that Officer Struble waited until after he gave Rodriguez the warning to conduct the dog sniff does not alter this analysis. Because "the use of a well-trained narcotics-detection dog . . . generally does not implicate legitimate privacy interests," "conducting a dog sniff would not change the character of a traffic stop that is lawful at its inception and otherwise executed in a reasonable manner." The stop here was "lawful at its inception and otherwise executed in a reasonable manner." As in *Caballes*, "conducting a dog sniff [did] not change the character of [the] traffic stop," *ibid.*, and thus no Fourth Amendment violation occurred.

II

Rather than adhere to the reasonableness requirement that we have repeatedly characterized as the "touchstone of the Fourth Amendment," the majority constructed a test of its own that is inconsistent with our precedents.

The majority's rule requires a traffic stop to "en[d] when tasks tied to the traffic infraction are — or reasonably should have been — completed." "If an officer can complete traffic-based inquiries expeditiously, then that is the amount of time reasonably required to complete the stop's mission" and he may hold the individual no longer. The majority's rule thus imposes a one-way ratchet for constitutional protection linked to the characteristics of the individual officer conducting the stop: If a driver is stopped by a particularly efficient officer, then he will be entitled to be released from the traffic stop after a shorter period of time than a driver stopped by a less efficient officer. Similarly, if a driver is stopped by an officer with access to technology that can shorten a records check, then he will be entitled to be released from the stop after a shorter period of time than an individual stopped by an officer without access to such technology.

I "cannot accept that the search and seizure protections of the Fourth Amendment are so variable and can be made to turn upon such trivialities." We have repeatedly explained that the reasonableness inquiry must not hinge on the characteristics of the individual officer conducting the seizure.

The majority's logic would produce similarly arbitrary results. Under its reasoning, a traffic stop made by a rookie could be executed in a reasonable manner, whereas the same traffic stop made by a knowledgeable, veteran officer *in precisely the same circumstances* might not, if in fact his knowledge and experience made him capable of completing the stop faster. We have long rejected interpretations of the Fourth Amendment that would produce such haphazard results, and I see no reason to depart from our consistent practice today.

III

Today's revision of our Fourth Amendment jurisprudence was also entirely unnecessary. Rodriguez suffered no Fourth Amendment violation here for an entirely independent reason: Officer Struble had reasonable suspicion to continue

4

to hold him for investigative purposes. Our precedents make clear that the Fourth Amendment permits an officer to conduct an investigative traffic stop when that officer has "a particularized and objective basis for suspecting the particular person stopped of criminal activity."

Officer Struble testified that he first became suspicious that Rodriguez was engaged in criminal activity for a number of reasons. When he approached the vehicle, he smelled an "overwhelming odor of air freshener coming from the vehicle," which is, in his experience, "a common attempt to conceal an odor that [people] don't want . . . to be smelled by the police." He also observed, upon approaching the front window on the passenger side of the vehicle, that Rodriguez's passenger, Scott Pollman, appeared nervous. Pollman pulled his hat down low, puffed nervously on a cigarette, and refused to make eye contact with him. The officer thought he was "more nervous than your typical passenger" who "do[esn't] have anything to worry about because [t]hey didn't commit a [traffic] violation."

Officer Struble's interactions with the vehicle's occupants only increased his suspicions. When he asked Rodriguez why he had driven onto the shoulder, Rodriguez claimed that he swerved to avoid a pothole. But that story could not be squared with Officer Struble's observation of the vehicle slowly driving off the road before being jerked back onto it. And when Officer Struble asked Pollman where they were coming from and where they were going, Pollman told him they were traveling from Omaha, Nebraska, back to Norfolk, Nebraska, after looking at a vehicle they were considering purchasing. Pollman told the officer that he had neither seen pictures of the vehicle nor confirmed title before the trip. As Officer Struble explained, it "seemed suspicious" to him "to drive . . . approximately two hours . . . late at night to see a vehicle sight unseen to possibly buy it," and to go from Norfolk to Omaha to look at it because "[u]sually people leave Omaha to go get vehicles, not the other way around" due to higher Omaha taxes.

These facts, taken together, easily meet our standard for reasonable suspicion. Taking into account all the relevant facts, Officer Struble possessed reasonable suspicion of criminal activity to conduct the dog sniff.

Justice ALITO, dissenting.

This is an unnecessary,1 impractical, and arbitrary decision. It addresses a purely hypothetical question: whether the traffic stop in this case *would be* unreasonable if the police officer, prior to leading a drug-sniffing dog around the exterior of petitioner's car, did not already have reasonable suspicion that the car contained drugs. In fact, however, the police officer *did have* reasonable suspicion, and, as a result, the officer was justified in detaining the occupants for the short period of time (seven or eight minutes) that is at issue.

Not only does the Court reach out to decide a question not really presented by the facts in this case, but the Court's answer to that question is arbitrary. The Court refuses to address the real Fourth Amendment question: whether the stop was unreasonably prolonged. Instead, the Court latches onto the fact that Officer Struble delivered the warning prior to the dog sniff and proclaims that the authority to detain based on a traffic stop ends when a citation or warning is handed over to the driver. The Court thus holds that the Fourth Amendment was violated, not because of the length of the stop, but simply because of the sequence in which Officer Struble chose to perform his tasks.

This holding is not only arbitrary; it is perverse since Officer Struble chose that sequence for the purpose of protecting his own safety and possibly the safety of others. Without prolonging the stop, Officer Struble could have conducted the dog sniff while one of the tasks that the Court regards as properly part of the traffic stop was still in progress, but that sequence would have entailed unnecessary risk.

The Court's holding therefore makes no practical sense. And nothing in the Fourth Amendment, which speaks of *reasonableness*, compels this arbitrary line.

The rule that the Court adopts will do little good going forward. It is unlikely to have any appreciable effect on the length of future traffic stops. Most officers will learn the prescribed sequence of events even if they cannot fathom the reason for that requirement. (I would love to be the proverbial fly on the wall when police instructors teach this rule to officers who make traffic stops.)

The Court has decided two other recent cases concerning the use of drug-sniffing dogs. In *Florida v. Jardines*, the Court held that bringing a drug-sniffing dog on to someone's property was a search within the meaning of the Fourth Amendment. As in *United States v. Jones* (casebook p. 38), the Court found that this was a trespass and that was sufficient for a search. In *Florida v. Harris*, the Court held that there are no special burdens on prosecutors and police in showing the reliability of a drug-sniffing dog as the basis for probable cause for a search.

Florida v. Jardines
133 S. Ct. 1409 (2013)

Justice SCALIA delivered the opinion of the Court.

We consider whether using a drug-sniffing dog on a homeowner's porch to investigate the contents of the home is a "search" within the meaning of the Fourth Amendment.

I

In 2006, Detective William Pedraja of the Miami-Dade Police Department received an unverified tip that marijuana was being grown in the home of respondent Joelis Jardines. One month later, the Department and the Drug Enforcement Administration sent a joint surveillance team to Jardines' home. Detective Pedraja was part of that team. He watched the home for fifteen minutes and saw no vehicles in the driveway or activity around the home, and could not see inside because the blinds were drawn. Detective Pedraja then approached Jardines' home accompanied by Detective Douglas Bartelt, a trained canine handler who had just arrived at the scene with his drug-sniffing dog. The dog was trained to detect the scent of marijuana, cocaine, heroin, and several other drugs, indicating the presence of any of these substances through particular behavioral changes recognizable by his handler.

Detective Bartelt had the dog on a six-foot leash, owing in part to the dog's "wild" nature and tendency to dart around erratically while searching. As the dog approached Jardines' front porch, he apparently sensed one of the odors he had been trained to detect, and began energetically exploring the area for the strongest point source of that odor. As Detective Bartelt explained, the dog "began tracking that airborne odor by . . . tracking back and forth," engaging in what is called "bracketing," "back and forth, back and forth." Detective Bartelt gave the dog "the full six feet of the leash plus whatever safe distance [he could] give him" to do this—he testified that he needed to give the dog "as much distance as I can." And Detective Pedraja stood back while this was occurring, so that he would not "get knocked over" when the dog was "spinning around trying to find" the source.

After sniffing the base of the front door, the dog sat, which is the trained behavior upon discovering the odor's strongest point. Detective Bartelt then pulled the dog away from the door and returned to his vehicle. He left the scene after informing Detective Pedraja that there had been a positive alert for narcotics.

On the basis of what he had learned at the home, Detective Pedraja applied for and received a warrant to search the residence. When the warrant was executed later that day, Jardines attempted to flee and was arrested; the search revealed marijuana plants, and he was charged with trafficking in cannabis.

We granted certiorari, limited to the question of whether the officers' behavior was a search within the meaning of the Fourth Amendment.

II

The [Fourth] Amendment establishes a simple baseline, one that for much of our history formed the exclusive basis for its protections: When "the Government obtains information by physically intruding" on persons, houses, papers, or effects, "a 'search' within the original meaning of the Fourth Amendment" has "undoubtedly occurred." *United States v. Jones* (2012). By reason of our decision in *Katz v. United States* (1967), property rights "are not the sole measure of Fourth Amendment violations," but though *Katz* may add to the baseline, it does not subtract anything from the Amendment's protections "when the Government *does* engage in [a] physical intrusion of a constitutionally protected area."

That principle renders this case a straightforward one. The officers were gathering information in an area belonging to Jardines and immediately surrounding his house—in the curtilage of the house, which we have held enjoys protection as part of the home itself. And they gathered that information by physically entering and occupying the area to engage in conduct not explicitly or implicitly permitted by the homeowner.

A

The Fourth Amendment "indicates with some precision the places and things encompassed by its protections": persons, houses, papers, and effects. The Fourth Amendment does not, therefore, prevent all investigations conducted on private property; for example, an officer may (subject to *Katz*) gather information in what we have called "open fields"—even if those fields are privately owned—because such fields are not enumerated in the Amendment's text.

But when it comes to the Fourth Amendment, the home is first among equals. At the Amendment's "very core" stands "the right of a man to retreat into his own home and there be free from unreasonable governmental intrusion." This right would be of little practical value if the State's agents could stand in a home's porch or side garden and trawl for evidence with impunity; the right to retreat would be significantly diminished if the police could enter a man's property to observe his repose from just outside the front window.

We therefore regard the area "immediately surrounding and associated with the home"—what our cases call the curtilage—as "part of the home itself for Fourth Amendment purposes." That principle has ancient and durable roots. This area around the home is "intimately linked to the home, both physically and psychologically," and is where "privacy expectations are most heightened."

While the boundaries of the curtilage are generally "clearly marked," the "conception defining the curtilage" is at any rate familiar enough that it is "easily understood from our daily experience." Here there is no doubt that the officers entered it: The front porch is the classic exemplar of an area adjacent to the home and "to which the activity of home life extends."

B

Since the officers' investigation took place in a constitutionally protected area, we turn to the question of whether it was accomplished through an unlicensed physical intrusion. *Entick v. Carrington* (K.B. 1765), a case "undoubtedly familiar" to "every American statesman" at the time of the Founding, states the general rule clearly: "[O]ur law holds the property of every man so sacred, that no man can set his foot upon his neighbour's close without his leave." As it is undisputed that the detectives had all four of their feet and all four of their companion's firmly planted on the constitutionally protected extension of Jardines' home, the only question is whether he had given his leave (even implicitly) for them to do so. He had not.

"A license may be implied from the habits of the country," notwithstanding the "strict rule of the English common law as to entry upon a close." We have accordingly recognized that "the knocker on the front door is treated as an invitation or license to attempt an entry, justifying ingress to the home by solicitors, hawkers and peddlers of all kinds." This implicit license typically permits the visitor to approach the home by the front path, knock promptly, wait briefly to be received, and then (absent invitation to linger longer) leave. Complying with the terms of that traditional invitation does not require fine-grained legal knowledge; it is generally managed without incident by the Nation's Girl Scouts and trick-or-treaters. Thus, a police officer not armed with a warrant may approach a home and knock, precisely because that is "no more than any private citizen might do."

But introducing a trained police dog to explore the area around the home in hopes of discovering incriminating evidence is something else. There is no customary invitation to do *that*. An invitation to engage in canine forensic investigation assuredly does not inhere in the very act of hanging a knocker. To find a visitor knocking on the door is routine (even if sometimes unwelcome); to spot that same visitor exploring the front path with a metal detector, or marching his bloodhound into the garden before saying hello and asking permission, would inspire most of us to—well, call the police. The scope of a license—express or implied—is limited not only to a particular area but also to a specific purpose. Consent at a traffic stop to an officer's checking out an anonymous tip that there is a body in the trunk does not permit the officer to rummage through the trunk for narcotics. Here, the background social norms that invite a visitor to the front door do not invite him there to conduct a search.

III

The State argues that investigation by a forensic narcotics dog by definition cannot implicate any legitimate privacy interest. [W]e need not decide whether the officers' investigation of Jardines' home violated his expectation of privacy under *Katz*. One virtue of the Fourth Amendment's property-rights baseline is that it keeps easy cases easy. That the officers learned what they learned only by physically intruding on Jardines' property to gather evidence is enough to establish that a search occurred.

The government's use of trained police dogs to investigate the home and its immediate surroundings is a "search" within the meaning of the Fourth Amendment.

Justice KAGAN, with whom Justice GINSBURG and Justice SOTOMAYOR join, concurring.

For me, a simple analogy clinches this case—and does so on privacy as well as property grounds. A stranger comes to the front door of your home carrying super-high-powered binoculars. He doesn't knock or say hello. Instead, he stands on the porch and uses the binoculars to peer through your windows, into your home's furthest corners. It doesn't take long (the binoculars are really very fine): In just a couple of minutes, his uncommon behavior allows him to learn details of your life you disclose to no one. Has your "visitor" trespassed on your property, exceeding the license you have granted to members of the public to, say, drop off the mail or distribute campaign flyers? Yes, he has. And has he also invaded your "reasonable expectation of privacy," by nosing into intimacies you sensibly thought protected from disclosure? Yes, of course, he has done that too.

That case is this case in every way that matters. Here, police officers came to Joelis Jardines' door with a super-sensitive instrument, which they deployed to detect things inside that they could not perceive unassisted. The equipment they used was animal, not mineral. But contra the dissent, that is of no significance in determining whether a search occurred. Detective Bartelt's dog was not your neighbor's pet, come to your porch on a leisurely stroll. They are to the poodle down the street as high-powered binoculars are to a piece of plain glass. Like the binoculars, a drug-detection dog is a specialized device for discovering objects not in plain view (or plain smell). And as in the hypothetical above, that device was aimed here at a home—the most private and inviolate (or so we expect) of all the places and things the Fourth Amendment protects. Was this activity a trespass? Yes, as the Court holds today. Was it also an invasion of privacy? Yes, that as well.

The Court today treats this case under a property rubric; I write separately to note that I could just as happily have decided it by looking to Jardines' privacy interests. I can think of only one divergence: If we had decided this case on privacy grounds, we would have realized that *Kyllo v. United States* (2001), already resolved it. The *Kyllo* Court held that police officers conducted a search when they used a thermal-imaging device to detect heat emanating from a private home, even though they committed no trespass.

With these further thoughts, suggesting that a focus on Jardines' privacy interests would make an "easy cas[e] easy" twice over, I join the Court's opinion in full.

Justice ALITO, with whom THE CHIEF JUSTICE, Justice KENNEDY, and Justice BREYER join, dissenting.

The Court's decision in this important Fourth Amendment case is based on a putative rule of trespass law that is nowhere to be found in the annals of Anglo-American jurisprudence.

The law of trespass generally gives members of the public a license to use a walkway to approach the front door of a house and to remain there for a brief time. This license is not limited to persons who intend to speak to an occupant or who actually do so. (Mail carriers and persons delivering packages and flyers are examples of individuals who may lawfully approach a front door without intending to converse.) Nor is the license restricted to categories of visitors whom an occupant of the dwelling is likely to welcome; as the Court acknowledges, this license applies even to "solicitors, hawkers and peddlers of all kinds." And the license even extends to police officers who wish to gather evidence against an occupant (by asking potentially incriminating questions).

According to the Court, however, the police officer in this case, Detective Bartelt, committed a trespass because he was accompanied during his otherwise lawful visit to the front door of respondent's house by his dog, Franky. Where is the authority evidencing such a rule? Dogs have been domesticated for about 12,000 years; they were ubiquitous in both this country and Britain at the time of the adoption of the Fourth Amendment; and their acute sense of smell has been used in law enforcement for centuries. Yet the Court has been unable to find a single case—from the United States or any other common-law nation—that supports the rule on which its decision is based. Thus, trespass law provides no support for the Court's holding today.

The Court's decision is also inconsistent with the reasonable-expectations-of-privacy test that the Court adopted in 1967. A reasonable person understands that odors emanating from a house may be detected from locations that are open to the public, and a reasonable person will not count on the strength of those odors remaining within the range that, while detectible by a dog, cannot be smelled by a human.

For these reasons, I would hold that no search within the meaning of the Fourth Amendment took place in this case, and I would reverse the decision below.

The conduct of the police officer in this case did not constitute a trespass and did not violate respondent's reasonable expectations of privacy. I would hold that this conduct was not a search, and I therefore respectfully dissent.

Florida v. Harris

133 S. Ct. 1050 (2013)

Justice KAGAN delivered the opinion of the Court.

In this case, we consider how a court should determine if the "alert" of a drug-detection dog during a traffic stop provides probable cause to search a vehicle. The Florida Supreme Court held that the State must in every case present an exhaustive set of records, including a log of the dog's performance in the field, to establish the dog's reliability. We think that demand inconsistent with the "flexible, common-sense standard" of probable cause.

I

William Wheetley is a K-9 Officer in the Liberty County, Florida Sheriff's Office. On June 24, 2006, he was on a routine patrol with Aldo, a German shepherd trained to detect certain narcotics (methamphetamine, marijuana, cocaine, heroin, and ecstasy). Wheetley pulled over respondent Clayton Harris's truck because it had an expired license plate. On approaching the driver's-side door, Wheetley saw that Harris was "visibly nervous," unable to sit still, shaking, and breathing rapidly. Wheetley also noticed an open can of beer in the truck's cup holder. Wheetley asked Harris for consent to search the truck, but Harris refused. At that point, Wheetley retrieved Aldo from the patrol car and walked him around Harris's truck for a "free air sniff." Aldo alerted at the driver's-side door handle—signaling, through a distinctive set of behaviors, that he smelled drugs there.

Wheetley concluded, based principally on Aldo's alert, that he had probable cause to search the truck. His search did not turn up any of the drugs Aldo was trained to detect. But it did reveal 200 loose pseudoephedrine pills, 8,000 matches, a bottle of hydrochloric acid, two containers of antifreeze, and a coffee filter full of iodine crystals—all ingredients for making methamphetamine. Wheetley accordingly arrested Harris, who admitted after proper *Miranda* warnings that he routinely "cooked" methamphetamine at his house and could not go "more than a few days without using" it. The State charged Harris with possessing pseudoephedrine for use in manufacturing methamphetamine.

While out on bail, Harris had another run-in with Wheetley and Aldo. This time, Wheetley pulled Harris over for a broken brake light. Aldo again sniffed the truck's exterior, and again alerted at the driver's-side door handle. Wheetley once more searched the truck, but on this occasion discovered nothing of interest.

Harris moved to suppress the evidence found in his truck on the ground that Aldo's alert had not given Wheetley probable cause for a search. At the hearing on that motion, Wheetley testified about both his and Aldo's training in drug detection. In 2004, Wheetley (and a different dog) completed a 160-hour course in narcotics detection offered by the Dothan, Alabama Police Department, while Aldo (and a different handler) completed a similar, 120-hour course given by the Apopka, Florida Police Department. That same year, Aldo received a one-year certification from Drug Beat, a private company that specializes in testing and certifying K-9 dogs. Wheetley and Aldo teamed up in 2005 and went through another, 40-hour refresher course in Dothan together. They also did four hours of training exercises each week to maintain their skills. Wheetley would hide drugs in certain vehicles or buildings while leaving others "blank" to determine whether Aldo alerted at the right places. According to Wheetley, Aldo's performance in those exercises was "really good." The State introduced "Monthly Canine Detection Training Logs" consistent with that testimony: They showed that Aldo always found hidden drugs and that he performed "satisfactorily" (the higher of two possible assessments) on each day of training.

On cross-examination, Harris's attorney chose not to contest the quality of Aldo's or Wheetley's training. She focused instead on Aldo's certification and his performance in the field, particularly the two stops of Harris's truck. Wheetley conceded that the certification (which, he noted, Florida law did not require) had expired the year before he pulled Harris over. Wheetley also acknowledged that he did not keep complete records of Aldo's performance in traffic stops or other field work; instead, he maintained records only of alerts resulting in arrests. But Wheetley defended Aldo's two alerts to Harris's seemingly narcotics-free truck: According to Wheetley, Harris probably transferred the odor of methamphetamine to the door handle, and Aldo responded to that "residual odor."

The trial court concluded that Wheetley had probable cause to search Harris's truck and so denied the motion to suppress. Harris then entered a no-contest plea while reserving the right to appeal the trial court's ruling. An intermediate state court summarily affirmed.

2. Searches and Seizures

The Florida Supreme Court reversed, holding that Wheetley lacked probable cause to search Harris's vehicle under the Fourth Amendment. "[W]hen a dog alerts," the court wrote, "the fact that the dog has been trained and certified is simply not enough to establish probable cause." To demonstrate a dog's reliability, the State needed to produce a wider array of evidence:

> "[T]he State must present . . . the dog's training and certification records, an explanation of the meaning of the particular training and certification, field performance records (including any unverified alerts), and evidence concerning the experience and training of the officer handling the dog, as well as any other objective evidence known to the officer about the dog's reliability."

The court particularly stressed the need for "evidence of the dog's performance history," including records showing "how often the dog has alerted in the field without illegal contraband having been found." That data, the court stated, could help to expose such problems as a handler's tendency (conscious or not) to "cue [a] dog to alert" and "a dog's inability to distinguish between residual odors and actual drugs." Accordingly, an officer like Wheetley who did not keep full records of his dog's field performance could never have the requisite cause to think "that the dog is a reliable indicator of drugs."

II

A police officer has probable cause to conduct a search when "the facts available to [him] would 'warrant a [person] of reasonable caution in the belief'" that contraband or evidence of a crime is present. The test for probable cause is not reducible to "precise definition or quantification." "Finely tuned standards such as proof beyond a reasonable doubt or by a preponderance of the evidence . . . have no place in the [probable-cause] decision." All we have required is the kind of "fair probability" on which "reasonable and prudent [people,] not legal technicians, act."

In evaluating whether the State has met this practical and common-sensical standard, we have consistently looked to the totality of the circumstances. We have rejected rigid rules, bright-line tests, and mechanistic inquiries in favor of a more flexible, all-things-considered approach.

The Florida Supreme Court flouted this established approach to determining probable cause. To assess the reliability of a drug-detection dog, the court created a strict evidentiary checklist, whose every item the State must tick off. Most prominently, an alert cannot establish probable cause under the Florida court's decision unless the State introduces comprehensive documentation of the dog's prior "hits" and "misses" in the field. (One wonders how the court would apply its test to a rookie dog.) No matter how much other proof the State offers of the dog's reliability, the absent field performance records will preclude a finding of probable cause. That is the antithesis of a totality-of-the-circumstances analysis.

Making matters worse, the decision below treats records of a dog's field performance as the gold standard in evidence, when in most cases they have relatively limited import. Errors may abound in such records. If a dog on patrol fails to alert to a car containing drugs, the mistake usually will go undetected because the officer will not initiate a search. Field data thus may not capture a dog's false negatives. Conversely (and more relevant here), if the dog alerts to a car in which the officer finds no narcotics, the dog may not have made a mistake at all. The dog may have detected substances that were too well hidden or present in quantities too small for the officer to locate. Or the dog may have smelled the residual odor of drugs previously in the vehicle or on the driver's person. Field data thus may markedly overstate a dog's real false positives. By contrast, those inaccuracies—in either direction—do not taint records of a dog's performance in standard training and certification settings. There, the designers of an assessment know where drugs are hidden and where they are not—and so where a dog should alert and where he should not. The better measure of a dog's reliability thus comes away from the field, in controlled testing environments.

For that reason, evidence of a dog's satisfactory performance in a certification or training program can itself provide sufficient reason to trust his alert. If a bona fide organization has certified a dog after testing his reliability in a controlled setting, a court can presume (subject to any conflicting evidence offered) that the dog's alert provides probable cause to search. The same is true, even in the absence of formal certification, if the dog has recently and successfully completed a training program that evaluated his proficiency in locating drugs. After all, law enforcement units have their own strong incentive to use effective training and certification programs, because only accurate drug-detection dogs enable officers to locate contraband without incurring unnecessary risks or wasting limited time and resources.

A defendant, however, must have an opportunity to challenge such evidence of a dog's reliability, whether by cross-examining the testifying officer or by introducing his own fact or expert witnesses. The defendant, for example, may contest the adequacy of a certification or training program, perhaps asserting that its standards are too lax or its methods faulty. So too, the defendant may examine how the dog (or handler) performed in the assessments made in those settings. Indeed, evidence of the dog's (or handler's) history in the field, although susceptible to the kind of misinterpretation we have discussed, may sometimes be relevant. And even assuming a dog is generally reliable, circumstances surrounding a particular alert may undermine the case for probable cause—if, say, the officer cued the dog (consciously or not), or if the team was working under unfamiliar conditions.

In short, a probable-cause hearing focusing on a dog's alert should proceed much like any other. The court should allow the parties to make their best case, consistent with the usual rules of criminal procedure. And the court should then evaluate the proffered evidence to decide what all the circumstances demonstrate.

2. Searches and Seizures

If the State has produced proof from controlled settings that a dog performs reliably in detecting drugs, and the defendant has not contested that showing, then the court should find probable cause. If, in contrast, the defendant has challenged the State's case (by disputing the reliability of the dog overall or of a particular alert), then the court should weigh the competing evidence. In all events, the court should not prescribe, as the Florida Supreme Court did, an inflexible set of evidentiary requirements. The question—similar to every inquiry into probable cause—is whether all the facts surrounding a dog's alert, viewed through the lens of common sense, would make a reasonably prudent person think that a search would reveal contraband or evidence of a crime. A sniff is up to snuff when it meets that test.

III

And here, Aldo's did. The record in this case amply supported the trial court's determination that Aldo's alert gave Wheetley probable cause to search Harris's truck.

The State, as earlier described, introduced substantial evidence of Aldo's training and his proficiency in finding drugs.

Because training records established Aldo's reliability in detecting drugs and Harris failed to undermine that showing, we agree with the trial court that Wheetley had probable cause to search Harris's truck.

The Requirement for Probable Cause (casebook p. 94)

3. What if the police make a mistake as to the law?

In *Heien v. North Carolina*, the Court held that a stop that results from a police officer's mistake as to the law does not violate the Fourth Amendment.

Heien v. North Carolina
135 S. Ct. 530 (2014)

Chief Justice ROBERTS delivered the opinion of the Court.

The Fourth Amendment prohibits "unreasonable searches and seizures." Under this standard, a search or seizure may be permissible even though the justification for the action includes a reasonable factual mistake. An officer might, for example, stop a motorist for traveling alone in a high-occupancy vehicle lane, only to discover upon approaching the car that two children are slumped over asleep in the back seat. The driver has not violated the law, but neither has the officer violated the Fourth Amendment.

But what if the police officer's reasonable mistake is not one of fact but of law? In this case, an officer stopped a vehicle because one of its two brake lights was out, but a court later determined that a single working brake light was all the law required. The question presented is whether such a mistake of law can nonetheless give rise to the reasonable suspicion necessary to uphold the seizure under the Fourth Amendment. We hold that it can. Because the officer's mistake about the brake-light law was reasonable, the stop in this case was lawful under the Fourth Amendment.

I

On the morning of April 29, 2009, Sergeant Matt Darisse of the Surry County Sheriff's Department sat in his patrol car near Dobson, North Carolina, observing northbound traffic on Interstate 77. Shortly before 8 a.m., a Ford Escort passed by. Darisse thought the driver looked "very stiff and nervous," so he pulled onto the interstate and began following the Escort. A few miles down the road, the Escort braked as it approached a slower vehicle, but only the left brake light came on. Noting the faulty right brake light, Darisse activated his vehicle's lights and pulled the Escort over.

Two men were in the car: Maynor Javier Vasquez sat behind the wheel, and petitioner Nicholas Brady Heien lay across the rear seat. Sergeant Darisse explained to Vasquez that as long as his license and registration checked out, he would receive only a warning ticket for the broken brake light. A records check revealed no problems with the documents, and Darisse gave Vasquez the warning ticket. But Darisse had become suspicious during the course of the stop — Vasquez appeared nervous, Heien remained lying down the entire time, and the two gave inconsistent answers about their destination. Darisse asked Vasquez if he would be willing to answer some questions. Vasquez assented, and Darisse asked whether the men were transporting various types of contraband. Told no, Darisse asked whether he could search the Escort. Vasquez said he had no objection, but told Darisse he should ask Heien, because Heien owned the car. Heien gave his consent, and Darisse, aided by a fellow officer who had since arrived, began a thorough search of the vehicle. In the side compartment of a duffle bag, Darisse found a sandwich bag containing cocaine. The officers arrested both men.

The State charged Heien with attempted trafficking in cocaine. Heien moved to suppress the evidence seized from the car, contending that the stop and search had violated the Fourth Amendment of the United States Constitution. After a hearing at which both officers testified and the State played a video recording of the stop, the trial court denied the suppression motion, concluding that the faulty brake light had given Sergeant Darisse reasonable suspicion to initiate the stop, and that Heien's subsequent consent to the search was valid. Heien pleaded guilty but reserved his right to appeal the suppression decision.

The North Carolina Court of Appeals reversed. The initial stop was not valid, the court held, because driving with only one working brake light was not actually

16

2. Searches and Seizures

a violation of North Carolina law. The relevant provision of the vehicle code provides that a car must be "equipped with a stop lamp on the rear of the vehicle. The stop lamp shall display a red or amber light visible from a distance of not less than 100 feet to the rear in normal sunlight, and shall be actuated upon application of the service (foot) brake. The stop lamp may be incorporated into a unit with one or more other rear lamps."

The State appealed, and the North Carolina Supreme Court reversed. *NC SC*

held as trial ct. did search valid

II

A traffic stop for a suspected violation of law is a "seizure" of the occupants of the vehicle and therefore must be conducted in accordance with the Fourth Amendment. All parties agree that to justify this type of seizure, officers need only "reasonable suspicion"—that is, "a particularized and objective basis for suspecting the particular person stopped" of breaking the law. The question here is whether reasonable suspicion can rest on a mistaken understanding of the scope of a legal prohibition. We hold that it can.

As the text indicates and we have repeatedly affirmed, "the ultimate touchstone of the Fourth Amendment is 'reasonableness.'" To be reasonable is not to be perfect, and so the Fourth Amendment allows for some mistakes on the part of government officials, giving them "fair leeway for enforcing the law in the community's protection." We have recognized that searches and seizures based on mistakes of fact can be reasonable. The warrantless search of a home, for instance, is reasonable if undertaken with the consent of a resident, and remains lawful when officers obtain the consent of someone who reasonably appears to be but is not in fact a resident. By the same token, if officers with probable cause to arrest a suspect mistakenly arrest an individual matching the suspect's description, neither the seizure nor an accompanying search of the arrestee would be unlawful. The limit is that "the mistakes must be those of reasonable men."

But reasonable men make mistakes of law, too, and such mistakes are no less compatible with the concept of reasonable suspicion. Reasonable suspicion arises from the combination of an officer's understanding of the facts and his understanding of the relevant law. The officer may be reasonably mistaken on either ground. Whether the facts turn out to be not what was thought, or the law turns out to be not what was thought, the result is the same: the facts are outside the scope of the law. There is no reason, under the text of the Fourth Amendment or our precedents, why this same result should be acceptable when reached by way of a reasonable mistake of fact, but not when reached by way of a similarly reasonable mistake of law.

Contrary to the suggestion of Heien and *amici*, our decision does not discourage officers from learning the law. The Fourth Amendment tolerates only *reasonable* mistakes, and those mistakes—whether of fact or of law—must be *objectively* reasonable. We do not examine the subjective understanding of the particular officer involved. And the inquiry is not as forgiving as the one employed

17

in the distinct context of deciding whether an officer is entitled to qualified immunity for a constitutional or statutory violation. Thus, an officer can gain no Fourth Amendment advantage through a sloppy study of the laws he is duty-bound to enforce.

Finally, Heien and *amici* point to the well-known maxim, "Ignorance of the law is no excuse," and contend that it is fundamentally unfair to let police officers get away with mistakes of law when the citizenry is accorded no such leeway. Though this argument has a certain rhetorical appeal, it misconceives the implication of the maxim. The true symmetry is this: Just as an individual generally cannot escape criminal liability based on a mistaken understanding of the law, so too the government cannot impose criminal liability based on a mistaken understanding of the law. If the law required two working brake lights, Heien could not escape a ticket by claiming he reasonably thought he needed only one; if the law required only one, Sergeant Darisse could not issue a valid ticket by claiming he reasonably thought drivers needed two. But just because mistakes of law cannot justify either the imposition or the avoidance of criminal liability, it does not follow that they cannot justify an investigatory stop. And Heien is not appealing a brake-light ticket; he is appealing a cocaine-trafficking conviction as to which there is no asserted mistake of fact or law.

Heien Argument

III

Here we have little difficulty concluding that the officer's error of law was reasonable. Although the North Carolina statute at issue refers to "*a* stop lamp," suggesting the need for only a single working brake light, it also provides that "[t]he stop lamp may be incorporated into a unit with one or more *other* rear lamps." The use of "other" suggests to the everyday reader of English that a "stop lamp" is a type of "rear lamp." And another subsection of the same provision requires that vehicles "have all originally equipped rear lamps or the equivalent in good working order," arguably indicating that if a vehicle has multiple "stop lamp[s]," all must be functional.

This "stop lamp" provision, moreover, had never been previously construed by North Carolina's appellate courts. It was thus objectively reasonable for an officer in Sergeant Darisse's position to think that Heien's faulty right brake light was a violation of North Carolina law. And because the mistake of law was reasonable, there was reasonable suspicion justifying the stop.

Justice KAGAN, with whom Justice GINSBURG joins, concurring.

I concur in full in the Court's opinion, which explains why certain mistakes of law can support the reasonable suspicion needed to stop a vehicle under the Fourth Amendment. In doing so, the Court correctly emphasizes that the "Fourth Amendment tolerates only ... *objectively* reasonable" mistakes of law. And the Court makes clear that the inquiry into whether an officer's mistake of law counts as objectively reasonable "is not as forgiving as the one employed in the distinct context of deciding whether an officer is entitled to qualified immunity." I write separately to elaborate briefly on those important limitations.

First, an officer's "subjective understanding" is irrelevant: As the Court notes, "[w]e do not examine" it at all. That means the government cannot defend an officer's mistaken legal interpretation on the ground that the officer was unaware of or untrained in the law. And it means that, contrary to the dissenting opinion in the court below, an officer's reliance on "an incorrect memo or training program from the police department" makes no difference to the analysis. Those considerations pertain to the officer's subjective understanding of the law and thus cannot help to justify a seizure.

Second, the inquiry the Court permits today is more demanding than the one courts undertake before awarding qualified immunity. Our modern qualified immunity doctrine protects "all but the plainly incompetent or those who knowingly violate the law."

A court tasked with deciding whether an officer's mistake of law can support a seizure thus faces a straightforward question of statutory construction. If the statute is genuinely ambiguous, such that overturning the officer's judgment requires hard interpretive work, then the officer has made a reasonable mistake. But if not, not. As the Solicitor General made the point at oral argument, the statute must pose a "really difficult" or "very hard question of statutory interpretation." And indeed, both North Carolina and the Solicitor General agreed that such cases will be "exceedingly rare."

Justice SOTOMAYOR, dissenting.

The Court is, of course, correct that "the ultimate touchstone of the Fourth Amendment is "reasonableness." But this broad statement simply sets the standard a court is to apply when it conducts its inquiry into whether the Fourth Amendment has been violated. It does not define the categories of inputs that courts are to consider when assessing the reasonableness of a search or seizure, each of which must be independently justified. What this case requires us to decide is whether a police officer's understanding of the law is an input into the reasonableness inquiry, or whether this inquiry instead takes the law as a given and assesses an officer's understanding of the facts against a fixed legal yardstick.

I would hold that determining whether a search or seizure is reasonable requires evaluating an officer's understanding of the facts against the actual state of the law.

Both our enunciation of the reasonableness inquiry and our justification for it thus have always turned on an officer's factual conclusions and an officer's expertise with respect to those factual conclusions. Neither has hinted at taking into account an officer's understanding of the law, reasonable or otherwise.

Departing from this tradition means further eroding the Fourth Amendment's protection of civil liberties in a context where that protection has already been worn down. Traffic stops like those at issue here can be "annoying, frightening, and perhaps humiliating." We have nevertheless held that an officer's subjective motivations do not render a traffic stop unlawful. *Whren v. United*

States (1996). But we assumed in *Whren* that when an officer acts on pretext, at least that pretext would be the violation of an actual law. Giving officers license to effect seizures so long as they can attach to their reasonable view of the facts some reasonable legal interpretation (or misinterpretation) that suggests a law has been violated significantly expands this authority. One wonders how a citizen seeking to be law-abiding and to structure his or her behavior to avoid these invasive, frightening, and humiliating encounters could do so.

In addition to these human consequences—including those for communities and for their relationships with the police—permitting mistakes of law to justify seizures has the perverse effect of preventing or delaying the clarification of the law. Under such an approach, courts need not interpret statutory language but can instead simply decide whether an officer's interpretation was reasonable.

Of course, if the law enforcement system could not function without permitting mistakes of law to justify seizures, one could at least argue that permitting as much is a necessary evil. But I have not seen any persuasive argument that law enforcement will be unduly hampered by a rule that precludes consideration of mistakes of law in the reasonableness inquiry. After all, there is no indication that excluding an officer's mistake of law from the reasonableness inquiry has created a problem for law enforcement in the overwhelming number of Circuits which have adopted that approach. If an officer makes a stop in good faith but it turns out that, as in this case, the officer was wrong about what the law proscribed or required, I know of no penalty that the officer would suffer.

In short, there is nothing in our case law requiring us to hold that a reasonable mistake of law can justify a seizure under the Fourth Amendment, and quite a bit suggesting just the opposite. I also see nothing to be gained from such a holding, and much to be lost.

While I appreciate that the Court has endeavored to set some bounds on the types of mistakes of law that it thinks will qualify as reasonable, and while I think that the set of reasonable mistakes of law ought to be narrowly circumscribed if they are to be countenanced at all, I am not at all convinced that the Court has done so in a clear way. It seems to me that the difference between qualified immunity's reasonableness standard—which the Court insists without elaboration does not apply here—and the Court's conception of reasonableness in this context—which remains undefined—will prove murky in application. I fear the Court's unwillingness to sketch a fuller view of what makes a mistake of law reasonable only presages the likely difficulty that courts will have applying the Court's decision in this case.

To my mind, the more administrable approach—and the one more consistent with our precedents and principles—would be to hold that an officer's mistake of law, no matter how reasonable, cannot support the individualized suspicion necessary to justify a seizure under the Fourth Amendment. I respectfully dissent.

D. The Warrant Requirement

3. What Are the Requirements in Executing Warrants?

a. How May Police Treat Those Who Are Present When a Warrant Is Being Executed? (casebook p. 122)

In *Michigan v. Summers* (1981) (casebook p. 122), the Supreme Court held that the police may detain an individual while a search is being conducted of the person's home. What, though, if the person is arrested a short distance from the home while the search is being conducted?

United States v. Bailey
133 S. Ct. 1031 (2013)

Justice KENNEDY delivered the opinion of the Court.

The Fourth Amendment guarantees the right to be free from unreasonable searches and seizures. A search may be of a person, a thing, or a place. So too a seizure may be of a person, a thing, or even a place. A search or a seizure may occur singly or in combination, and in differing sequence. In some cases the validity of one determines the validity of the other. The instant case involves the search of a place (an apartment dwelling) and the seizure of a person. But here, though it is acknowledged that the search was lawful, it does not follow that the seizure was lawful as well. The seizure of the person is quite in question. The issue to be resolved is whether the seizure of the person was reasonable when he was stopped and detained at some distance away from the premises to be searched when the only justification for the detention was to ensure the safety and efficacy of the search.

I

At 8:45 p.m. on July 28, 2005, local police obtained a warrant to search a residence for a .380-caliber handgun. The residence was a basement apartment at 103 Lake Drive, in Wyandanch, New York. A confidential informant had told police he observed the gun when he was at the apartment to purchase drugs from "a heavy set black male with short hair" known as "Polo." As the search unit began preparations for executing the warrant, two officers, Detectives Richard Sneider and Richard Gorbecki, were conducting surveillance in an unmarked car outside the residence. About 9:56 p.m., Sneider and Gorbecki observed two men—later identified as petitioner Chunon Bailey and Bryant Middleton—leave the gated area above the basement apartment and enter a car parked in the driveway. Both matched the general physical description of "Polo" provided by the informant. There was no indication that the men were aware of the officers' presence or had any knowledge of the impending search. The detectives watched the car leave the driveway. They waited for it to go a few hundred yards down the street and followed. The detectives informed the search team of their intent to follow and detain the departing occupants. The search team then executed the search warrant at the apartment.

Detectives Sneider and Gorbecki tailed Bailey's car for about a mile—and for about five minutes—before pulling the vehicle over in a parking lot by a fire station. They ordered Bailey and Middleton out of the car and did a patdown search of both men. The officers found no weapons but discovered a ring of keys in Bailey's pocket. Bailey identified himself and said he was coming from his home at 103 Lake Drive. His driver's license, however, showed his address as Bayshore, New York, the town where the confidential informant told the police the suspect, "Polo," used to live. Bailey's passenger, Middleton, said Bailey was giving him a ride home and confirmed they were coming from Bailey's residence at 103 Lake Drive. The officers put both men in handcuffs. When Bailey asked why, Gorbecki stated that they were being detained incident to the execution of a search warrant at 103 Lake Drive. Bailey responded: "I don't live there. Anything you find there ain't mine, and I'm not cooperating with your investigation."

The detectives called for a patrol car to take Bailey and Middleton back to the Lake Drive apartment. Detective Sneider drove the unmarked car back, while Detective Gorbecki used Bailey's set of keys to drive Bailey's car back to the search scene. By the time the group returned to 103 Lake Drive, the search team had discovered a gun and drugs in plain view inside the apartment. Bailey and Middleton were placed under arrest, and Bailey's keys were seized incident to the arrest. Officers later discovered that one of Bailey's keys opened the door of the basement apartment.

At trial Bailey moved to suppress the apartment key and the statements he made when stopped by Detectives Sneider and Gorbecki. That evidence, Bailey argued, derived from an unreasonable seizure. The District Court held that Bailey's detention was permissible under *Michigan v. Summers* (1981), as a detention incident to the execution of a search warrant. In the alternative, it held that Bailey's detention was lawful as an investigatory detention supported by reasonable suspicion under *Terry v. Ohio* (1968).

II

In *Summers*, the Court defined an important category of cases in which detention is allowed without probable cause to arrest for a crime. It permitted officers executing a search warrant "to detain the occupants of the premises while a proper search is conducted." The rule in *Summers* extends farther than some earlier exceptions because it does not require law enforcement to have particular suspicion that an individual is involved in criminal activity or poses a specific danger to the officers. [In] *Muehler v. Mena* (2005), applying the rule in *Summers*,

2. Searches and Seizures

the Court stated: "An officer's authority to detain incident to a search is categorical; it does not depend on the 'quantum of proof justifying detention or the extent of the intrusion to be imposed by the seizure.'" The rule announced in *Summers* allows detention incident to the execution of a search warrant "because the character of the additional intrusion caused by detention is slight and because the justifications for detention are substantial."

A

In *Summers*, the Court recognized three important law enforcement interests that, taken together, justify the detention of an occupant who is on the premises during the execution of a search warrant: officer safety, facilitating the completion of the search, and preventing flight.

In sum, of the three law enforcement interests identified to justify the detention in *Summers*, none applies with the same or similar force to the detention of recent occupants beyond the immediate vicinity of the premises to be searched. Any of the individual interests is also insufficient, on its own, to justify an expansion of the rule in *Summers* to permit the detention of a former occupant, wherever he may be found away from the scene of the search. This would give officers too much discretion. The categorical authority to detain incident to the execution of a search warrant must be limited to the immediate vicinity of the premises to be searched.

B

In *Summers*, the Court recognized the authority to detain occupants incident to the execution of a search warrant not only in light of the law enforcement interests at stake but also because the intrusion on personal liberty was limited. The Court held detention of a current occupant "represents only an incremental intrusion on personal liberty when the search of a home has been authorized by a valid warrant." Because the detention occurs in the individual's own home, "it could add only minimally to the public stigma associated with the search itself and would involve neither the inconvenience nor the indignity associated with a compelled visit to the police station."

Where officers arrest an individual away from his home, however, there is an additional level of intrusiveness. A public detention, even if merely incident to a search, will resemble a full-fledged arrest. As demonstrated here, detention beyond the immediate vicinity can involve an initial detention away from the scene and a second detention at the residence. In between, the individual will suffer the additional indignity of a compelled transfer back to the premises, giving all the appearances of an arrest. The detention here was more intrusive than a usual detention at the search scene. Bailey's car was stopped; he was ordered to step out and was detained in full public view; he was handcuffed, transported in a marked patrol car, and detained further outside the apartment. These facts illustrate that detention away from a premises where police are already present often will be more intrusive than detentions at the scene.

C

Summers recognized that a rule permitting the detention of occupants on the premises during the execution of a search warrant, even absent individualized suspicion, was reasonable and necessary in light of the law enforcement interests in conducting a safe and efficient search. Because this exception grants substantial authority to police officers to detain outside of the traditional rules of the Fourth Amendment, it must be circumscribed.

A spatial constraint defined by the immediate vicinity of the premises to be searched is therefore required for detentions incident to the execution of a search warrant. The police action permitted here—the search of a residence—has a spatial dimension, and so a spatial or geographical boundary can be used to determine the area within which both the search and detention incident to that search may occur. Limiting the rule in *Summers* to the area in which an occupant poses a real threat to the safe and efficient execution of a search warrant ensures that the scope of the detention incident to a search is confined to its underlying justification. Once an occupant is beyond the immediate vicinity of the premises to be searched, the search-related law enforcement interests are diminished and the intrusiveness of the detention is more severe.

Here, petitioner was detained at a point beyond any reasonable understanding of the immediate vicinity of the premises in question; and so this case presents neither the necessity nor the occasion to further define the meaning of immediate vicinity. In closer cases courts can consider a number of factors to determine whether an occupant was detained within the immediate vicinity of the premises to be searched, including the lawful limits of the premises, whether the occupant was within the line of sight of his dwelling, the ease of reentry from the occupant's location, and other relevant factors.

Confining an officer's authority to detain under *Summers* to the immediate vicinity of a premises to be searched is a proper limit because it accords with the rationale of the rule.

III

Detentions incident to the execution of a search warrant are reasonable under the Fourth Amendment because the limited intrusion on personal liberty is outweighed by the special law enforcement interests at stake. Once an individual has left the immediate vicinity of a premises to be searched, however, detentions must be justified by some other rationale. In this respect it must be noted that the District Court, as an alternative ruling, held that stopping petitioner was lawful under *Terry*. This opinion expresses no view on that issue. It will be open, on remand, for the Court of Appeals to address the matter and to determine whether, assuming the *Terry* stop was valid, it yielded information that justified the detention the officers then imposed.

2. Searches and Seizures

Justice BREYER, with whom Justice THOMAS and Justice ALITO join, dissenting.

Did the police act reasonably when they followed (for 0.7 miles), and then detained, two men who left a basement apartment as the police were about to enter to execute a search warrant for a gun? The Court of Appeals for the Second Circuit found that the police action was reasonable because (1) the "premises [were] subject to a valid search warrant," (2) the detained persons were "seen leaving those premises," and (3) "the detention [was] effected *as soon as reasonably practicable.*" In light of the risks of flight, of evidence destruction, and of human injury present in this and similar cases, I would follow the approach of the Court of Appeals and uphold its determination.

The Court of Appeals rested its holding upon well-supported District Court findings. The police stopped the men "at the earliest practicable location that was consistent with the safety and security of the officers and the public." "[D]etention in open view outside the residence" would have subjected the officers "to additional dangers during the execution of the search," and it would have "potentially frustrat[ed] the whole purpose of the search due to destruction of evidence." It also could have "jeopardize[d] the search or endanger[ed] the lives of the officers . . . by allowing any other occupants inside the residence, who might see or hear the detention of the individual outside the residence as he was leaving, to have some time to (1) destroy or hide incriminating evidence just before the police are about to enter for the search; (2) flee through a back door or window; or (3) arm themselves in preparation for a violent confrontation with the police when they entered to conduct the search."

Moreover, the police stopped the men's car "at the first spot where they determined it was safe to conduct the stop," namely after the car, which had traveled a few blocks along busier streets and intersections, turned off on a quieter side road.

There is, however, one further consideration, namely an administrative consideration. A bright line will sometimes help police more easily administer Fourth Amendment rules, while also helping to ensure that the police do not go beyond the bounds of the reasonable. The majority, however, offers no easily administered bright line. It describes its line as one drawn at "the immediate vicinity of the premises to be searched," to be determined by "a number of factors . . . including [but not limited to] the lawful limits of the premises, whether the occupant was within the line of sight of his dwelling, the ease of reentry from the occupant's location, and other relevant factors." The majority's line invites case-by-case litigation although, divorced as it is from interests that directly motivate the Fourth Amendment, it offers no clear case-by-case guidance.

In any event, as the lower courts pointed out, considerations related to the risks of flight, of evidence destruction, and of physical danger overcome any administrative advantages. Consider *why* the officers here waited until the occupants had left the block to stop them: They did so because the occupants might have been armed.

Indeed, even if those emerging occupants were not armed (and even if the police knew it), those emerging occupants might have seen the officers outside the house. And they might have alerted others inside the house where, as we now know (and the officers had probable cause to believe), there was a gun lying on the floor in plain view. Suppose those inside the house, once alerted, had tried to flee with the evidence. Suppose they had destroyed the evidence. Suppose that one of them had picked up the gun and fired when the officers entered. Suppose that an individual inside the house (perhaps under the influence of drugs) had grabbed the gun and begun to fire through the window, endangering police, neighbors, or families passing by.

Considerations of this kind reveal the dangers inherent in the majority's effort to draw a semi-bright line. And they show the need here and in this class of cases to test the constitutionality of the details of a search warrant's execution by taking more directly into account concerns related to safety, evidence, and flight, *i.e.*, the kinds of concerns more directly related to the Fourth Amendment's "ultimate touchstone of . . . reasonableness."

In sum, I believe that the majority has substituted a line based on indeterminate geography for a line based on realistic considerations related to basic Fourth Amendment concerns such as privacy, safety, evidence destruction, and flight. In my view, these latter considerations should govern the Fourth Amendment determination at issue here. I consequently dissent.

E. Exceptions to the Warrant Requirement

1. Exigent Circumstances

d. *Limits on Exigent Circumstances* (casebook p. 157)

In *Missouri v. McNeely*, the government argued that in all driving under the influence cases there are exigent circumstances that allow taking blood without a consent and without a warrant because alcohol is quickly metabolized in the body.

The Supreme Court disagreed.

Missouri v. McNeely
133 S. Ct. 1552 (2013)

Justice SOTOMAYOR announced the judgment of the Court and delivered the opinion of the Court with respect to Parts I, II-A, II-B, and IV, and an opinion with respect to Parts II-C and III, in which Justice SCALIA, Justice GINSBURG, and Justice KAGAN join.

In (1966), this Court upheld a warrantless blood test of an individual arrested for driving under the influence of alcohol because the officer "might reasonably have believed that he was confronted with an emergency, in which the delay necessary to obtain a warrant, under the circumstances, threatened the destruction of evidence." The question presented here is whether the natural metabolization of alcohol in the bloodstream presents a *per se* exigency that justifies an exception to the Fourth Amendment's warrant requirement for non-consensual blood testing in all drunk-driving cases. We conclude that it does not, and we hold, consistent with general Fourth Amendment principles, that exigency in this context must be determined case by case based on the totality of the circumstances.

I

While on highway patrol at approximately 2:08 a.m., a Missouri police officer stopped Tyler McNeely's truck after observing it exceed the posted speed limit and repeatedly cross the centerline. The officer noticed several signs that McNeely was intoxicated, including McNeely's bloodshot eyes, his slurred speech, and the smell of alcohol on his breath. McNeely acknowledged to the officer that he had consumed "a couple of beers" at a bar, and he appeared unsteady on his feet when he exited the truck. After McNeely performed poorly on a battery of field-sobriety tests and declined to use a portable breath-test device to measure his blood alcohol concentration (BAC), the officer placed him under arrest.

The officer began to transport McNeely to the station house. But when McNeely indicated that he would again refuse to provide a breath sample, the officer changed course and took McNeely to a nearby hospital for blood testing. The officer did not attempt to secure a warrant. Upon arrival at the hospital, the officer asked McNeely whether he would consent to a blood test. Reading from a standard implied consent form, the officer explained to McNeely that under state law refusal to submit voluntarily to the test would lead to the immediate revocation of his driver's license for one year and could be used against him in a future prosecution. McNeely nonetheless refused. The officer then directed a hospital lab technician to take a blood sample, and the sample was secured at approximately 2:35 a.m. Subsequent laboratory testing measured McNeely's BAC at 0.154 percent, which was well above the legal limit of 0.08 percent.

McNeely was charged with driving while intoxicated (DWI). He moved to suppress the results of the blood test, arguing in relevant part that, under the circumstances, taking his blood for chemical testing without first obtaining a search warrant violated his rights under the Fourth Amendment. The trial court agreed. The Missouri Supreme Court affirmed.

II

A

Our cases have held that a warrantless search of the person is reasonable only if it falls within a recognized exception. That principle applies to the type of search at issue in this case, which involved a compelled physical intrusion beneath McNeely's skin and into his veins to obtain a sample of his blood for use as evidence in a criminal investigation. Such an invasion of bodily integrity implicates an individual's "most personal and deep-rooted expectations of privacy."

We first considered the Fourth Amendment restrictions on such searches in *Schmerber California* (1966), . . . where, as in this case, a blood sample was drawn from a defendant suspected of driving while under the influence of alcohol. Noting that "[s]earch warrants are ordinarily required for searches of dwellings," we reasoned that "absent an emergency, no less could be required where intrusions into the human body are concerned," even when the search was conducted following a lawful arrest.

As noted, the warrant requirement is subject to exceptions. "One well-recognized exception," and the one at issue in this case, "applies when the exigencies of the situation make the needs of law enforcement so compelling that a warrantless search is objectively reasonable under the Fourth Amendment."

To determine whether a law enforcement officer faced an emergency that justified acting without a warrant, this Court looks to the totality of circumstances.

Our decision in *Schmerber* applied this totality of the circumstances approach. In that case, the petitioner had suffered injuries in an automobile accident and was taken to the hospital. While he was there receiving treatment, a police officer arrested the petitioner for driving while under the influence of alcohol and ordered a blood test over his objection. After explaining that the warrant requirement applied generally to searches that intrude into the human body, we concluded that the warrantless blood test "in the present case" was nonetheless permissible because the officer "might reasonably have believed that he was confronted with an emergency, in which the delay necessary to obtain a warrant, under the circumstances, threatened 'the destruction of evidence.'"

B

The State properly recognizes that the reasonableness of a warrantless search under the exigency exception to the warrant requirement must be evaluated based on the totality of the circumstances. But the State nevertheless seeks a *per se* rule for blood testing in drunk-driving cases. The State contends that whenever an officer has probable cause to believe an individual has been driving under the influence of alcohol, exigent circumstances will necessarily exist because BAC evidence is inherently evanescent. As a result, the State claims that so long as the officer has probable cause and the blood test is conducted in a reasonable manner, it is categorically reasonable for law enforcement to obtain the blood sample without a warrant.

It is true that as a result of the human body's natural metabolic processes, the alcohol level in a person's blood begins to dissipate once the alcohol is fully absorbed and continues to decline until the alcohol is eliminated. Testimony before the trial court in this case indicated that the percentage of alcohol in an individual's blood typically decreases by approximately 0.015 percent to 0.02

percent per hour once the alcohol has been fully absorbed. Regardless of the exact elimination rate, it is sufficient for our purposes to note that because an individual's alcohol level gradually declines soon after he stops drinking, a significant delay in testing will negatively affect the probative value of the results. This fact was essential to our holding in *Schmerber*, as we recognized that, under the circumstances, further delay in order to secure a warrant after the time spent investigating the scene of the accident and transporting the injured suspect to the hospital to receive treatment would have threatened the destruction of evidence.

But it does not follow that we should depart from careful case-by-case assessment of exigency and adopt the categorical rule proposed by the State and its *amici*. In those drunk-driving investigations where police officers can reasonably obtain a warrant before a blood sample can be drawn without significantly undermining the efficacy of the search, the Fourth Amendment mandates that they do so. We do not doubt that some circumstances will make obtaining a warrant impractical such that the dissipation of alcohol from the bloodstream will support an exigency justifying a properly conducted warrantless blood test. That, however, is a reason to decide each case on its facts, as we did in *Schmerber*, not to accept the "considerable overgeneralization" that a *per se* rule would reflect.

The context of blood testing is different in critical respects from other destruction-of-evidence cases in which the police are truly confronted with a "'now or never'" situation. In contrast to, for example, circumstances in which the suspect has control over easily disposable evidence, BAC evidence from a drunk-driving suspect naturally dissipates over time in a gradual and relatively predictable manner. Moreover, because a police officer must typically transport a drunk-driving suspect to a medical facility and obtain the assistance of someone with appropriate medical training before conducting a blood test, some delay between the time of the arrest or accident and the time of the test is inevitable regardless of whether police officers are required to obtain a warrant.

The State's proposed *per se* rule also fails to account for advances in the 47 years since *Schmerber* was decided that allow for the more expeditious processing of warrant applications, particularly in contexts like drunk-driving investigations where the evidence offered to establish probable cause is simple. The Federal Rules of Criminal Procedure were amended in 1977 to permit federal magistrate judges to issue a warrant based on sworn testimony communicated by telephone. As amended, the law now allows a federal magistrate judge to consider "information communicated by telephone or other reliable electronic means." States have also innovated. Well over a majority of States allow police officers or prosecutors to apply for search warrants remotely through various means, including telephonic or radio communication, electronic communication such as e-mail, and video conferencing. And in addition to technology-based developments, jurisdictions have found other ways to streamline the warrant process, such as by using standard-form warrant applications for drunk-driving investigations.

We by no means claim that telecommunications innovations have, will, or should eliminate all delay from the warrant-application process. Warrants inevitably take some time for police officers or prosecutors to complete and for magistrate judges to review. Telephonic and electronic warrants may still require officers to follow time-consuming formalities designed to create an adequate record, such as preparing a duplicate warrant before calling the magistrate judge. See Fed. Rule Crim. Proc. 4.1(b)(3). And improvements in communications technology do not guarantee that a magistrate judge will be available when an officer needs a warrant after making a late-night arrest. But technological developments that enable police officers to secure warrants more quickly, and do so without undermining the neutral magistrate judge's essential role as a check on police discretion, are relevant to an assessment of exigency. That is particularly so in this context, where BAC evidence is lost gradually and relatively predictably.

Of course, there are important countervailing concerns. While experts can work backwards from the BAC at the time the sample was taken to determine the BAC at the time of the alleged offense, longer intervals may raise questions about the accuracy of the calculation. For that reason, exigent circumstances justifying a warrantless blood sample may arise in the regular course of law enforcement due to delays from the warrant application process. But adopting the State's *per se* approach would improperly ignore the current and future technological developments in warrant procedures, and might well diminish the incentive for jurisdictions "to pursue progressive approaches to warrant acquisition that preserve the protections afforded by the warrant while meeting the legitimate interests of law enforcement."

In short, while the natural dissipation of alcohol in the blood may support a finding of exigency in a specific case, as it did in *Schmerber*, it does not do so categorically. Whether a warrantless blood test of a drunk-driving suspect is reasonable must be determined case by case based on the totality of the circumstances.

C

In an opinion concurring in part and dissenting in part, The Chief Justice agrees that the State's proposed *per se* rule is overbroad because "[f]or exigent circumstances to justify a warrantless search . . . there must . . . be 'no time to secure a warrant.'" But The Chief Justice then goes on to suggest his own categorical rule under which a warrantless blood draw is permissible if the officer could not secure a warrant (or reasonably believed he could not secure a warrant) in the time it takes to transport the suspect to a hospital or similar facility and obtain medical assistance. Although we agree that delay inherent to the blood-testing process is relevant to evaluating exigency, we decline to substitute The Chief Justice's modified *per se* rule for our traditional totality of the circumstances analysis.

For one thing, making exigency completely dependent on the window of time between an arrest and a blood test produces odd consequences. Under The Chief Justice's rule, if a police officer serendipitously stops a suspect near an emergency room, the officer may conduct a nonconsensual warrantless blood draw even if all agree that a warrant could be obtained with very little delay under the circumstances (perhaps with far less delay than an average ride to the hospital in the jurisdiction). The rule would also distort law enforcement incentives. As with the State's *per se* rule, The Chief Justice's rule might discourage efforts to expedite the warrant process because it categorically authorizes warrantless blood draws so long as it takes more time to secure a warrant than to obtain medical assistance. On the flip side, making the requirement of independent judicial oversight turn exclusively on the amount of time that elapses between an arrest and BAC testing could induce police departments and individual officers to minimize testing delay to the detriment of other values.

III

The remaining arguments advanced in support of a *per se* exigency rule are unpersuasive.

The State and several of its *amici*, including the United States, express concern that a case-by-case approach to exigency will not provide adequate guidance to law enforcement officers deciding whether to conduct a blood test of a drunk-driving suspect without a warrant. The Chief Justice and the dissent also raise this concern. While the desire for a bright-line rule is understandable, the Fourth Amendment will not tolerate adoption of an overly broad categorical approach that would dilute the warrant requirement in a context where significant privacy interests are at stake. Moreover, a case-by-case approach is hardly unique within our Fourth Amendment jurisprudence. Numerous police actions are judged based on fact-intensive, totality of the circumstances analyses rather than according to categorical rules, including in situations that are more likely to require police officers to make difficult split-second judgments.

"No one can seriously dispute the magnitude of the drunken driving problem or the States' interest in eradicating it." Certainly we do not. While some progress has been made, drunk driving continues to exact a terrible toll on our society. See NHTSA, Traffic Safety Facts, 2011 Data 1 (No. 811700, Dec. 2012) (reporting that 9,878 people were killed in alcohol-impaired driving crashes in 2011, an average of one fatality every 53 minutes).

But the general importance of the government's interest in this area does not justify departing from the warrant requirement without showing exigent circumstances that make securing a warrant impractical in a particular case. To the extent that the State and its *amici* contend that applying the traditional Fourth Amendment totality-of-the-circumstances analysis to determine whether an exigency justified a warrantless search will undermine the governmental interest in preventing and prosecuting drunk-driving offenses, we are not convinced.

As an initial matter, States have a broad range of legal tools to enforce their drunk-driving laws and to secure BAC evidence without undertaking warrantless nonconsensual blood draws. For example, all 50 States have adopted implied consent laws that require motorists, as a condition of operating a motor vehicle within the State, to consent to BAC testing if they are arrested or otherwise detained on suspicion of a drunk-driving offense. Such laws impose significant consequences when a motorist withdraws consent; typically the motorist's driver's license is immediately suspended or revoked, and most States allow the motorist's refusal to take a BAC test to be used as evidence against him in a subsequent criminal prosecution.

IV

The State argued before this Court that the fact that alcohol is naturally metabolized by the human body creates an exigent circumstance in every case. The State did not argue that there were exigent circumstances in this particular case because a warrant could not have been obtained within a reasonable amount of time. In his testimony before the trial court, the arresting officer did not identify any other factors that would suggest he faced an emergency or unusual delay in securing a warrant.

Here and in its own courts the State based its case on an insistence that a driver who declines to submit to testing after being arrested for driving under the influence of alcohol is always subject to a nonconsensual blood test without any precondition for a warrant. That is incorrect.

Because this case was argued on the broad proposition that drunk-driving cases present a *per se* exigency, the arguments and the record do not provide the Court with an adequate analytic framework for a detailed discussion of all the relevant factors that can be taken into account in determining the reasonableness of acting without a warrant. It suffices to say that the metabolization of alcohol in the bloodstream and the ensuing loss of evidence are among the factors that must be considered in deciding whether a warrant is required. No doubt, given the large number of arrests for this offense in different jurisdictions nationwide, cases will arise when anticipated delays in obtaining a warrant will justify a blood test without judicial authorization, for in every case the law must be concerned that evidence is being destroyed. But that inquiry ought not to be pursued here where the question is not properly before this Court.

We hold that in drunk-driving investigations, the natural dissipation of alcohol in the bloodstream does not constitute an exigency in every case sufficient to justify conducting a blood test without a warrant.

Chief Justice ROBERTS, with whom Justice BREYER and Justice ALITO join, concurring in part and dissenting in part.

A police officer reading this Court's opinion would have no idea — no idea — what the Fourth Amendment requires of him, once he decides to obtain a blood sample from a drunk driving suspect who has refused a breathalyzer test. I have no quarrel with the Court's "totality of the circumstances" approach as a general matter; that is what our cases require. But the circumstances in drunk driving cases are often typical, and the Court should be able to offer guidance on how police should handle cases like the one before us.

2. Searches and Seizures

In my view, the proper rule is straightforward. Our cases establish that there is an exigent circumstances exception to the warrant requirement. That exception applies when there is a compelling need to prevent the imminent destruction of important evidence, and there is no time to obtain a warrant. The natural dissipation of alcohol in the bloodstream constitutes not only the imminent but ongoing destruction of critical evidence. That would qualify as an exigent circumstance, except that there may be time to secure a warrant before blood can be drawn. If there is, an officer must seek a warrant. If an officer could reasonably conclude that there is not, the exigent circumstances exception applies by its terms, and the blood may be drawn without a warrant.

The reasonable belief that critical evidence is being destroyed gives rise to a compelling need for blood draws in cases like this one. Here, in fact, there is not simply a belief that any alcohol in the bloodstream will be destroyed; it is a biological certainty. Alcohol dissipates from the bloodstream at a rate of 0.01 percent to 0.025 percent per hour. Evidence is literally disappearing by the minute. That certainty makes this case an even stronger one than usual for application of the exigent circumstances exception.

And that evidence is important. A serious and deadly crime is at issue. According to the Department of Transportation, in 2011, one person died every 53 minutes due to drinking and driving. No surprise then that drinking and driving is punished severely, including with jail time. McNeely, for instance, faces up to four years in prison.

Evidence of a driver's blood alcohol concentration (BAC) is crucial to obtain convictions for such crimes. All 50 States and the District of Columbia have laws providing that it is *per se* illegal to drive with a BAC of 0.08 percent or higher. Most States also have laws establishing additional penalties for drivers who drive with a "high BAC," often defined as 0.15 percent or above. BAC evidence clearly matters. And when drivers refuse breathalyzers, as McNeely did here, a blood draw becomes necessary to obtain that evidence.

The need to prevent the imminent destruction of BAC evidence is no less compelling because the incriminating alcohol dissipates over a limited period of time, rather than all at once. As noted, the concentration of alcohol can make a difference not only between guilt and innocence, but between different crimes and different degrees of punishment. The officer is unlikely to know precisely when the suspect consumed alcohol or how much; all he knows is that critical evidence is being steadily lost. Fire can spread gradually, but that does not lessen the need and right of the officers to respond immediately.

McNeely contends that there is no compelling need for a warrantless blood draw, because if there is some alcohol left in the blood by the time a warrant is obtained, the State can use math and science to work backwards and identify a defendant's BAC at the time he was driving. But that's not good enough. We have indicated that exigent circumstances justify warrantless entry when drugs are about to be flushed down the toilet. We have not said that, because there could well be drug paraphernalia elsewhere in the home, or because a defendant's co-conspirator might testify to the amount of drugs involved, the drugs themselves are not crucial and there is no compelling need for warrantless entry.

The same approach should govern here. There is a compelling need to search because alcohol—the nearly conclusive evidence of a serious crime—is dissipating from the bloodstream. The need is no less compelling because the police might be able to acquire second-best evidence some other way.

For exigent circumstances to justify a warrantless search, however, there must also be "no time to secure a warrant." As noted, the fact that alcohol dissipates gradually from the bloodstream does not diminish the compelling need for a search—critical evidence is still disappearing. But the fact that the dissipation persists for some time means that the police—although they may not be able to do anything about it right away—may still be able to respond to the ongoing destruction of evidence later on.

There might, therefore, be time to obtain a warrant in many cases. As the Court explains, police can often request warrants rather quickly these days. At least 30 States provide for electronic warrant applications. In many States, a police officer can call a judge, convey the necessary information, and be authorized to affix the judge's signature to a warrant.

In a case such as this, applying the exigent circumstances exception to the general warrant requirement of the Fourth Amendment seems straightforward: If there is time to secure a warrant before blood can be drawn, the police must seek one. If an officer could reasonably conclude that there is not sufficient time to seek and receive a warrant, or he applies for one but does not receive a response before blood can be drawn, a warrantless blood draw may ensue.

Justice THOMAS, dissenting.

This case requires the Court to decide whether the Fourth Amendment prohibits an officer from obtaining a blood sample without a warrant when there is probable cause to believe that a suspect has been driving under the influence of alcohol. Because the body's natural metabolization of alcohol inevitably destroys evidence of the crime, it constitutes an exigent circumstance. As a result, I would hold that a warrantless blood draw does not violate the Fourth Amendment.

Once police arrest a suspect for drunk driving, each passing minute eliminates probative evidence of the crime. The human liver eliminates alcohol from the bloodstream at a rate of approximately 0.015 percent to 0.020 percent per hour, with some heavy drinkers as high as 0.022 percent per hour, depending on, among other things, a person's sex, weight, body type, and drinking history.

The rapid destruction of evidence acknowledged by the parties, the majority, and *Schmerber*'s exigency determination occurs in *every* situation where police have probable cause to arrest a drunk driver. In turn, that destruction of evidence implicates the exigent-circumstances doctrine.

2. Searches and Seizures

A hypothetical involving classic exigent circumstances further illustrates the point. Officers are watching a warehouse and observe a worker carrying bundles from the warehouse to a large bonfire and throwing them into the blaze. The officers have probable cause to believe the bundles contain marijuana. Because there is only one person carrying the bundles, the officers believe it will take hours to completely destroy the drugs. During that time the officers likely could obtain a warrant. But it is clear that the officers need not sit idly by and watch the destruction of evidence while they wait for a warrant. The fact that it will take time for the evidence to be destroyed and that *some* evidence may remain by the time the officers secure a warrant are not relevant to the exigency. However, the ever-diminishing quantity of drugs may have an impact on the severity of the crime and the length of the sentence. Conducting a warrantless search of the warehouse in this situation would be entirely reasonable.

The same obtains in the drunk-driving context. Just because it will take time for the evidence to be completely destroyed does not mean there is no exigency.

In light of *Missouri v. McNeely*, may a state make it a crime for a person to refuse to consent to a blood or breath test? The Court held that it is permissible for the state to require a person to submit to a breath test, but not a blood test.

Birchfield v. North Dakota
136 S. Ct. 2160 (2016)

Justice ALITO delivered the opinion of the Court.

Drunk drivers take a grisly toll on the Nation's roads, claiming thousands of lives, injuring many more victims, and inflicting billions of dollars in property damage every year. To fight this problem, all States have laws that prohibit motorists from driving with a blood alcohol concentration (BAC) that exceeds a specified level. But determining whether a driver's BAC is over the legal limit requires a test, and many drivers stopped on suspicion of drunk driving would not submit to testing if given the option. So every State also has long had what are termed "implied consent laws." These laws impose penalties on motorists who refuse to undergo testing when there is sufficient reason to believe they are violating the State's drunk-driving laws.

In the past, the typical penalty for noncompliance was suspension or revocation of the motorist's license. The cases now before us involve laws that go beyond that and make it a crime for a motorist to refuse to be tested after being lawfully arrested for driving while impaired. The question presented is whether such laws violate the Fourth Amendment's prohibition against unreasonable searches.

I

The most common and economical method of calculating BAC is by means of a machine that measures the amount of alcohol in a person's breath. Today, such devices can detect the presence of alcohol more quickly and accurately than before, typically using infrared technology rather than a chemical reaction. And in practice all breath testing machines used for evidentiary purposes must be approved by the National Highway Traffic Safety Administration. These machines are generally regarded as very reliable because the federal standards require that the devices produce accurate and reproducible test results at a variety of BAC levels, from the very low to the very high.

Measurement of BAC based on a breath test requires the cooperation of the person being tested. The subject must take a deep breath and exhale through a mouthpiece that connects to the machine. Typically the test subject must blow air into the device " 'for a period of several seconds' " to produce an adequate breath sample, and the process is sometimes repeated so that analysts can compare multiple samples to ensure the device's accuracy. Modern breath test machines are designed to capture so-called "deep lung" or alveolar air. Air from the alveolar region of the lungs provides the best basis for determining the test subject's BAC, for it is in that part of the lungs that alcohol vapor and other gases are exchanged between blood and breath.

When a standard infrared device is used, the whole process takes only a few minutes from start to finish. Most evidentiary breath tests do not occur next to the vehicle, at the side of the road, but in a police station, where the controlled environment is especially conducive to reliable testing, or in some cases in the officer's patrol vehicle or in special mobile testing facilities.

Because the cooperation of the test subject is necessary when a breath test is administered and highly preferable when a blood sample is taken, the enactment of laws defining intoxication based on BAC made it necessary for States to find a way of securing such cooperation. So-called "implied consent" laws were enacted to achieve this result. They provided that cooperation with BAC testing was a condition of the privilege of driving on state roads and that the privilege would be rescinded if a suspected drunk driver refused to honor that condition. Suspension or revocation of the motorist's driver's license remains the standard legal consequence of refusal. In addition, evidence of the motorist's refusal is admitted as evidence of likely intoxication in a drunk-driving prosecution.

In recent decades, the States and the Federal Government have toughened drunk-driving laws, and those efforts have corresponded to a dramatic decrease in alcohol-related fatalities. As of the early 1980's, the number of annual fatalities averaged 25,000; by 2014, the most recent year for which statistics are available, the number had fallen to below 10,000. One legal change has been further lowering the BAC standard from 0.10% to 0.08%. In addition, many States now impose increased penalties for recidivists and for drivers with a BAC level that exceeds a higher threshold.

2. Searches and Seizures

Many other States have taken a similar approach, but this new structure threatened to undermine the effectiveness of implied consent laws. If the penalty for driving with a greatly elevated BAC or for repeat violations exceeds the penalty for refusing to submit to testing, motorists who fear conviction for the more severely punished offenses have an incentive to reject testing. And in some States, the refusal rate is high. On average, over one-fifth of all drivers asked to submit to BAC testing in 2011 refused to do so.

To combat the problem of test refusal, some States have begun to enact laws making it a crime to refuse to undergo testing.

II

Petitioner Danny Birchfield accidentally drove his car off a North Dakota highway on October 10, 2013. A state trooper arrived and watched as Birchfield unsuccessfully tried to drive back out of the ditch in which his car was stuck. The trooper approached, caught a strong whiff of alcohol, and saw that Birchfield's eyes were bloodshot and watery. Birchfield spoke in slurred speech and struggled to stay steady on his feet. At the trooper's request, Birchfield agreed to take several field sobriety tests and performed poorly on each. He had trouble reciting sections of the alphabet and counting backwards in compliance with the trooper's directions.

The state trooper arrested Birchfield for driving while impaired, gave the usual *Miranda* warnings, again advised him of his obligation under North Dakota law to undergo BAC testing, and informed him, as state law requires that refusing to take the test would expose him to criminal penalties.Although faced with the prospect of prosecution under this law, Birchfield refused to let his blood be drawn.

On August 5, 2012, Minnesota police received a report of a problem at a South St. Paul boat launch. Three apparently intoxicated men had gotten their truck stuck in the river while attempting to pull their boat out of the water. When police arrived, witnesses informed them that a man in underwear had been driving the truck. That man proved to be William Robert Bernard, Jr., petitioner in the second of these cases. Bernard admitted that he had been drinking but denied driving the truck (though he was holding its keys) and refused to perform any field sobriety tests. After noting that Bernard's breath smelled of alcohol and that his eyes were bloodshot and watery, officers arrested Bernard for driving while impaired.

Back at the police station, officers read Bernard Minnesota's implied consent advisory, which like North Dakota's informs motorists that it is a crime under state law to refuse to submit to a legally required BAC test. The officers asked Bernard to take a breath test. After he refused, prosecutors charged him with test refusal in the first degree because he had four prior impaired-driving convictions.

A police officer spotted our third petitioner, Steve Michael Beylund, driving the streets of Bowman, North Dakota, on the night of August 10, 2013. The officer saw Beylund try unsuccessfully to turn into a driveway. In the process, Beylund's car nearly hit a stop sign before coming to a stop still partly on the public road. The officer walked up to the car and saw that Beylund had an empty wine glass in the center console next to him. Noticing that Beylund also smelled of alcohol, the officer asked him to step out of the car. As Beylund did so, he struggled to keep his balance. The officer arrested Beylund for driving while impaired and took him to a nearby hospital. There he read Beylund North Dakota's implied consent advisory, informing him that test refusal in these circumstances is itself a crime. Unlike the other two petitioners in these cases, Beylund agreed to have his blood drawn and analyzed. A nurse took a blood sample, which revealed a blood alcohol concentration of 0.250%, more than three times the legal limit.

Given the test results, Beylund's driver's license was suspended for two years after an administrative hearing. Beylund appealed the hearing officer's decision to a North Dakota District Court, principally arguing that his consent to the blood test was coerced by the officer's warning that refusing to consent would itself be a crime.

III

As our summary of the facts and proceedings in these three cases reveals, the cases differ in some respects. Petitioners Birchfield and Beylund were told that they were obligated to submit to a blood test, whereas petitioner Bernard was informed that a breath test was required.

Despite these differences, success for all three petitioners depends on the proposition that the criminal law ordinarily may not compel a motorist to submit to the taking of a blood sample or to a breath test unless a warrant authorizing such testing is issued by a magistrate. If, on the other hand, such warrantless searches comport with the Fourth Amendment, it follows that a State may criminalize the refusal to comply with a demand to submit to the required testing, just as a State may make it a crime for a person to obstruct the execution of a valid search warrant.

IV

The [Fourth] Amendment prohibits "unreasonable searches," and our cases establish that the taking of a blood sample or the administration of a breath test is a search. The question, then, is whether the warrantless searches at issue here were reasonable.

In the three cases now before us, the drivers were searched or told that they were required to submit to a search after being placed under arrest for drunk driving. We therefore consider how the search-incident-to-arrest doctrine applies to breath and blood tests incident to such arrests.

V

We begin by considering the impact of breath and blood tests on individual privacy interests, and we will discuss each type of test in turn.

2. Searches and Seizures

1

Years ago we said that breath tests do not "implicat[e] significant privacy concerns." That remains so today. First, the physical intrusion is almost negligible. Breath tests "do not require piercing the skin" and entail "a minimum of inconvenience." As Minnesota describes its version of the breath test, the process requires the arrestee to blow continuously for 4 to 15 seconds into a straw-like mouthpiece that is connected by a tube to the test machine. The effort is no more demanding than blowing up a party balloon.

Petitioner Bernard argues, however, that the process is nevertheless a significant intrusion because the arrestee must insert the mouthpiece of the machine into his or her mouth. But there is nothing painful or strange about this requirement. The use of a straw to drink beverages is a common practice and one to which few object. Nor, contrary to Bernard, is the test a significant intrusion because it does not capture an ordinary exhalation of the kind that routinely is exposed to the public but instead requires a sample of alveolar (deep lung) air. Humans have never been known to assert a possessory interest in or any emotional attachment to *any* of the air in their lungs. The air that humans exhale is not part of their bodies. Exhalation is a natural process—indeed, one that is necessary for life. Humans cannot hold their breath for more than a few minutes, and all the air that is breathed into a breath analyzing machine, including deep lung air, sooner or later would be exhaled even without the test.

Second, breath tests are capable of revealing only one bit of information, the amount of alcohol in the subject's breath. A breath test results in a BAC reading on a machine, nothing more. No sample of anything is left in the possession of the police.

Finally, participation in a breath test is not an experience that is likely to cause any great enhancement in the embarrassment that is inherent in any arrest. The act of blowing into a straw is not inherently embarrassing, nor are evidentiary breath tests administered in a manner that causes embarrassment. Again, such tests are normally administered in private at a police station, in a patrol car, or in a mobile testing facility, out of public view. Moreover, once placed under arrest, the individual's expectation of privacy is necessarily diminished.

For all these reasons, a breath test does not "implicat[e] significant privacy concerns."

2

Blood tests are a different matter. They "require piercing the skin" and extract a part of the subject's body. And while humans exhale air from their lungs many times per minute, humans do not continually shed blood. It is true, of course, that people voluntarily submit to the taking of blood samples as part of a physical examination, and the process involves little pain or risk. Nevertheless, for many, the process is not one they relish. It is significantly more intrusive than blowing into a tube. In addition, a blood test, unlike a breath test, places in the hands of law enforcement authorities a sample that can be preserved and from which it is possible to extract information beyond a simple BAC reading. Even if the law enforcement agency is precluded from testing the blood for any purpose other than to measure BAC, the potential remains and may result in anxiety for the person tested.

C

Having assessed the impact of breath and blood testing on privacy interests, we now look to the States' asserted need to obtain BAC readings for persons arrested for drunk driving. The States and the Federal Government have a "paramount interest . . . in preserving the safety of . . . public highways." Although the number of deaths and injuries caused by motor vehicle accidents has declined over the years, the statistics are still staggering. Alcohol consumption is a leading cause of traffic fatalities and injuries. During the past decade, annual fatalities in drunk-driving accidents ranged from 13,582 deaths in 2005 to 9,865 deaths in 2011. The most recent data report a total of 9,967 such fatalities in 2014—on average, one death every 53 minutes.

Justice Sotomayor's partial dissent suggests that States' interests in fighting drunk driving are satisfied once suspected drunk drivers are arrested, since such arrests take intoxicated drivers off the roads where they might do harm. But of course States are not solely concerned with neutralizing the threat posed by a drunk driver who has already gotten behind the wheel. They also have a compelling interest in creating effective "deterrent[s] to drunken driving" so such individuals make responsible decisions and do not become a threat to others in the first place.

Petitioners and Justice Sotomayor next suggest that requiring a warrant for BAC testing in every case in which a motorist is arrested for drunk driving would not impose any great burden on the police or the courts. But of course the same argument could be made about searching through objects found on the arrestee's possession, which our cases permit even in the absence of a warrant. What about the cigarette package in *Robinson*? What if a motorist arrested for drunk driving has a flask in his pocket? What if a motorist arrested for driving while under the influence of marijuana has what appears to be a marijuana cigarette on his person? What about an unmarked bottle of pills?

If a search warrant were required for every search incident to arrest that does not involve exigent circumstances, the courts would be swamped. And even if we arbitrarily singled out BAC tests incident to arrest for this special treatment, as it appears the dissent would do, the impact on the courts would be considerable. The number of arrests every year for driving under the influence is enormous—more than 1.1 million in 2014. Particularly in sparsely populated areas, it would be no small task for courts to field a large new influx of warrant applications that could come on any day of the year and at any hour. In many jurisdictions, judicial officers have the authority to issue warrants only within their own districts, and in rural areas, some districts may have only a small number of judicial officers.

2.   Searches and Seizures

Having assessed the effect of BAC tests on privacy interests and the need for such tests, we conclude that the Fourth Amendment permits warrantless breath tests incident to arrests for drunk driving. The impact of breath tests on privacy is slight, and the need for BAC testing is great.

We reach a different conclusion with respect to blood tests. Blood tests are significantly more intrusive, and their reasonableness must be judged in light of the availability of the less invasive alternative of a breath test. Respondents have offered no satisfactory justification for demanding the more intrusive alternative without a warrant.

Neither respondents nor their *amici* dispute the effectiveness of breath tests in measuring BAC. Breath tests have been in common use for many years. Their results are admissible in court and are widely credited by juries, and respondents do not dispute their accuracy or utility. What, then, is the justification for warrantless blood tests?

One advantage of blood tests is their ability to detect not just alcohol but also other substances that can impair a driver's ability to operate a car safely. A breath test cannot do this, but police have other measures at their disposal when they have reason to believe that a motorist may be under the influence of some other substance (for example, if a breath test indicates that a clearly impaired motorist has little if any alcohol in his blood). Nothing prevents the police from seeking a warrant for a blood test when there is sufficient time to do so in the particular circumstances or from relying on the exigent circumstances exception to the warrant requirement when there is not.

A blood test also requires less driver participation than a breath test. In order for a technician to take a blood sample, all that is needed is for the subject to remain still, either voluntarily or by being immobilized. Thus, it is possible to extract a blood sample from a subject who forcibly resists, but many States reasonably prefer not to take this step.

It is true that a blood test, unlike a breath test, may be administered to a person who is unconscious (perhaps as a result of a crash) or who is unable to do what is needed to take a breath test due to profound intoxication or injuries. But we have no reason to believe that such situations are common in drunk-driving arrests, and when they arise, the police may apply for a warrant if need be.

A breath test may also be ineffective if an arrestee deliberately attempts to prevent an accurate reading by failing to blow into the tube for the requisite length of time or with the necessary force. But courts have held that such conduct qualifies as a refusal to undergo testing, and it may be prosecuted as such. And again, a warrant for a blood test may be sought.

Because breath tests are significantly less intrusive than blood tests and in most cases amply serve law enforcement interests, we conclude that a breath test, but not a blood test, may be administered as a search incident to a lawful arrest for drunk driving. As in all cases involving reasonable searches incident to arrest, a warrant is not needed in this situation.

Justice SOTOMAYOR, with whom Justice GINSBURG joins, concurring in part and dissenting in part.

The Court today considers three consolidated cases. I join the majority's disposition of *Birchfield v. North Dakota*, and *Beylund v. Levi* in which the Court holds that the search-incident-to-arrest exception to the Fourth Amendment's warrant requirement does not permit warrantless blood tests. But I dissent from the Court's disposition of *Bernard v. Minnesota*, in which the Court holds that the same exception permits warrantless breath tests. Because no governmental interest categorically makes it impractical for an officer to obtain a warrant before measuring a driver's alcohol level, the Fourth Amendment prohibits such searches without a warrant, unless exigent circumstances exist in a particular case.

The States do not challenge *McNeely*'s holding that a categorical exigency exception is not necessary to accommodate the governmental interests associated with the dissipation of blood alcohol after drunk-driving arrests. They instead seek to exempt breath tests from the warrant requirement categorically under the search-incident-to-arrest doctrine. The majority agrees. Both are wrong.

As discussed above, regardless of the exception a State requests, the Court's traditional framework asks whether, in light of the privacy interest at stake, a legitimate governmental interest ever requires conducting breath searches without a warrant—and, if so, whether that governmental interest is adequately addressed by a case-by-case exception or requires a categorical exception to the warrant requirement. That framework directs the conclusion that a categorical search-incident-to-arrest rule for breath tests is unnecessary to address the States' governmental interests in combating drunk driving.

Beginning with the governmental interests, there can be no dispute that States must have tools to combat drunk driving. But neither the States nor the Court has demonstrated that "obtaining a warrant" in cases not already covered by the exigent circumstances exception "is likely to frustrate the governmental purpose[s] behind [this] search."

First, the Court cites the governmental interest in protecting the public from drunk drivers. But it is critical to note that once a person is stopped for drunk driving and arrested, he no longer poses an immediate threat to the public. Because the person is already in custody prior to the administration of the breath test, there can be no serious claim that the time it takes to obtain a warrant would increase the danger that drunk driver poses to fellow citizens.

Second, the Court cites the governmental interest in preventing the destruction or loss of evidence. But neither the Court nor the States identify any practical reasons why obtaining a warrant after making an arrest and before conducting a breath test compromises the quality of the evidence obtained. To the contrary, the delays inherent in administering reliable breath tests generally provide ample time to obtain a warrant.

There is a common misconception that breath tests are conducted roadside, immediately after a driver is arrested. While some preliminary testing is conducted roadside, reliability concerns with roadside tests confine their use in most circumstances to establishing probable cause for an arrest. The standard evidentiary breath test is conducted after a motorist is arrested and transported to a police station, governmental building, or mobile testing facility where officers can access reliable, evidence-grade breath testing machinery. Transporting the motorist to the equipment site is not the only potential delay in the process, however. Officers must also observe the subject for 15 to 20 minutes to ensure that "residual mouth alcohol," which can inflate results and expose the test to an evidentiary challenge at trial, has dissipated and that the subject has not inserted any food or drink into his mouth. In many States, including Minnesota, officers must then give the motorist a window of time within which to contact an attorney before administering a test. Finally, if a breath test machine is not already active, the police officer must set it up. North Dakota's Intoxilyzer 8000 machine can take as long as 30 minutes to "warm-up."

Because of these necessary steps, the standard breath test is conducted well after an arrest is effectuated. The Minnesota Court of Appeals has explained that nearly all breath tests "involve a time lag of 45 minutes to two hours." Both North Dakota and Minnesota give police a 2-hour period from the time the motorist was pulled over within which to administer a breath test.

During this built-in window, police can seek warrants. That is particularly true in light of "advances" in technology that now permit "the more expeditious processing of warrant applications." Moreover, counsel for North Dakota explained at oral argument that the State uses a typical "on-call" system in which some judges are available even during off-duty times.

Where "an officer can . . . secure a warrant while" the motorist is being transported and the test is being prepared, this Court has said that "there would be no plausible justification for an exception to the warrant requirement." Neither the Court nor the States provide any evidence to suggest that, in the normal course of affairs, obtaining a warrant and conducting a breath test will exceed the allotted 2-hour window.

Third, the Court and the States cite a governmental interest in minimizing the costs of gathering evidence of drunk driving. But neither has demonstrated that requiring police to obtain warrants for breath tests would impose a sufficiently significant burden on state resources to justify the elimination of the Fourth Amendment's warrant requirement.

Assuming that North Dakota police officers do not obtain warrants for any drunk-driving arrests today, and assuming that they would need to obtain a warrant for every drunk-driving arrest tomorrow, each of the State's 82 judges and magistrate judges would need to issue fewer than two extra warrants per week. Minnesota has nearly the same ratio of judges to drunk-driving arrests, and so would face roughly the same burden. These back-of-the-envelope numbers suggest that the burden of obtaining a warrant before conducting a breath test would be small in both States.

But even these numbers *overstate* the burden by a significant degree. States only need to obtain warrants for drivers who refuse testing and a significant majority of drivers voluntarily consent to breath tests, even in States without criminal penalties for refusal. In North Dakota, only 21% of people refuse breath tests and in Minnesota, only 12% refuse. Each of their judges and magistrate judges would need to issue fewer than one extra warrant a week. That bears repeating: The Court finds a categorical exception to the warrant requirement because each of a State's judges and magistrate judges would need to issue less than one extra warrant a week.

Fourth, the Court alludes to the need to collect evidence conveniently. But mere convenience in investigating drunk driving cannot itself justify an exception to the warrant requirement. This Court has never said that mere convenience in gathering evidence justifies an exception to the warrant requirement.

After evaluating the governmental and privacy interests at stake here, the final step is to determine whether any situations in which warrants would interfere with the States' legitimate governmental interests should be accommodated through a case-by-case or categorical exception to the warrant requirement.

As shown, because there are so many circumstances in which obtaining a warrant will not delay the administration of a breath test or otherwise compromise any governmental interest cited by the States, it should be clear that allowing a categorical exception to the warrant requirement is a "considerable overgeneralization" here.

Here, the Court lacks even the pretense of attempting to situate breath searches within the narrow and weighty law enforcement needs that have historically justified the limited use of warrantless searches. I fear that if the Court continues down this road, the Fourth Amendment's warrant requirement will become nothing more than a suggestion.

Justice Thomas, concurring in judgment in part and dissenting in part.

The compromise the Court reaches today is not a good one. By deciding that some (but not all) warrantless tests revealing the blood alcohol concentration (BAC) of an arrested driver are constitutional, the Court contorts the search-incident-to-arrest exception to the Fourth Amendment's warrant requirement. The far simpler answer to the question presented is the one rejected in (2013). Here, the tests revealing the BAC of a driver suspected of driving drunk are constitutional under the exigent-circumstances exception to the warrant requirement.

I

Today's decision chips away at a well-established exception to the warrant requirement. Until recently, we have admonished that "[a] police officer's determination as to how and where to search the person of a suspect whom he has arrested is necessarily a quick *ad hoc* judgment which the Fourth Amendment does not require to be broken down in each instance into an analysis of each step in the search." Under our precedents, a search incident to lawful arrest "require[d] no additional justification."

2.   Searches and Seizures

The Court justifies its result—an arbitrary line in the sand between blood and breath tests—by balancing the invasiveness of the particular type of search against the government's reasons for the search. Such case-by-case balancing is bad for the People, who "through ratification, have already weighed the policy tradeoffs that constitutional rights entail." It is also bad for law enforcement officers, who depend on predictable rules to do their job, as Members of this Court have exhorted in the past.

Today's application of the search-incident-to-arrest exception is bound to cause confusion in the lower courts. The Court's choice to allow some (but not all) BAC searches is undeniably appealing, for it both reins in the pernicious problem of drunk driving and also purports to preserve some Fourth Amendment protections. But that compromise has little support under this Court's existing precedents.

The better (and far simpler) way to resolve these cases is by applying the *per se* rule that I proposed in *McNeely*. Under that approach, both warrantless breath and blood tests are constitutional because "the natural metabolization of [BAC] creates an exigency once police have probable cause to believe the driver is drunk. It naturally follows that police may conduct a search in these circumstances."

The Court in *McNeely* rejected that bright-line rule and instead adopted a totality-of-the-circumstances test examining whether the facts of a particular case presented exigent circumstances justifying a warrantless search. The Court ruled that "the natural dissipation of alcohol in the blood" could not "categorically" create an "exigency" in every case. The destruction of "BAC evidence from a drunk-driving suspect" that "naturally dissipates over time in a gradual and relatively predictable manner," according to the Court, was qualitatively different from the destruction of evidence in "circumstances in which the suspect has control over easily disposable evidence."

The Court was wrong in *McNeely*, and today's compromise is perhaps an inevitable consequence of that error. Both searches contemplated by the state laws at issue in these cases would be constitutional under the exigent-circumstances exception to the warrant requirement. I respectfully concur in the judgment in part and dissent in part.

4.   Searches Incident to Arrest (casebook p. 174)

In *Riley v. California*, the Court considered the important question of whether police, without a warrant, may search the contents of a cellphone that is found on a person when it is found in a search incident to arrest. In considering this, the Court clarified the permissible scope of searches incident to arrest and also the protection for informational privacy in the context of cellphones.

Riley v. California
134 S. Ct. 2473 (2014)

Chief Justice ROBERTS delivered the opinion of the Court.

Issue

These two cases raise a common question: whether the police may, without a warrant, search digital information on a cell phone seized from an individual who has been arrested.

I

In the first case, petitioner David Riley was stopped by a police officer for driving with expired registration tags. In the course of the stop, the officer also learned that Riley's license had been suspended. The officer impounded Riley's car, pursuant to department policy, and another officer conducted an inventory search of the car. Riley was arrested for possession of concealed and loaded firearms when that search turned up two handguns under the car's hood.

An officer searched Riley incident to the arrest and found items associated with the "Bloods" street gang. He also seized a cell phone from Riley's pants pocket. According to Riley's uncontradicted assertion, the phone was a "smart phone," a cell phone with a broad range of other functions based on advanced computing capability, large storage capacity, and Internet connectivity. The officer accessed information on the phone and noticed that some words (presumably in text messages or a contacts list) were preceded by the letters "CK"—a label that, he believed, stood for "Crip Killers," a slang term for members of the Bloods gang.

evidence from phone

At the police station about two hours after the arrest, a detective specializing in gangs further examined the contents of the phone. The detective testified that he "went through" Riley's phone "looking for evidence, because . . . gang members will often video themselves with guns or take pictures of themselves with the guns." Although there was "a lot of stuff" on the phone, particular files that "caught [the detective's] eye" included videos of young men sparring while someone yelled encouragement using the moniker "Blood." The police also found photographs of Riley standing in front of a car they suspected had been involved in a shooting a few weeks earlier.

Prior to trial, Riley moved to suppress all evidence that the police had obtained from his cell phone. The trial court rejected that argument.

In the second case, a police officer performing routine surveillance observed respondent Brima Wurie make an apparent drug sale from a car. Officers subsequently arrested Wurie and took him to the police station. At the station, the officers seized two cell phones from Wurie's person. The one at issue here was a "flip phone," a kind of phone that is flipped open for use and that generally has a smaller range of features than a smart phone. Five to ten minutes after arriving at the station, the officers noticed that the phone was repeatedly receiving calls from

2. Searches and Seizures

a source identified as "my house" on the phone's external screen. A few minutes later, they opened the phone and saw a photograph of a woman and a baby set as the phone's wallpaper. They pressed one button on the phone to access its call log, then another button to determine the phone number associated with the "my house" label. They next used an online phone directory to trace that phone number to an apartment building.

When the officers went to the building, they saw Wurie's name on a mailbox and observed through a window a woman who resembled the woman in the photograph on Wurie's phone. They secured the apartment while obtaining a search warrant and, upon later executing the warrant, found and seized 215 grams of crack cocaine, marijuana, drug paraphernalia, a firearm and ammunition, and cash.

He moved to suppress the evidence obtained from the search of the apartment, arguing that it was the fruit of an unconstitutional search of his cell phone. The District Court denied the motion. A divided panel of the First Circuit reversed the denial of Wurie's motion to suppress and vacated Wurie's convictions for possession with intent to distribute and possession of a firearm as a felon.

2nd Case

II

As the text [of the Fourth Amendment] makes clear, "the ultimate touchstone of the Fourth Amendment is 'reasonableness.'" Our cases have determined that "[w]here a search is undertaken by law enforcement officials to discover evidence of criminal wrongdoing, ... reasonableness generally requires the obtaining of a judicial warrant." Such a warrant ensures that the inferences to support a search are "drawn by a neutral and detached magistrate instead of being judged by the officer engaged in the often competitive enterprise of ferreting out crime." In the absence of a warrant, a search is reasonable only if it falls within a specific exception to the warrant requirement.

The two cases before us concern the reasonableness of a warrantless search incident to a lawful arrest. In 1914, this Court first acknowledged in dictum "the right on the part of the Government, always recognized under English and American law, to search the person of the accused when legally arrested to discover and seize the fruits or evidences of crime." Since that time, it has been well accepted that such a search constitutes an exception to the warrant requirement. Indeed, the label "exception" is something of a misnomer in this context, as warrantless searches incident to arrest occur with far greater frequency than searches conducted pursuant to a warrant.

Although the existence of the exception for such searches has been recognized for a century, its scope has been debated for nearly as long. Three related precedents set forth the rules governing such searches:

The first, *Chimel v. California* (1969), laid the groundwork for most of the existing search incident to arrest doctrine. The Court crafted the following rule for assessing the reasonableness of a search incident to arrest:

reasoning for Exception

> "When an arrest is made, it is reasonable for the arresting officer to search the person arrested in order to remove any weapons that the latter might seek to use in order to resist arrest or effect his escape. Otherwise, the officer's safety might well be endangered, and the arrest itself frustrated. In addition, it is entirely reasonable for the arresting officer to search for and seize any evidence on the arrestee's person in order to prevent its concealment or destruction. . . . There is ample justification, therefore, for a search of the arrestee's person and the area 'within his immediate control'—construing that phrase to mean the area from within which he might gain possession of a weapon or destructible evidence."

The extensive warrantless search of Chimel's home did not fit within this exception, because it was not needed to protect officer safety or to preserve evidence.

Four years later, in *United States v. Robinson* (1973), the Court applied the *Chimel* analysis in the context of a search of the arrestee's person. A police officer had arrested Robinson for driving with a revoked license. The officer conducted a patdown search and felt an object that he could not identify in Robinson's coat pocket. He removed the object, which turned out to be a crumpled cigarette package, and opened it. Inside were 14 capsules of heroin.

This Court [rejected] the notion that "case-by-case adjudication" was required to determine "whether or not there was present one of the reasons supporting the authority for a search of the person incident to a lawful arrest." As the Court explained, "[t]he authority to search the person incident to a lawful custodial arrest, while based upon the need to disarm and to discover evidence, does not depend on what a court may later decide was the probability in a particular arrest situation that weapons or evidence would in fact be found upon the person of the suspect." Instead, a "custodial arrest of a suspect based on probable cause is a reasonable intrusion under the Fourth Amendment; that intrusion being lawful, a search incident to the arrest requires no additional justification."

The Court thus concluded that the search of Robinson was reasonable even though there was no concern about the loss of evidence, and the arresting officer had no specific concern that Robinson might be armed. In doing so, the Court did not draw a line between a search of Robinson's person and a further examination of the cigarette pack found during that search. It merely noted that, "[h]aving in the course of a lawful search come upon the crumpled package of cigarettes, [the officer] was entitled to inspect it." A few years later, the Court clarified that this exception was limited to "personal property . . . immediately associated with the person of the arrestee."

The search incident to arrest trilogy concludes with *Arizona v. Gant,* which analyzed searches of an arrestee's vehicle. *Gant,* like *Robinson,* recognized that the *Chimel* concerns for officer safety and evidence preservation underlie the search incident to arrest exception. As a result, the Court concluded that *Chimel* could authorize police to search a vehicle "only when the arrestee is unsecured and within reaching distance of the passenger compartment at the time of the search." *Gant* added, however, an independent exception for a warrantless search of a vehicle's passenger compartment "when it is 'reasonable to believe evidence relevant to the crime of arrest might be found in the vehicle.'"

III

These cases require us to decide how the search incident to arrest doctrine applies to modern cell phones, which are now such a pervasive and insistent part of daily life that the proverbial visitor from Mars might conclude they were an important feature of human anatomy. A smart phone of the sort taken from Riley was unheard of ten years ago; a significant majority of American adults now own such phones. Even less sophisticated phones like Wurie's, which have already faded in popularity since Wurie was arrested in 2007, have been around for less than 15 years. Both phones are based on technology nearly inconceivable just a few decades ago, when *Chimel* and *Robinson* were decided.

Absent more precise guidance from the founding era, we generally determine whether to exempt a given type of search from the warrant requirement "by assessing, on the one hand, the degree to which it intrudes upon an individual's privacy and, on the other, the degree to which it is needed for the promotion of legitimate governmental interests." *[handwritten: balancing test]*

But while *Robinson*'s categorical rule strikes the appropriate balance in the context of physical objects, neither of its rationales has much force with respect to digital content on cell phones. On the government interest side, *Robinson* concluded that the two risks identified in *Chimel*—harm to officers and destruction of evidence—are present in all custodial arrests. There are no comparable risks when the search is of digital data. In addition, *Robinson* regarded any privacy interests retained by an individual after arrest as significantly diminished by the fact of the arrest itself. Cell phones, however, place vast quantities of personal information literally in the hands of individuals. A search of the information on a cell phone bears little resemblance to the type of brief physical search considered in *Robinson*.

We therefore decline to extend *Robinson* to searches of data on cell phones, and hold instead that officers must generally secure a warrant before conducting such a search.

A

We first consider each *Chimel* concern in turn.

Digital data stored on a cell phone cannot itself be used as a weapon to harm an arresting officer or to effectuate the arrestee's escape. Law enforcement officers remain free to examine the physical aspects of a phone to ensure that it will not be used as a weapon—say, to determine whether there is a razor blade hidden between the phone and its case. Once an officer has secured a phone and eliminated any potential physical threats, however, data on the phone can endanger no one.

Perhaps the same might have been said of the cigarette pack seized from Robinson's pocket. Once an officer gained control of the pack, it was unlikely that Robinson could have accessed the pack's contents. But unknown physical objects may always pose risks, no matter how slight, during the tense atmosphere of a custodial arrest. The officer in *Robinson* testified that he could not identify the objects in the cigarette pack but knew they were not cigarettes. Given that, a further search was a reasonable protective measure. No such unknowns exist with respect to digital data.

The United States and California both suggest that a search of cell phone data might help ensure officer safety in more indirect ways, for example by alerting officers that confederates of the arrestee are headed to the scene. There is undoubtedly a strong government interest in warning officers about such possibilities, but neither the United States nor California offers evidence to suggest that their concerns are based on actual experience. The proposed consideration would also represent a broadening of *Chimel*'s concern that an *arrestee himself* might grab a weapon and use it against an officer "to resist arrest or effect his escape." And any such threats from outside the arrest scene do not "lurk[ ] in all custodial arrests." Accordingly, the interest in protecting officer safety does not justify dispensing with the warrant requirement across the board.

The United States and California focus primarily on the second *Chimel* rationale: preventing the destruction of evidence.

Both Riley and Wurie concede that officers could have seized and secured their cell phones to prevent destruction of evidence while seeking a warrant. And once law enforcement officers have secured a cell phone, there is no longer any risk that the arrestee himself will be able to delete incriminating data from the phone.

The United States and California argue that information on a cell phone may nevertheless be vulnerable to two types of evidence destruction unique to digital data-remote wiping and data encryption. Remote wiping occurs when a phone, connected to a wireless network, receives a signal that erases stored data. This can happen when a third party sends a remote signal or when a phone is preprogrammed to delete data upon entering or leaving certain geographic areas (so-called "geofencing"). Encryption is a security feature that some modern cell phones use in addition to password protection. When such phones lock, data becomes protected by sophisticated encryption that renders a phone all but "unbreakable" unless police know the password.

As an initial matter, these broader concerns about the loss of evidence are distinct from *Chimel*'s focus on a defendant who responds to arrest by trying to conceal or destroy evidence within his reach. With respect to remote wiping, the Government's primary concern turns on the actions of third parties who are not present at the scene of arrest. And data encryption is even further afield. There, the Government focuses on the ordinary operation of a phone's security features, apart from *any* active attempt by a defendant or his associates to conceal or destroy evidence upon arrest.

We have also been given little reason to believe that either problem is prevalent. The briefing reveals only a couple of anecdotal examples of remote wiping triggered by an arrest. Similarly, the opportunities for officers to search a password-protected phone before data becomes encrypted are quite limited. Law enforcement officers are very unlikely to come upon such a phone in an unlocked state because most phones lock at the touch of a button or, as a default, after some very short period of inactivity. This may explain why the encryption argument was not made until the merits stage in this Court, and has never been considered by the Courts of Appeals.

Moreover, in situations in which an arrest might trigger a remote-wipe attempt or an officer discovers an unlocked phone, it is not clear that the ability to conduct a warrantless search would make much of a difference. The need to effect the arrest, secure the scene, and tend to other pressing matters means that law enforcement officers may well not be able to turn their attention to a cell phone right away. Cell phone data would be vulnerable to remote wiping from the time an individual anticipates arrest to the time any eventual search of the phone is completed, which might be at the station house hours later. Likewise, an officer who seizes a phone in an unlocked state might not be able to begin his search in the short time remaining before the phone locks and data becomes encrypted.

In any event, as to remote wiping, law enforcement is not without specific means to address the threat. Remote wiping can be fully prevented by disconnecting a phone from the network. There are at least two simple ways to do this: First, law enforcement officers can turn the phone off or remove its battery. Second, if they are concerned about encryption or other potential problems, they can leave a phone powered on and place it in an enclosure that isolates the phone from radio waves. They are essentially sandwich bags made of aluminum foil: cheap, lightweight, and easy to use. They may not be a complete answer to the problem, but at least for now they provide a reasonable response.

B

The United States asserts that a search of all data stored on a cell phone is "materially indistinguishable" from searches of physical items. That is like saying a ride on horseback is materially indistinguishable from a flight to the moon. Both are ways of getting from point A to point B, but little else justifies lumping them together. Modern cell phones, as a category, implicate privacy concerns far beyond those implicated by the search of a cigarette pack, a wallet, or a purse.

Cell phones differ in both a quantitative and a qualitative sense from other objects that might be kept on an arrestee's person. The term "cell phone" is itself misleading shorthand; many of these devices are in fact minicomputers that also happen to have the capacity to be used as a telephone. They could just as easily be called cameras, video players, rolodexes, calendars, tape recorders, libraries, diaries, albums, televisions, maps, or newspapers.

One of the most notable distinguishing features of modern cell phones is their immense storage capacity. Before cell phones, a search of a person was limited by physical realities and tended as a general matter to constitute only a narrow intrusion on privacy. Most people cannot lug around every piece of mail they have received for the past several months, every picture they have taken, or every book or article they have read — nor would they have any reason to attempt to do so. And if they did, they would have to drag behind them a trunk of the sort held to require a search warrant in *Chadwick*, rather than a container the size of the cigarette package in *Robinson*.

But the possible intrusion on privacy is not physically limited in the same way when it comes to cell phones. The current top-selling smart phone has a standard capacity of 16 gigabytes (and is available with up to 64 gigabytes). Sixteen gigabytes translates to millions of pages of text, thousands of pictures, or hundreds of videos. Cell phones couple that capacity with the ability to store many different types of information: Even the most basic phones that sell for less than $20 might hold photographs, picture messages, text messages, Internet browsing history, a calendar, a thousand-entry phone book, and so on. We expect that the gulf between physical practicability and digital capacity will only continue to widen in the future.

The storage capacity of cell phones has several interrelated consequences for privacy. First, a cell phone collects in one place many distinct types of information — an address, a note, a prescription, a bank statement, a video — that reveal much more in combination than any isolated record. Second, a cell phone's capacity allows even just one type of information to convey far more than previously possible. The sum of an individual's private life can be reconstructed through a thousand photographs labeled with dates, locations, and descriptions; the same cannot be said of a photograph or two of loved ones tucked into a wallet. Third, the data on a phone can date back to the purchase of the phone, or even earlier. A person might carry in his pocket a slip of paper reminding him to call Mr. Jones; he would not carry a record of all his communications with Mr. Jones for the past several months, as would routinely be kept on a phone.

Finally, there is an element of pervasiveness that characterizes cell phones but not physical records. Prior to the digital age, people did not typically carry a cache of sensitive personal information with them as they went about their day. Now it is the person who is not carrying a cell phone, with all that it contains, who is the exception. According to one poll, nearly three-quarters of smart phone users report being within five feet of their phones most of the time, with 12% admitting that they even use their phones in the shower. A decade ago police officers searching an arrestee might have occasionally stumbled across a highly personal item such as a diary. But those discoveries were likely to be few and far between. Today, by contrast, it is no exaggeration to say that many of the more than 90% of American adults who own a cell phone keep on their person a digital record of nearly every aspect of their lives — from the mundane to the intimate. Allowing the police to scrutinize such records on a routine basis is quite different from allowing them to search a personal item or two in the occasional case.

Although the data stored on a cell phone is distinguished from physical records by quantity alone, certain types of data are also qualitatively different. An Internet search and browsing history, for example, can be found on an Internet-enabled phone and could reveal an individual's private interests or concerns—perhaps a search for certain symptoms of disease, coupled with frequent visits to WebMD. Data on a cell phone can also reveal where a person has been. Historic location information is a standard feature on many smart phones and can reconstruct someone's specific movements down to the minute, not only around town but also within a particular building.

Mobile application software on a cell phone, or "apps," offer a range of tools for managing detailed information about all aspects of a person's life. There are apps for Democratic Party news and Republican Party news; apps for alcohol, drug, and gambling addictions; apps for sharing prayer requests; apps for tracking pregnancy symptoms; apps for planning your budget; apps for every conceivable hobby or pastime; apps for improving your romantic life. There are popular apps for buying or selling just about anything, and the records of such transactions may be accessible on the phone indefinitely. There are over a million apps available in each of the two major app stores; the phrase "there's an app for that" is now part of the popular lexicon. The average smart phone user has installed 33 apps, which together can form a revealing montage of the user's life.

To further complicate the scope of the privacy interests at stake, the data a user views on many modern cell phones may not in fact be stored on the device itself. Treating a cell phone as a container whose contents may be searched incident to an arrest is a bit strained as an initial matter. But the analogy crumbles entirely when a cell phone is used to access data located elsewhere, at the tap of a screen. That is what cell phones, with increasing frequency, are designed to do by taking advantage of "cloud computing." Cloud computing is the capacity of Internet-connected devices to display data stored on remote servers rather than on the device itself. Cell phone users often may not know whether particular information is stored on the device or in the cloud, and it generally makes little difference. Moreover, the same type of data may be stored locally on the device for one user and in the cloud for another.

The United States concedes that the search incident to arrest exception may not be stretched to cover a search of files accessed remotely—that is, a search of files stored in the cloud. Such a search would be like finding a key in a suspect's pocket and arguing that it allowed law enforcement to unlock and search a house. But officers searching a phone's data would not typically know whether the information they are viewing was stored locally at the time of the arrest or has been pulled from the cloud.

Although the Government recognizes the problem, its proposed solutions are unclear. It suggests that officers could disconnect a phone from the network before searching the device—the very solution whose feasibility it contested with respect to the threat of remote wiping. Alternatively, the Government proposes that law enforcement agencies "develop protocols to address" concerns raised by cloud computing. Probably a good idea, but the Founders did not fight a revolution to gain the right to government agency protocols. The possibility that a search might extend well beyond papers and effects in the physical proximity of an arrestee is yet another reason that the privacy interests here dwarf those in *Robinson*.

C

Apart from their arguments for a direct extension of *Robinson*, the United States and California offer various fallback options for permitting warrantless cell phone searches under certain circumstances. Each of the proposals is flawed and contravenes our general preference to provide clear guidance to law enforcement through categorical rules.

The United States first proposes that the *Gant* standard be imported from the vehicle context, allowing a warrantless search of an arrestee's cell phone whenever it is reasonable to believe that the phone contains evidence of the crime of arrest. But *Gant* relied on "circumstances unique to the vehicle context" to endorse a search solely for the purpose of gathering evidence. [T]hose unique circumstances are "a reduced expectation of privacy" and "heightened law enforcement needs" when it comes to motor vehicles. For reasons that we have explained, cell phone searches bear neither of those characteristics.

At any rate, a *Gant* standard would prove no practical limit at all when it comes to cell phone searches. In the vehicle context, *Gant* generally protects against searches for evidence of past crimes. In the cell phone context, however, it is reasonable to expect that incriminating information will be found on a phone regardless of when the crime occurred.

We also reject the United States' final suggestion that officers should always be able to search a phone's call log, as they did in Wurie's case. The Government relies on *Smith v. Maryland* (1979), which held that no warrant was required to use a pen register at telephone company premises to identify numbers dialed by a particular caller. The Court in that case, however, concluded that the use of a pen register was not a "search" at all under the Fourth Amendment. There is no dispute here that the officers engaged in a search of Wurie's cell phone. Moreover, call logs typically contain more than just phone numbers; they include any identifying information that an individual might add, such as the label "my house" in Wurie's case.

Finally, at oral argument California suggested a different limiting principle, under which officers could search cell phone data if they could have obtained the same information from a pre-digital counterpart. But the fact that a search in the pre-digital era could have turned up a photograph or two in a wallet does not justify a search of thousands of photos in a digital gallery. The fact that someone could have tucked a paper bank statement in a pocket does not justify a search of every bank statement from the last five years. And to make matters worse, such an analogue test would allow law enforcement to search a range of items contained on a phone, even though people would be unlikely to carry such a variety of information in physical form.

IV

We cannot deny that our decision today will have an impact on the ability of law enforcement to combat crime. Cell phones have become important tools in facilitating coordination and communication among members of criminal enterprises, and can provide valuable incriminating information about dangerous criminals. Privacy comes at a cost.

Our holding, of course, is not that the information on a cell phone is immune from search; it is instead that a warrant is generally required before such a search, even when a cell phone is seized incident to arrest. Our cases have historically recognized that the warrant requirement is "an important working part of our machinery of government," not merely "an inconvenience to be somehow 'weighed' against the claims of police efficiency." Recent technological advances similar to those discussed here have, in addition, made the process of obtaining a warrant itself more efficient.

Moreover, even though the search incident to arrest exception does not apply to cell phones, other case-specific exceptions may still justify a warrantless search of a particular phone. "One well-recognized exception applies when "'the exigencies of the situation" make the needs of law enforcement so compelling that [a] warrantless search is objectively reasonable under the Fourth Amendment.'" Such exigencies could include the need to prevent the imminent destruction of evidence in individual cases, to pursue a fleeing suspect, and to assist persons who are seriously injured or are threatened with imminent injury.

In light of the availability of the exigent circumstances exception, there is no reason to believe that law enforcement officers will not be able to address some of the more extreme hypotheticals that have been suggested: a suspect texting an accomplice who, it is feared, is preparing to detonate a bomb, or a child abductor who may have information about the child's location on his cell phone.

Modern cell phones are not just another technological convenience. With all they contain and all they may reveal, they hold for many Americans "the privacies of life," The fact that technology now allows an individual to carry such information in his hand does not make the information any less worthy of the protection for which the Founders fought. Our answer to the question of what police must do before searching a cell phone seized incident to an arrest is accordingly simple — get a warrant.

Justice ALITO, concurring in part and concurring in the judgment.

I agree with the Court that law enforcement officers, in conducting a lawful search incident to arrest, must generally obtain a warrant before searching information stored or accessible on a cell phone. I write separately to address two points.

1st

First, I am not convinced at this time that the ancient rule on searches incident to arrest is based exclusively (or even primarily) on the need to protect the safety of arresting officers and the need to prevent the destruction of evidence.

2nd

This brings me to my second point. While I agree with the holding of the Court, I would reconsider the question presented here if either Congress or state legislatures, after assessing the legitimate needs of law enforcement and the privacy interests of cell phone owners, enact legislation that draws reasonable distinctions based on categories of information or perhaps other variables.

Modern cell phones are of great value for both lawful and unlawful purposes. They can be used in committing many serious crimes, and they present new and difficult law enforcement problems. At the same time, because of the role that these devices have come to play in contemporary life, searching their contents implicates very sensitive privacy interests that this Court is poorly positioned to understand and evaluate.

In light of these developments, it would be very unfortunate if privacy protection in the 21st century were left primarily to the federal courts using the blunt instrument of the Fourth Amendment. Legislatures, elected by the people, are in a better position than we are to assess and respond to the changes that have already occurred and those that almost certainly will take place in the future.

7. Consent (casebook p. 201)

In *Georgia v. Randolph* (casebook p. 208), the Court held that if two co-occupants of a dwelling are both present and one refuses consent for a search, the police do not have valid consent. The obvious question is what if the police wait until the non-consenting occupant is no longer present; can the police then get valid consent from the other occupant? That was the issue in *Fernandez v. California*.

Fernandez v. California
134 S. Ct. 1126 (2014)

Justice ALITO delivered the opinion of the Court.

Our cases firmly establish that police officers may search jointly occupied premises if one of the occupants consents. In *Georgia v. Randolph* (2006), we recognized a narrow exception to this rule, holding that the consent of one occupant is insufficient when another occupant is present and objects to the search. In this case, we consider whether *Randolph* applies if the objecting occupant is absent when another occupant consents. Our opinion in *Randolph* took great pains to emphasize that its holding was limited to situations in which the objecting occupant is physically present. We therefore refuse to extend *Randolph* to the very different situation in this case, where consent was provided by an abused woman well after her male partner had been removed from the apartment they shared.

I

The events involved in this case occurred in Los Angeles in October 2009. After observing Abel Lopez cash a check, petitioner Walter Fernandez approached Lopez and asked about the neighborhood in which he lived. When Lopez responded that he was from Mexico, Fernandez laughed and told Lopez that he was in territory ruled by the "D.F.S.," *i.e.*, the "Drifters" gang. Petitioner then pulled out a knife and pointed it at Lopez' chest. Lopez raised his hand in self-defense, and petitioner cut him on the wrist.

Lopez ran from the scene and called 911 for help, but petitioner whistled, and four men emerged from a nearby apartment building and attacked Lopez. After knocking him to the ground, they hit and kicked him and took his cell phone and his wallet, which contained $400 in cash.

A police dispatch reported the incident and mentioned the possibility of gang involvement, and two Los Angeles police officers, Detective Clark and Officer Cirrito, drove to an alley frequented by members of the Drifters. A man who appeared scared walked by the officers and said: "'[T]he guy is in the apartment.'" The officers then observed a man run through the alley and into the building to which the man was pointing. A minute or two later, the officers heard sounds of screaming and fighting coming from that building.

After backup arrived, the officers knocked on the door of the apartment unit from which the screams had been heard. Roxanne Rojas answered the door. She was holding a baby and appeared to be crying. Her face was red, and she had a large bump on her nose. The officers also saw blood on her shirt and hand from what appeared to be a fresh injury. Rojas told the police that she had been in a fight. Officer Cirrito asked if anyone else was in the apartment, and Rojas said that her 4-year-old son was the only other person present.

After Officer Cirrito asked Rojas to step out of the apartment so that he could conduct a protective sweep, petitioner appeared at the door wearing only boxer shorts. Apparently agitated, petitioner stepped forward and said, "You don't have any right to come in here. I know my rights.'" Suspecting that petitioner had assaulted Rojas, the officers removed him from the apartment and then placed him under arrest. Lopez identified petitioner as his initial attacker, and petitioner was taken to the police station for booking.

Approximately one hour after petitioner's arrest, Detective Clark returned to the apartment and informed Rojas that petitioner had been arrested. Detective Clark requested and received both oral and written consent from Rojas to search the premises. In the apartment, the police found Drifters gang paraphernalia, a butterfly knife, clothing worn by the robbery suspect, and ammunition. Rojas' young son also showed the officers where petitioner had hidden a sawed-off shotgun.

II

The Fourth Amendment prohibits unreasonable searches and seizures and provides that a warrant may not be issued without probable cause, but "the text of the Fourth Amendment does not specify when a search warrant must be obtained." Our cases establish that a warrant is generally required for a search of a home, but "the ultimate touchstone of the Fourth Amendment is 'reasonableness.'" And certain categories of permissible warrantless searches have long been recognized.

Consent searches occupy one of these categories. "Consent searches are part of the standard investigatory techniques of law enforcement agencies" and are "a constitutionally permissible and wholly legitimate aspect of effective police activity." It would be unreasonable—indeed, absurd—to require police officers to obtain a warrant when the sole owner or occupant of a house or apartment voluntarily consents to a search. The owner of a home has a right to allow others to enter and examine the premises, and there is no reason why the owner should not be permitted to extend this same privilege to police officers if that is the owner's choice. Where the owner believes that he or she is under suspicion, the owner may want the police to search the premises so that their suspicions are dispelled. This may be particularly important where the owner has a strong interest in the apprehension of the perpetrator of a crime and believes that the suspicions of the police are deflecting the course of their investigation. An owner may want the police to search even where they lack probable cause, and if a warrant were always required, this could not be done. And even where the police could establish probable cause, requiring a warrant despite the owner's consent would needlessly inconvenience everyone involved—not only the officers and the magistrate but also the occupant of the premises, who would generally either be compelled or would feel a need to stay until the search was completed.

While it is clear that a warrantless search is reasonable when the sole occupant of a house or apartment consents, what happens when there are two or more occupants? Must they all consent? Must they all be asked? Is consent by one occupant enough? The Court faced that problem 40 years ago in *United States v. Matlock* (1974). In that case, Matlock and a woman named Graff were living together in a house that was also occupied by several of Graff's siblings and by her mother, who had rented the house. While in the front yard of the house, Matlock was arrested for bank robbery and was placed in a squad car. Although the police could have easily asked him for consent to search the room that he and Graff shared, they did not do so. Instead, they knocked on the door and obtained Graff's permission to search. The search yielded incriminating evidence, which the defendant sought to suppress, but this Court held that Graff's consent justified the warrantless search. As the Court put it, "the consent of one who possesses common authority over premises or effects is valid as against the absent, noncon-senting person with whom that authority is shared."

While consent by one resident of jointly occupied premises is generally sufficient to justify a warrantless search, we recognized a narrow exception to this rule in *Georgia v. Randolph* (2006). In that case, police officers responded to the Randolphs' home after receiving a report of a domestic dispute. When the officers arrived, Janet Randolph informed the officers that her estranged husband, Scott Randolph, was a cocaine user and that there were "items of drug evidence" in the house. The officers first asked Scott for consent to search, but he "unequivo-cally refused." The officers then turned to Janet, and she consented to the search, which produced evidence that was later used to convict Scott for possession of cocaine.

Without questioning the prior holdings in *Matlock* and *Rodriguez*, this Court held that Janet Randolph's consent was insufficient under the circumstances to justify the warrantless search. The Court reiterated the proposition that a person who shares a residence with others assumes the risk that "any one of them may admit visitors, with the consequence that a guest obnoxious to one may neverthe-less be admitted in his absence by another." But the Court held that "*a physically present inhabitant's* express refusal of consent to a police search [of his home] is dispositive as to him, regardless of the consent of a fellow occupant."

The Court's opinion went to great lengths to make clear that its holding was limited to situations in which the objecting occupant is present. Again and again, the opinion of the Court stressed this controlling factor.

III

In this case, petitioner was not present when Rojas consented, but petitioner still contends that *Randolph* is controlling. He advances two main arguments. First, he claims that his absence should not matter since he was absent only because the police had taken him away. Second, he maintains that it was sufficient that he objected to the search while he was still present. Such an objection, he says, should remain in effect until the objecting party "no longer wishes to keep the police out of his home." Neither of these arguments is sound.

We first consider the argument that the presence of the objecting occupant is not necessary when the police are responsible for his absence. In *Randolph*, the Court suggested in dictum that consent by one occupant might not be sufficient if "there is evidence that the police have removed the potentially objecting tenant from the entrance for the sake of avoiding a possible objection." We do not believe the statement should be read to suggest that improper motive may invalidate objectively justified removal. Hence, it does not govern here.

The *Randolph* dictum is best understood not to require an inquiry into the subjective intent of officers who detain or arrest a potential objector but instead to refer to situations in which the removal of the potential objector is not objectively reasonable. As petitioner acknowledges, our Fourth Amendment cases "have repeatedly rejected" a subjective approach.

Petitioner does not claim that the *Randolph* Court meant to break from this consistent practice, and we do not think that it did. And once it is recognized that the test is one of objective reasonableness, petitioner's argument collapses. He does not contest the fact that the police had reasonable grounds for removing him from the apartment so that they could speak with Rojas, an apparent victim of domestic violence, outside of petitioner's potentially intimidating presence. In fact, he does not even contest the existence of probable cause to place him under arrest. We therefore hold that an occupant who is absent due to a lawful detention or arrest stands in the same shoes as an occupant who is absent for any other reason.

This conclusion does not "make a mockery of *Randolph*, "as petitioner protests. It simply accepts *Randolph* on its own terms. The *Randolph* holding unequivocally requires the presence of the objecting occupant in every situation other than the one mentioned in the dictum discussed above.

This brings us to petitioner's second argument, that his objection, made at the threshold of the premises that the police wanted to search, remained effective until he changed his mind and withdrew his objection. This argument is inconsistent with *Randolph*'s reasoning in at least two important ways. First, the argument cannot be squared with the "widely shared social expectations" or "customary social usage" upon which the *Randolph* holding was based. When the objecting occupant is standing at the threshold saying "stay out," a friend or visitor invited to enter by another occupant can expect at best an uncomfortable scene and at worst violence if he or she tries to brush past the objector. But when the objector is not on the scene (and especially when it is known that the objector will not return during the course of the visit), the friend or visitor is much more likely to accept the invitation to enter. Thus, petitioner's argument is inconsistent with *Randolph*'s reasoning.

Second, petitioner's argument would create the very sort of practical complications that *Randolph* sought to avoid. The rule that petitioner would have us adopt would produce a plethora of practical problems. For one thing, there is the question of duration. Petitioner argues that an objection, once made, should last until it is withdrawn by the objector, but such a rule would be unreasonable. Suppose that a husband and wife owned a house as joint tenants and that the husband, after objecting to a search of the house, was convicted and sentenced to a 15-year prison term. Under petitioner's proposed rule, the wife would be unable to consent to a search of the house 10 years after the date on which her husband objected. We refuse to stretch *Randolph* to such strange lengths.

Nor are we persuaded to hold that an objection lasts for a "reasonable" time. "[I]t is certainly unusual for this Court to set forth precise time limits governing police action," and what interval of time would be reasonable in this context? A week? A month? A year? Ten years?

2. Searches and Seizures

Petitioner's rule would also require the police and ultimately the courts to determine whether, after the passage of time, an objector still had "common authority" over the premises, and this would often be a tricky question. Suppose that an incarcerated objector and a consenting co-occupant were joint tenants on a lease. If the objector, after incarceration, stopped paying rent, would he still have "common authority," and would his objection retain its force? Would it be enough that his name remained on the lease? Would the result be different if the objecting and consenting lessees had an oral month-to-month tenancy?

Another problem concerns the procedure needed to register a continuing objection. Would it be necessary for an occupant to object while police officers are at the door? If presence at the time of consent is not needed, would an occupant have to be present at the premises when the objection was made? Could an objection be made pre-emptively? Could a person like Scott Randolph, suspecting that his estranged wife might invite the police to view his drug stash and paraphernalia, register an objection in advance? Could this be done by posting a sign in front of the house? Could a standing objection be registered by serving notice on the chief of police?

Finally, there is the question of the particular law enforcement officers who would be bound by an objection. Would this set include just the officers who were present when the objection was made? Would it also apply to other officers working on the same investigation? Would it extend to officers who were unaware of the objection? How about officers assigned to different but arguably related cases? Would it be limited by law enforcement agency?

If *Randolph* is taken at its word—that it applies only when the objector is standing in the door saying "stay out" when officers propose to make a consent search—all of these problems disappear.

Petitioner argues strenuously that his expansive interpretation of *Randolph* would not hamper law enforcement because in most cases where officers have probable cause to arrest a physically present objector they also have probable cause to search the premises that the objector does not want them to enter, but this argument misunderstands the constitutional status of consent searches. A warrantless consent search is reasonable and thus consistent with the Fourth Amendment irrespective of the availability of a warrant. Even with modern technological advances, the warrant procedure imposes burdens on the officers who wish to search, the magistrate who must review the warrant application, and the party willing to give consent. When a warrantless search is justified, requiring the police to obtain a warrant may "unjustifiably interfer[e] with legitimate law enforcement strategies." Such a requirement may also impose an unmerited burden on the person who consents to an immediate search, since the warrant application procedure entails delay. Putting the exception the Court adopted in *Randolph* to one side, the lawful occupant of a house or apartment should have the right to invite the police to enter the dwelling and conduct a search. Any other rule would trample on the rights of the occupant who is willing to consent.

Denying someone in Rojas' position the right to allow the police to enter *her* home would also show disrespect for her independence. Having beaten Rojas, petitioner would bar her from controlling access to her own home until such time as he chose to relent. The Fourth Amendment does not give him that power.

Justice SCALIA, concurring.

Like Justice Thomas, I believe *Georgia v. Randolph* was wrongly decided. I nonetheless join the Court's opinion because it is a faithful application of *Randolph*. I write separately to address the argument that the search of petitioner's shared apartment violated the Fourth Amendment because he had a right under property law to exclude the police.

I would therefore find this a more difficult case if it were established that property law did not give petitioner's cotenant the right to admit visitors over petitioner's objection. That difficulty does not arise, however, because the authorities cited by the *amicus* association fail to establish that a guest would commit a trespass if one of two joint tenants invited the guest to enter and the other tenant forbade the guest to do so. Indeed, what limited authority there is on the subject points to the opposite conclusion. There accordingly is no basis for us to conclude that the police infringed on any property right of petitioner's when they entered the premises with his cotenant's consent.

Justice THOMAS, concurring.

I join the opinion of the Court, which faithfully applies *Georgia v. Randolph*. I write separately to make clear the extent of my disagreement with *Randolph*.

I dissented in *Randolph* because the facts of that case did not implicate a Fourth Amendment search and never should have been analyzed as such.

Justice GINSBURG, with whom Justice SOTOMAYOR and Justice KAGAN join, dissenting.

Instead of adhering to the warrant requirement, today's decision tells the police they may dodge it, nevermind ample time to secure the approval of a neutral magistrate. Suppressing the warrant requirement, the Court shrinks to petite size our holding in *Georgia v. Randolph*, that "a physically present inhabitant's express refusal of consent to a police search [of his home] is dispositive as to him, regardless of the consent of a fellow occupant."

I

This case calls for a straightforward application of *Randolph*. The police officers in *Randolph* were confronted with a scenario closely resembling the situation presented here. After Walter Fernandez, while physically present at his home, rebuffed the officers' request to come in, the police removed him from the premises and then arrested him, albeit with cause to believe he had assaulted his cohabitant, Roxanne Rojas. At the time of the arrest, Rojas said nothing to contradict Fernandez' refusal. About an hour later, however, and with no attempt to obtain a search warrant, the police returned to the apartment and prevailed upon Rojas to sign a consent form authorizing search of the premises.

The circumstances triggering "the Fourth Amendment's traditional hostility to police entry into a home without a warrant," are at least as salient here as they were in *Randolph*. In both cases, "[t]he search at issue was a search solely for evidence"; "[t]he objecting party," while on the premises, "made his objection [to police entry] known clearly and directly to the officers seeking to enter the [residence]"; and "the officers might easily have secured the premises and sought a warrant permitting them to enter." Here, moreover, with the objector in custody, there was scant danger to persons on the premises, or risk that evidence might be destroyed or concealed, pending request for, and receipt of, a warrant.

Despite these marked similarities, the Court removes this case from *Randolph*'s ambit. The Court does so principally by seizing on the fact that Fernandez, unlike Scott Randolph, was no longer present and objecting when the police obtained the co-occupant's consent. But Fernandez *was* present when he stated his objection to the would-be searchers in no uncertain terms. The officers could scarcely have forgotten, one hour later, that Fernandez refused consent while physically present. That express, on-premises objection should have been "dispositive as to him."

Next, the Court cautions, applying *Randolph* to these facts would pose "a plethora of practical problems." For instance, the Court asks, must a cotenant's objection, once registered, be respected indefinitely? Yet it blinks reality to suppose that Fernandez, by withholding consent, could stop police in their tracks eternally. To mount the prosecution eventuating in a conviction, of course, the State would first need to obtain incriminating evidence, and could get it easily simply by applying for a warrant. Warrant in police hands, the Court's practical problems disappear.

Indeed, as the Court acknowledges, reading *Randolph* to require continuous physical presence poses administrative difficulties of its own. Does an occupant's refusal to consent lose force as soon as she absents herself from the doorstep, even if only for a moment? Are the police free to enter the instant after the objector leaves the door to retire for a nap, answer the phone, use the bathroom, or speak to another officer outside? Hypothesized practical considerations, in short, provide no cause for today's drastic reduction of *Randolph*'s holding and attendant disregard for the warrant requirement.

II

In its zeal to diminish *Randolph*, today's decision overlooks the warrant requirement's venerable role as the "bulwark of Fourth Amendment protection." Reducing *Randolph* to a "narrow exception," the Court declares the main rule to be that "consent by one resident of jointly occupied premises is generally sufficient to justify a warrantless search." That declaration has it backwards, for consent searches themselves are a "'jealously and carefully drawn' exception" to "the Fourth Amendment rule ordinarily prohibiting the warrantless entry of a person's house as unreasonable *per se*."

In this case, the police could readily have obtained a warrant to search the shared residence. The Court does not dispute this, but instead disparages the warrant requirement as inconvenient, burdensome, entailing delay "[e]ven with modern technological advances." Shut from the Court's sight is the ease and speed with which search warrants nowadays can be obtained.

Although the police have probable cause and could obtain a warrant with dispatch, if they can gain the consent of someone other than the suspect, why should the law insist on the formality of a warrant? Because the Framers saw the neutral magistrate as an essential part of the criminal process shielding all of us, good or bad, saint or sinner, from unchecked police activity.

A final word is in order about the Court's reference to Rojas' autonomy, which, in its view, is best served by allowing her consent to trump an abusive cohabitant's objection. Rojas' situation is not distinguishable from Janet Randolph's in this regard. If a person's health and safety are threatened by a domestic abuser, exigent circumstances would justify immediate removal of the abuser from the premises, as happened here. As the Court understood in *Randolph*, however, the specter of domestic abuse hardly necessitates the diminution of the Fourth Amendment rights at stake here.

For the reasons stated, I would honor the Fourth Amendment's warrant requirement and hold that Fernandez' objection to the search did not become null upon his arrest and removal from the scene.

8. Searches When There Are Special Needs? (casebook p. 212)

h. (new) DNA Testing of Those Arrested

May the police take DNA from those arrested for purposes of investigating crimes other than the one for which the person was arrested?

Maryland v. King
133 S. Ct. 1958 (2013)

Justice KENNEDY delivered the opinion of the Court.

In 2003 a man concealing his face and armed with a gun broke into a woman's home in Salisbury, Maryland. He raped her. The police were unable to identify or apprehend the assailant based on any detailed description or other evidence they then had, but they did obtain from the victim a sample of the perpetrator's DNA.

2. Searches and Seizures

In 2009 Alonzo King was arrested in Wicomico County, Maryland, and charged with first- and second-degree assault for menacing a group of people with a shotgun. As part of a routine booking procedure for serious offenses, his DNA sample was taken by applying a cotton swab or filter paper—known as a buccal swab—to the inside of his cheeks. The DNA was found to match the DNA taken from the Salisbury rape victim. King was tried and convicted for the rape. Additional DNA samples were taken from him and used in the rape trial, but there seems to be no doubt that it was the DNA from the cheek sample taken at the time he was booked in 2009 that led to his first having been linked to the rape and charged with its commission.

The Court of Appeals of Maryland, on review of King's rape conviction, ruled that the DNA taken when King was booked for the 2009 charge was an unlawful seizure because obtaining and using the cheek swab was an unreasonable search of the person. It set the rape conviction aside. This Court granted certiorari and now reverses the judgment of the Maryland court.

I

When King was arrested on April 10, 2009, for menacing a group of people with a shotgun and charged in state court with both first- and second-degree assault, he was processed for detention in custody at the Wicomico County Central Booking facility. Booking personnel used a cheek swab to take the DNA sample from him pursuant to provisions of the Maryland DNA Collection Act (or Act).

On July 13, 2009, King's DNA record was uploaded to the Maryland DNA database, and three weeks later, on August 4, 2009, his DNA profile was matched to the DNA sample collected in the unsolved 2003 rape case. Once the DNA was matched to King, detectives presented the forensic evidence to a grand jury, which indicted him for the rape. Detectives obtained a search warrant and took a second sample of DNA from King, which again matched the evidence from the rape.

II

The advent of DNA technology is one of the most significant scientific advancements of our era. The full potential for use of genetic markers in medicine and science is still being explored, but the utility of DNA identification in the criminal justice system is already undisputed. Since the first use of forensic DNA analysis to catch a rapist and murderer in England in 1986, see J. Butler, Fundamentals of Forensic DNA Typing 5 (2009) (hereinafter Butler), law enforcement, the defense bar, and the courts have acknowledged DNA testing's "unparalleled ability both to exonerate the wrongly convicted and to identify the guilty. It has the potential to significantly improve both the criminal justice system and police investigative practices."

The current standard for forensic DNA testing relies on an analysis of the chromosomes located within the nucleus of all human cells. "The DNA material in chromosomes is composed of 'coding' and 'noncoding' regions. The coding regions are known as *genes* and contain the information necessary for a cell to make proteins. . . . Non-protein-coding regions . . . are not related directly to making proteins, [and] have been referred to as 'junk' DNA." The adjective "junk" may mislead the layperson, for in fact this is the DNA region used with near certainty to identify a person. The term apparently is intended to indicate that this particular noncoding region, while useful and even dispositive for purposes like identity, does not show more far-reaching and complex characteristics like genetic traits.

Many of the patterns found in DNA are shared among all people, so forensic analysis focuses on "repeated DNA sequences scattered throughout the human genome," known as "short tandem repeats" (STRs). The alternative possibilities for the size and frequency of these STRs at any given point along a strand of DNA are known as "alleles," *id.*, at 25; and multiple alleles are analyzed in order to ensure that a DNA profile matches only one individual. Future refinements may improve present technology, but even now STR analysis makes it "possible to determine whether a biological tissue matches a suspect with near certainty."

The Act authorizes Maryland law enforcement authorities to collect DNA samples from "an individual who is charged with . . . a crime of violence or an attempt to commit a crime of violence; or . . . burglary or an attempt to commit burglary." Maryland law defines a crime of violence to include murder, rape, first-degree assault, kidnaping, arson, sexual assault, and a variety of other serious crimes. Once taken, a DNA sample may not be processed or placed in a database before the individual is arraigned (unless the individual consents). It is at this point that a judicial officer ensures that there is probable cause to detain the arrestee on a qualifying serious offense. If "all qualifying criminal charges are determined to be unsupported by probable cause . . . the DNA sample shall be immediately destroyed." DNA samples are also destroyed if "a criminal action begun against the individual . . . does not result in a conviction," "the conviction is finally reversed or vacated and no new trial is permitted," or "the individual is granted an unconditional pardon."

The Act also limits the information added to a DNA database and how it may be used. Specifically, "[o]nly DNA records that directly relate to the identification of individuals shall be collected and stored." No purpose other than identification is permissible: "A person may not willfully test a DNA sample for information that does not relate to the identification of individuals as specified in this subtitle." Tests for familial matches are also prohibited.

Respondent's DNA was collected in this case using a common procedure known as a "buccal swab." "Buccal cell collection involves wiping a small piece of filter paper or a cotton swab similar to a Q-tip against the inside cheek of an individual's mouth to collect some skin cells." The procedure is quick and painless. The swab touches inside an arrestee's mouth, but it requires no "surgical intrusio[n] beneath the skin," and it poses no "threa[t] to the health or safety" of arrestees.

B

Respondent's identification as the rapist resulted in part through the operation of a national project to standardize collection and storage of DNA profiles. Authorized by Congress and supervised by the Federal Bureau of Investigation, the Combined DNA Index System (CODIS) connects DNA laboratories at the local, state, and national level. Since its authorization in 1994, the CODIS system has grown to include all 50 States and a number of federal agencies. CODIS collects DNA profiles provided by local laboratories taken from arrestees, convicted offenders, and forensic evidence found at crime scenes.

All 50 States require the collection of DNA from felony convicts, and respondent does not dispute the validity of that practice. Twenty-eight States and the Federal Government have adopted laws similar to the Maryland Act authorizing the collection of DNA from some or all arrestees. Although those statutes vary in their particulars, such as what charges require a DNA sample, their similarity means that this case implicates more than the specific Maryland law. At issue is a standard, expanding technology already in widespread use throughout the Nation.

III

A

Although the DNA swab procedure used here presents a question the Court has not yet addressed, the framework for deciding the issue is well established. It can be agreed that using a buccal swab on the inner tissues of a person's cheek in order to obtain DNA samples is a search. Virtually any "intrusio[n] into the human body," *Schmerber v. California* (1966), will work an invasion of "'cherished personal security' that is subject to constitutional scrutiny."

A buccal swab is a far more gentle process than a venipuncture to draw blood. It involves but a light touch on the inside of the cheek; and although it can be deemed a search within the body of the arrestee, it requires no "surgical intrusions beneath the skin." The fact than an intrusion is negligible is of central relevance to determining reasonableness, although it is still a search as the law defines that term.

B

To say that the Fourth Amendment applies here is the beginning point, not the end of the analysis. "[T]he Fourth Amendment's proper function is to constrain, not against all intrusions as such, but against intrusions which are not justified in the circumstances, or which are made in an improper manner." "As the text of the Fourth Amendment indicates, the ultimate measure of the constitutionality of a governmental search is 'reasonableness.'" In giving content to the inquiry whether an intrusion is reasonable, the Court has preferred "some quantum of individualized suspicion . . . [as] a prerequisite to a constitutional search or seizure. But the Fourth Amendment imposes no irreducible requirement of such suspicion."

The Maryland DNA Collection Act provides that, in order to obtain a DNA sample, all arrestees charged with serious crimes must furnish the sample on a buccal swab applied, as noted, to the inside of the cheeks. The arrestee is already in valid police custody for a serious offense supported by probable cause. The DNA collection is not subject to the judgment of officers whose perspective might be "colored by their primary involvement in 'the often competitive enterprise of ferreting out crime.'" Here, the search effected by the buccal swab of respondent falls within the category of cases this Court has analyzed by reference to the proposition that the "touchstone of the Fourth Amendment is reasonableness, not individualized suspicion."

Even if a warrant is not required, a search is not beyond Fourth Amendment scrutiny; for it must be reasonable in its scope and manner of execution. Urgent government interests are not a license for indiscriminate police behavior. To say that no warrant is required is merely to acknowledge that "rather than employing a *per se* rule of unreasonableness, we balance the privacy-related and law enforcement-related concerns to determine if the intrusion was reasonable." This application of "traditional standards of reasonableness" requires a court to weigh "the promotion of legitimate governmental interests" against "the degree to which [the search] intrudes upon an individual's privacy." An assessment of reasonableness to determine the lawfulness of requiring this class of arrestees to provide a DNA sample is central to the instant case.

IV

A

The legitimate government interest served by the Maryland DNA Collection Act is one that is well established: the need for law enforcement officers in a safe and accurate way to process and identify the persons and possessions they must take into custody. It is beyond dispute that "probable cause provides legal justification for arresting a person suspected of crime, and for a brief period of detention to take the administrative steps incident to arrest." Also uncontested is the "right on the part of the Government, always recognized under English and American law, to search the person of the accused when legally arrested."

The "routine administrative procedure[s] at a police station house incident to booking and jailing the suspect" derive from different origins and have different constitutional justifications than, say, the search of a place; for the search of a place not incident to an arrest depends on the "fair probability that contraband or evidence of a crime will be found in a particular place." The interests are further different when an individual is formally processed into police custody. Then "the law is in the act of subjecting the body of the accused to its physical dominion." When probable cause exists to remove an individual from the normal channels of society and hold him in legal custody, DNA identification plays a critical role in serving those interests.

2. Searches and Seizures

First, "[i]n every criminal case, it is known and must be known who has been arrested and who is being tried." An individual's identity is more than just his name or Social Security number, and the government's interest in identification goes beyond ensuring that the proper name is typed on the indictment. Identity has never been considered limited to the name on the arrestee's birth certificate. In fact, a name is of little value compared to the real interest in identification at stake when an individual is brought into custody. "It is a well recognized aspect of criminal conduct that the perpetrator will take unusual steps to conceal not only his conduct, but also his identity. Disguises used while committing a crime may be supplemented or replaced by changed names, and even changed physical features."

A suspect's criminal history is a critical part of his identity that officers should know when processing him for detention. Police already seek this crucial identifying information. They use routine and accepted means as varied as comparing the suspect's booking photograph to sketch artists' depictions of persons of interest, showing his mugshot to potential witnesses, and of course making a computerized comparison of the arrestee's fingerprints against electronic databases of known criminals and unsolved crimes. In this respect the only difference between DNA analysis and the accepted use of fingerprint databases is the unparalleled accuracy DNA provides.

The task of identification necessarily entails searching public and police records based on the identifying information provided by the arrestee to see what is already known about him. The DNA collected from arrestees is an irrefutable identification of the person from whom it was taken. Like a fingerprint, the 13 CODIS loci are not themselves evidence of any particular crime, in the way that a drug test can by itself be evidence of illegal narcotics use. A DNA profile is useful to the police because it gives them a form of identification to search the records already in their valid possession. In this respect the use of DNA for identification is no different than matching an arrestee's face to a wanted poster of a previously unidentified suspect; or matching tattoos to known gang symbols to reveal a criminal affiliation; or matching the arrestee's fingerprints to those recovered from a crime scene. DNA is another metric of identification used to connect the arrestee with his or her public persona, as reflected in records of his or her actions that are available to the police. Those records may be linked to the arrestee by a variety of relevant forms of identification, including name, alias, date and time of previous convictions and the name then used, photograph, Social Security number, or CODIS profile. These data, found in official records, are checked as a routine matter to produce a more comprehensive record of the suspect's complete identity. Finding occurrences of the arrestee's CODIS profile in outstanding cases is consistent with this common practice. It uses a different form of identification than a name or fingerprint, but its function is the same.

Second, law enforcement officers bear a responsibility for ensuring that the custody of an arrestee does not create inordinate "risks for facility staff, for the existing detainee population, and for a new detainee." DNA identification can provide untainted information to those charged with detaining suspects and detaining the property of any felon. For these purposes officers must know the type of person whom they are detaining, and DNA allows them to make critical choices about how to proceed.

Third, looking forward to future stages of criminal prosecution, "the Government has a substantial interest in ensuring that persons accused of crimes are available for trials." A person who is arrested for one offense but knows that he has yet to answer for some past crime may be more inclined to flee the instant charges, lest continued contact with the criminal justice system expose one or more other serious offenses. For example, a defendant who had committed a prior sexual assault might be inclined to flee on a burglary charge, knowing that in every State a DNA sample would be taken from him after his conviction on the burglary charge that would tie him to the more serious charge of rape. In addition to subverting the administration of justice with respect to the crime of arrest, this ties back to the interest in safety; for a detainee who absconds from custody presents a risk to law enforcement officers, other detainees, victims of previous crimes, witnesses, and society at large.

Fourth, an arrestee's past conduct is essential to an assessment of the danger he poses to the public, and this will inform a court's determination whether the individual should be released on bail. DNA identification of a suspect in a violent crime provides critical information to the police and judicial officials in making a determination of the arrestee's future dangerousness.

Finally, in the interests of justice, the identification of an arrestee as the perpetrator of some heinous crime may have the salutary effect of freeing a person wrongfully imprisoned for the same offense. "[P]rompt [DNA] testing . . . would speed up apprehension of criminals before they commit additional crimes, and prevent the grotesque detention of . . . innocent people." J. Dwyer, P. Neufeld, & B. Scheck, Actual Innocence 245 (2000).

B

DNA identification represents an important advance in the techniques used by law enforcement to serve legitimate police concerns for as long as there have been arrests, concerns the courts have acknowledged and approved for more than a century. Law enforcement agencies routinely have used scientific advancements in their standard procedures for the identification of arrestees.

Perhaps the most direct historical analogue to the DNA technology used to identify respondent is the familiar practice of fingerprinting arrestees. From the advent of this technique, courts had no trouble determining that fingerprinting was a natural part of "the administrative steps incident to arrest."

DNA identification is an advanced technique superior to fingerprinting in many ways, so much so that to insist on fingerprints as the norm would make little sense to either the forensic expert or a layperson. The additional intrusion upon the arrestee's privacy beyond that associated with fingerprinting is not significant, and DNA is a markedly more accurate form of identifying arrestees. A suspect who has changed his facial features to evade photographic identification or even one who has undertaken the more arduous task of altering his fingerprints cannot escape the revealing power of his DNA.

In sum, there can be little reason to question "the legitimate interest of the government in knowing for an absolute certainty the identity of the person arrested, in knowing whether he is wanted elsewhere, and in ensuring his identification in the event he flees prosecution." In the balance of reasonableness required by the Fourth Amendment, therefore, the Court must give great weight both to the significant government interest at stake in the identification of arrestees and to the unmatched potential of DNA identification to serve that interest.

V

By comparison to this substantial government interest and the unique effectiveness of DNA identification, the intrusion of a cheek swab to obtain a DNA sample is a minimal one. True, a significant government interest does not alone suffice to justify a search. The government interest must outweigh the degree to which the search invades an individual's legitimate expectations of privacy. In considering those expectations in this case, however, the necessary predicate of a valid arrest for a serious offense is fundamental.

In this critical respect, the search here at issue differs from the sort of programmatic searches of either the public at large or a particular class of regulated but otherwise law-abiding citizens that the Court has previously labeled as "'special needs'" searches. Once an individual has been arrested on probable cause for a dangerous offense that may require detention before trial, however, his or her expectations of privacy and freedom from police scrutiny are reduced. DNA identification like that at issue here thus does not require consideration of any unique needs that would be required to justify searching the average citizen. The special needs cases, though in full accord with the result reached here, do not have a direct bearing on the issues presented in this case, because unlike the search of a citizen who has not been suspected of a wrong, a detainee has a reduced expectation of privacy.

In addition the processing of respondent's DNA sample's 13 CODIS loci did not intrude on respondent's privacy in a way that would make his DNA identification unconstitutional.

First, as already noted, the CODIS loci come from noncoding parts of the DNA that do not reveal the genetic traits of the arrestee. While science can always progress further, and those progressions may have Fourth Amendment consequences, alleles at the CODIS loci "are not at present revealing information beyond identification." The argument that the testing at issue in this case reveals any private medical information at all is open to dispute.

And even if non-coding alleles could provide some information, they are not in fact tested for that end. It is undisputed that law enforcement officers analyze DNA for the sole purpose of generating a unique identifying number against which future samples may be matched. This parallels a similar safeguard based on actual practice in the school drug-testing context, where the Court deemed it "significant that the tests at issue here look only for drugs, and not for whether the student is, for example, epileptic, pregnant, or diabetic." If in the future police analyze samples to determine, for instance, an arrestee's predisposition for a particular disease or other hereditary factors not relevant to identity, that case would present additional privacy concerns not present here.

Finally, the Act provides statutory protections that guard against further invasion of privacy. As noted above, the Act requires that "[o]nly DNA records that directly relate to the identification of individuals shall be collected and stored." No purpose other than identification is permissible.

In light of the context of a valid arrest supported by probable cause respondent's expectations of privacy were not offended by the minor intrusion of a brief swab of his cheeks. By contrast, that same context of arrest gives rise to significant state interests in identifying respondent not only so that the proper name can be attached to his charges but also so that the criminal justice system can make informed decisions concerning pretrial custody. Upon these considerations the Court concludes that DNA identification of arrestees is a reasonable search that can be considered part of a routine booking procedure. When officers make an arrest supported by probable cause to hold for a serious offense and they bring the suspect to the station to be detained in custody, taking and analyzing a cheek swab of the arrestee's DNA is, like fingerprinting and photographing, a legitimate police booking procedure that is reasonable under the Fourth Amendment.

Justice SCALIA, with whom Justice GINSBURG, Justice SOTOMAYOR, and Justice KAGAN join, dissenting.

The Fourth Amendment forbids searching a person for evidence of a crime when there is no basis for believing the person is guilty of the crime or is in possession of incriminating evidence. That prohibition is categorical and without exception; it lies at the very heart of the Fourth Amendment. Whenever this Court has allowed a suspicionless search, it has insisted upon a justifying motive apart from the investigation of crime.

It is obvious that no such noninvestigative motive exists in this case. The Court's assertion that DNA is being taken, not to solve crimes, but to *identify* those in the State's custody, taxes the credulity of the credulous. And the Court's comparison of Maryland's DNA searches to other techniques, such as fingerprinting, can seem apt only to those who know no more than today's opinion has chosen to tell them about how those DNA searches actually work.

I

At the time of the Founding, Americans despised the British use of so-called "general warrants" — warrants not grounded upon a sworn oath of a specific infraction by a particular individual, and thus not limited in scope and application.

2. Searches and Seizures

Although there is a "closely guarded category of constitutionally permissible suspicionless searches," that has never included searches designed to serve "the normal need for law enforcement." Even the common name for suspicionless searches—"special needs" searches—itself reflects that they must be justified, *always*, by concerns "other than crime detection."

So while the Court is correct to note that there are instances in which we have permitted searches without individualized suspicion, "[i]n none of these cases . . . did we indicate approval of a [search] whose primary purpose was to detect evidence of ordinary criminal wrongdoing." That limitation is crucial. It is only when a governmental purpose aside from crime-solving is at stake that we engage in the free-form "reasonableness" inquiry that the Court indulges at length today. To put it another way, both the legitimacy of the Court's method and the correctness of its outcome hinge entirely on the truth of a single proposition: that the primary purpose of these DNA searches is something other than simply discovering evidence of criminal wrongdoing. As I detail below, that proposition is wrong.

The Court alludes at several points to the fact that King was an arrestee, and arrestees may be validly searched incident to their arrest. But the Court does not really *rest* on this principle, and for good reason: The objects of a search incident to arrest must be either (1) weapons or evidence that might easily be destroyed, or (2) evidence relevant to the crime of arrest. Neither is the object of the search at issue here.

At any rate, all this discussion is beside the point. No matter the degree of invasiveness, suspicionless searches are *never* allowed if their principal end is ordinary crime-solving. A search incident to arrest either serves other ends (such as officer safety, in a search for weapons) or is not suspicionless (as when there is reason to believe the arrestee possesses evidence relevant to the crime of arrest).

Sensing (correctly) that it needs more, the Court elaborates at length the ways that the search here served the special purpose of "identifying" King. But that seems to me quite wrong—unless what one means by "identifying" someone is "searching for evidence that he has committed crimes unrelated to the crime of his arrest." If identifying someone means finding out what unsolved crimes he has committed, then identification is indistinguishable from the ordinary law-enforcement aims that have never been thought to justify a suspicionless search. Searching every lawfully stopped car, for example, might turn up information about unsolved crimes the driver had committed, but no one would say that such a search was aimed at "identifying" him, and no court would hold such a search lawful.

The portion of the Court's opinion that explains the identification rationale is strangely silent on the actual workings of the DNA search at issue here. To know those facts is to be instantly disabused of the notion that what happened had anything to do with identifying King.

King was arrested on April 10, 2009, on charges unrelated to the case before us. That same day, April 10, the police searched him and seized the DNA evidence at issue here. What happened next? Reading the Court's opinion, particularly its insistence that the search was necessary to know "who [had] been arrested," one might guess that King's DNA was swiftly processed and his identity thereby confirmed—perhaps against some master database of known DNA profiles, as is done for fingerprints. After all, was not the suspicionless search here crucial to avoid "inordinate risks for facility staff" or to "existing detainee population"? Surely, then—*surely*—the State of Maryland got cracking on those grave risks immediately, by rushing to identify King with his DNA as soon as possible.

Nothing could be further from the truth. Maryland officials did not even begin the process of testing King's DNA that day. Or, actually, the next day. Or the day after that. And that was for a simple reason: Maryland law forbids them to do so. A "DNA sample collected from an individual charged with a crime . . . *may not* be tested or placed in the statewide DNA data base system prior to the first scheduled arraignment date." And King's first appearance in court was not until three days after his arrest. (I suspect, though, that they did not wait three days to ask his name or take his fingerprints.)

It gets worse. King's DNA sample was not received by the Maryland State Police's Forensic Sciences Division until April 23, 2009—two weeks after his arrest. It sat in that office, ripening in a storage area, until the custodians got around to mailing it to a lab for testing on June 25, 2009—two months after it was received, and nearly *three* since King's arrest. After it was mailed, the data from the lab tests were not available for several more weeks, until July 13, 2009, which is when the test results were entered into Maryland's DNA database, *together with information identifying the person from whom the sample was taken*. Meanwhile, bail had been set, King had engaged in discovery, and he had requested a speedy trial—presumably not a trial of John Doe. It was not until August 4, 2009—four months after King's arrest—that the forwarded sample transmitted (*without* identifying information) from the Maryland DNA database to the Federal Bureau of Investigation's national database was matched with a sample taken from the scene of an unrelated crime years earlier.

In fact, if anything was "identified" at the moment that the DNA database returned a match, it was not King—his identity was already known. (The docket for the original criminal charges lists his full name, his race, his sex, his height, his weight, his date of birth, and his address.) Rather, what the August 4 match "identified" was *the previously-taken sample from the earlier crime*. That sample was genuinely mysterious to Maryland; the State knew that it had probably been left by the victim's attacker, but nothing else. King was not identified by his association with the sample; rather, the sample was identified by its association with King. The Court effectively destroys its own "identification" theory when it acknowledges that the object of this search was "to see what [was] already known about [King]." King was who he was, and volumes of his biography could not make him any more or any less King. No minimally competent speaker of English would say, upon noticing a known arrestee's similarity "to a wanted poster of a previously unidentified suspect," that the *arrestee* had thereby been identified. It was the previously unidentified suspect who had been identified—just as, here, it was the previously unidentified rapist.

So, to review: DNA testing does not even begin until after arraignment and bail decisions are already made. The samples sit in storage for months, and take weeks to test. When they are tested, they are checked against the Unsolved Crimes Collection—rather than the Convict and Arrestee Collection, which could be used to identify them. The Act forbids the Court's purpose (identification), but prescribes as its purpose what our suspicionless-search cases forbid ("official investigation into a crime"). Against all of that, it is safe to say that if the Court's identification theory is not wrong, there is no such thing as error.

II

The Court also attempts to bolster its identification theory with a series of inapposite analogies. Is not taking DNA samples the same, asks the Court, as taking a person's photograph? No—because that is not a Fourth Amendment search at all. It does not involve a physical intrusion onto the person, and we have never held that merely taking a person's photograph invades any recognized "expectation of privacy."

But is not the practice of DNA searches, the Court asks, the same as taking "Bertillon" measurements—noting an arrestee's height, shoe size, and so on, on the back of a photograph? No, because that system was not, in the ordinary case, used to solve unsolved crimes. It is possible, I suppose, to imagine situations in which such measurements might be useful to generate leads. (If witnesses described a very tall burglar, all the "tall man" cards could then be pulled.) But the obvious primary purpose of such measurements, as the Court's description of them makes clear, was to verify that, for example, the person arrested today is the same person that was arrested a year ago. Which is to say, Bertillon measurements were *actually* used as a system of identification, and drew their primary usefulness from that task.

It is on the fingerprinting of arrestees, however, that the Court relies most heavily. The Court does not actually say whether it believes that taking a person's fingerprints is a Fourth Amendment search, and our cases provide no ready answer to that question. Even assuming so, however, law enforcement's post-arrest use of fingerprints could not be more different from its post-arrest use of DNA. Fingerprints of arrestees are taken primarily to identify them (though that process sometimes solves crimes); the DNA of arrestees is taken to solve crimes (and nothing else).

The Court asserts that the taking of fingerprints was "constitutional for generations prior to the introduction" of the FBI's rapid computer-matching system. *Ante*, at 1977. This bold statement is bereft of citation to authority because there is none for it. The "great expansion in fingerprinting came before the modern era of Fourth Amendment jurisprudence," and so we were never asked to decide the legitimacy of the practice.

Today, it can fairly be said that fingerprints really are used to identify people — so well, in fact, that there would be no need for the expense of a separate, wholly redundant DNA confirmation of the same information. What DNA adds — what makes it a valuable weapon in the law-enforcement arsenal — is the ability to solve unsolved crimes, by matching old crime-scene evidence against the profiles of people whose identities are already known. That is what was going on when King's DNA was taken, and we should not disguise the fact. Solving unsolved crimes is a noble objective, but it occupies a lower place in the American pantheon of noble objectives than the protection of our people from suspicionless law-enforcement searches. The Fourth Amendment must prevail.

The Court disguises the vast (and scary) scope of its holding by promising a limitation it cannot deliver. The Court repeatedly says that DNA testing, and entry into a national DNA registry, will not befall thee and me, dear reader, but only those arrested for "serious offense[s]." I cannot imagine what principle could possibly justify this limitation, and the Court does not attempt to suggest any. If one believes that DNA will "identify" someone arrested for assault, he must believe that it will "identify" someone arrested for a traffic offense. This Court does not base its judgments on senseless distinctions. At the end of the day, *logic will out.* When there comes before us the taking of DNA from an arrestee for a traffic violation, the Court will predictably (and quite rightly) say, "We can find no significant difference between this case and *King*." Make no mistake about it: As an entirely predictable consequence of today's decision, your DNA can be taken and entered into a national DNA database if you are ever arrested, rightly or wrongly, and for whatever reason.

The most regrettable aspect of the suspicionless search that occurred here is that it proved to be quite unnecessary. All parties concede that it would have been entirely permissible, as far as the Fourth Amendment is concerned, for Maryland to take a sample of King's DNA as a consequence of his conviction for second-degree assault. So the ironic result of the Court's error is this: The only arrestees to whom the outcome here will ever make a difference are those who *have been acquitted* of the crime of arrest (so that their DNA could not have been taken upon conviction). In other words, this Act manages to burden uniquely the sole group for whom the Fourth Amendment's protections ought to be most jealously guarded: people who are innocent of the State's accusations.

Today's judgment will, to be sure, have the beneficial effect of solving more crimes; then again, so would the taking of DNA samples from anyone who flies on an airplane (surely the Transportation Security Administration needs to know the "identity" of the flying public), applies for a driver's license, or attends a public school. Perhaps the construction of such a genetic panopticon is wise. But I doubt that the proud men who wrote the charter of our liberties would have been so eager to open their mouths for royal inspection.

2. Searches and Seizures

I therefore dissent, and hope that today's incursion upon the Fourth Amendment, like an earlier one, will some day be repudiated.

1. Administrative searches (casebook p. 212)

In *City of Los Angeles v. Patel*, the Court considered the constitutionality of a city's ordinance that allowed police to examine the registers of hotels and motels at any time. The Court declared the law facially unconstitutional, emphasizing the need for some neutral review before hotel or motel operators could be punished for not allowing police examinations.

City of Los Angeles v. Patel
135 S. Ct. ___ (2015)

Justice SOTOMAYOR delivered the opinion of the Court.

Respondents brought a Fourth Amendment challenge to a provision of the Los Angeles Municipal Code that compels "[e]very operator of a hotel to keep a record" containing specified information concerning guests and to make this record "available to any officer of the Los Angeles Police Department for inspection" on demand. The questions presented are whether facial challenges to statutes can be brought under the Fourth Amendment and, if so, whether this provision of the Los Angeles Municipal Code is facially invalid. We hold facial challenges can be brought under the Fourth Amendment. We further hold that the provision of the Los Angeles Municipal Code that requires hotel operators to make their registries available to the police on demand is facially unconstitutional because it penalizes them for declining to turn over their records without affording them any opportunity for precompliance review.

I

Los Angeles Municipal Code (LAMC) §41.49 requires hotel operators to record information about their guests, including: the guest's name and address; the number of people in each guest's party; the make, model, and license plate number of any guest's vehicle parked on hotel property; the guest's date and time of arrival and scheduled departure date; the room number assigned to the guest; the rate charged and amount collected for the room; and the method of payment. Guests without reservations, those who pay for their rooms with cash, and any guests who rent a room for less than 12 hours must present photographic identification at the time of check-in, and hotel operators are required to record the number and expiration date of that document. For those guests who check in using an electronic kiosk, the hotel's records must also contain the guest's credit card information. This information can be maintained in either electronic or paper form, but it must be "kept on the hotel premises in the guest reception or guest check-in area or in an office adjacent" thereto for a period of 90 days.

Section 41.49(3)(a)—the only provision at issue here—states, in pertinent part, that hotel guest records "shall be made available to any officer of the Los Angeles Police Department for inspection," provided that "[w]henever possible, the inspection shall be conducted at a time and in a manner that minimizes any interference with the operation of the business." A hotel operator's failure to make his or her guest records available for police inspection is a misdemeanor punishable by up to six months in jail and a $1,000 fine.

II

We first clarify that facial challenges under the Fourth Amendment are not categorically barred or especially disfavored. A facial challenge is an attack on a statute itself as opposed to a particular application. While such challenges are "the most difficult . . . to mount successfully," the Court has never held that these claims cannot be brought under any otherwise enforceable provision of the Constitution. Instead, the Court has allowed such challenges to proceed under a diverse array of constitutional provisions.

Fourth Amendment challenges to statutes authorizing warrantless searches are no exception. Petitioner principally contends that facial challenges to statutes authorizing warrantless searches must fail because such searches will never be unconstitutional in all applications. In particular, the City points to situations where police are responding to an emergency, where the subject of the search consents to the intrusion, and where police are acting under a court-ordered warrant. While petitioner frames this argument as an objection to respondents' challenge in this case, its logic would preclude facial relief in every Fourth Amendment challenge to a statute authorizing warrantless searches. For this reason alone, the City's argument must fail: The Court's precedents demonstrate not only that facial challenges to statutes authorizing warrantless searches can be brought, but also that they can succeed.

Moreover, the City's argument misunderstands how courts analyze facial challenges. Under the most exacting standard the Court has prescribed for facial challenges, a plaintiff must establish that a "law is unconstitutional in all of its applications." But when assessing whether a statute meets this standard, the Court has considered only applications of the statute in which it actually authorizes or prohibits conduct.

Similarly, when addressing a facial challenge to a statute authorizing warrantless searches, the proper focus of the constitutional inquiry is searches that the law actually authorizes, not those for which it is irrelevant. If exigency or a warrant justifies an officer's search, the subject of the search must permit it to proceed irrespective of whether it is authorized by statute. Statutes authorizing warrantless searches also do no work where the subject of a search has consented. Accordingly, the constitutional "applications" that petitioner claims prevent facial relief here are irrelevant to our analysis because they do not involve actual applications of the statute.

III

Turning to the merits of the particular claim before us, we hold that §41.49(3)(a) is facially unconstitutional because it fails to provide hotel operators with an opportunity for precompliance review.

[T]he Court has repeatedly held that " 'searches conducted outside the judicial process, without prior approval by [a] judge or [a] magistrate [judge], are *per se* unreasonable . . . subject only to a few specifically established and well-delineated exceptions.'" This rule "applies to commercial premises as well as to homes." Search regimes where no warrant is ever required may be reasonable where "'special needs . . . make the warrant and probable-cause requirement impracticable,'" and where the "primary purpose" of the searches is "[d]istinguishable from the general interest in crime control." Here, we assume that the searches authorized by §41.49 serve a "special need" other than conducting criminal investigations: They ensure compliance with the recordkeeping requirement, which in turn deters criminals from operating on the hotels' premises. The Court has referred to this kind of search as an "administrative searc[h]." Thus, we consider whether §41.49 falls within the administrative search exception to the warrant requirement.

The Court has held that absent consent, exigent circumstances, or the like, in order for an administrative search to be constitutional, the subject of the search must be afforded an opportunity to obtain precompliance review before a neutral decisionmaker. And, we see no reason why this minimal requirement is inapplicable here. While the Court has never attempted to prescribe the exact form an opportunity for precompliance review must take, the City does not even attempt to argue that §41.49(3)(a) affords hotel operators any opportunity whatsoever. Section 41.49(3)(a) is, therefore, facially invalid.

A hotel owner who refuses to give an officer access to his or her registry can be arrested on the spot. The Court has held that business owners cannot reasonably be put to this kind of choice.

Absent an opportunity for precompliance review, the ordinance creates an intolerable risk that searches authorized by it will exceed statutory limits, or be used as a pretext to harass hotel operators and their guests. Even if a hotel has been searched 10 times a day, every day, for three months, without any violation being found, the operator can only refuse to comply with an officer's demand to turn over the registry at his or her own peril.

To be clear, we hold only that a hotel owner must be afforded an *opportunity* to have a neutral decisionmaker review an officer's demand to search the registry before he or she faces penalties for failing to comply. Actual review need only occur in those rare instances where a hotel operator objects to turning over the registry. Moreover, this opportunity can be provided without imposing onerous burdens on those charged with an administrative scheme's enforcement. For instance, respondents accept that the searches authorized by §41.49(3)(a) would be constitutional if they were performed pursuant to an administrative subpoena. These subpoenas, which are typically a simple form, can be issued by the individual seeking the record—here, officers in the field—without probable cause that a regulation is being infringed. Issuing a subpoena will usually be the full extent of an officer's burden because "the great majority of businessmen can be expected in normal course to consent to inspection without warrant." Indeed, the City has cited no evidence suggesting that without an ordinance authorizing on-demand searches, hotel operators would regularly refuse to cooperate with the police.

Finally, we underscore the narrow nature of our holding. Respondents have not challenged and nothing in our opinion calls into question those parts of §41.49 that require hotel operators to maintain guest registries containing certain information. And, even absent legislative action to create a procedure along the lines discussed above, police will not be prevented from obtaining access to these documents. As they often do, hotel operators remain free to consent to searches of their registries and police can compel them to turn them over if they have a proper administrative warrant—including one that was issued *ex parte*—or if some other exception to the warrant requirement applies, including exigent circumstances.

Rather than arguing that §41.49(3)(a) is constitutional under the general administrative search doctrine, the City and Justice Scalia contend that hotels are "closely regulated," and that the ordinance is facially valid under the more relaxed standard that applies to searches of this category of businesses. They are wrong on both counts.

Over the past 45 years, the Court has identified only four industries that "have such a history of government oversight that no reasonable expectation of privacy . . . could exist for a proprietor over the stock of such an enterprise." Simply listing these industries refutes petitioner's argument that hotels should be counted among them. Unlike liquor sales, firearms dealing, mining, or running an automobile junkyard, nothing inherent in the operation of hotels poses a clear and significant risk to the public welfare.

To classify hotels as pervasively regulated would permit what has always been a narrow exception to swallow the rule.

Justice SCALIA, with whom the Chief Justice and Justice THOMAS join, dissenting.

The city of Los Angeles, like many jurisdictions across the country, has a law that requires motels, hotels, and other places of overnight accommodation (here-inafter motels) to keep a register containing specified information about their guests. The purpose of this recordkeeping requirement is to deter criminal conduct, on the theory that criminals will be unwilling to carry on illicit activities in motel rooms if they must provide identifying information at check-in. Because this deterrent effect will only be accomplished if motels actually do require guests to provide the required information, the ordinance also authorizes police to conduct random spot checks of motels' guest registers to ensure that they are properly maintained. The ordinance limits these spot checks to the four corners of the register, and does not authorize police to enter any nonpublic area of the motel. To the extent possible, police must conduct these spot checks at times that will minimize any disruption to a motel's business.

The parties do not dispute the governmental interests at stake. Motels not only provide housing to vulnerable transient populations, they are also a particularly attractive site for criminal activity ranging from drug dealing and prostitution to human trafficking. Offering privacy and anonymity on the cheap, they have been employed as prisons for migrants smuggled across the border and held for ransom, and rendezvous sites where child sex workers meet their clients on threat of violence from their procurers.

Nevertheless, the Court today concludes that Los Angeles's ordinance is "unreasonable" inasmuch as it permits police to flip through a guest register to ensure it is being filled out without first providing an opportunity for the motel operator to seek judicial review. Because I believe that such a limited inspection of a guest register is eminently reasonable under the circumstances presented, I dissent.

I assume that respondents may bring a facial challenge to the City's ordinance under the Fourth Amendment. Even so, their claim must fail because, as discussed *infra*, the law is constitutional in most, if not all, of its applications.

One exception to normal warrant requirements applies to searches of closely regulated businesses. "[W]hen an entrepreneur embarks upon such a business, he has voluntarily chosen to subject himself to a full arsenal of governmental regulation," and so a warrantless search to enforce those regulations is not unreasonable. Recognizing that warrantless searches of closely regulated businesses may nevertheless *become* unreasonable if arbitrarily conducted, we have required laws authorizing such searches to satisfy three criteria: (1) There must be a "'substantial' government interest that informs the regulatory scheme pursuant to which the inspection is made"; (2) "the warrantless inspections must be 'necessary to further [the] regulatory scheme'"; and (3) " 'the statute's inspection program, in terms of the certainty and regularity of its application, [must] provid[e] a constitutionally adequate substitute for a warrant.'" Los Angeles's ordinance easily meets these standards.

In determining whether a business is closely regulated, this Court has looked to factors including the duration of the regulatory tradition; the comprehensiveness of the regulatory regime; and the imposition of similar regulations by other jurisdictions. These factors are not talismans, but shed light on the expectation of privacy the owner of a business may reasonably have, which in turn affects the reasonableness of a warrantless search.

Reflecting the unique public role of motels and their commercial forebears, governments have long subjected these businesses to unique public duties, and have established inspection regimes to ensure compliance. As Blackstone observed, "Inns, in particular, being intended for the lodging and receipt of travellers, may be indicted, suppressed, and the inn-keepers fined, if they refuse to entertain a traveller without a very sufficient cause: for thus to frustrate the end of their institution is held to be disorderly behavior." 4 W. Blackstone, Commentaries on the Laws of England 168 (1765). Justice Story similarly recognized "[t]he soundness of the public policy of subjecting particular classes of persons to extraordinary responsibility, in cases where an extraordinary confidence is necessarily reposed in them, and there is an extraordinary temptation to fraud, or danger of plunder." J. Story, Commentaries on the Law of Bailments §464, pp. 487–488 (5th ed. 1851).

Finally, this ordinance is not an outlier. The City has pointed us to more than 100 similar register-inspection laws in cities and counties across the country, and that is far from exhaustive. In all, municipalities in at least 41 States have laws similar to Los Angeles's, and at least 8 States have their own laws authorizing register inspections.

The City's ordinance easily satisfies the remaining requirements: It furthers a substantial governmental interest, it is necessary to achieving that interest, and it provides an adequate substitute for a search warrant.

Neither respondents nor the Court question the substantial interest of the City in deterring criminal activity. The private pain and public costs imposed by drug dealing, prostitution, and human trafficking are beyond contention, and motels provide an obvious haven for those who trade in human misery.

Warrantless inspections are also necessary to advance this interest. Although the Court acknowledges that law enforcement can enter a motel room without a warrant when exigent circumstances exist, the whole reason criminals use motel rooms in the first place is that they offer privacy and secrecy, so that police will never come to discover these exigencies. The recordkeeping requirement, which all parties admit is permissible, therefore operates by *deterring* crime. Criminals, who depend on the anonymity that motels offer, will balk when confronted with a motel's demand that they produce identification. And a motel's evasion of the recordkeeping requirement fosters crime.

Respondents and the Court acknowledge that *inspections* are necessary to achieve the purposes of the recordkeeping regime, but insist that *warrantless* inspections are not. They have to acknowledge, however, that the motel operators who conspire with drug dealers and procurers may demand precompliance judicial review simply as a pretext to buy time for making fraudulent entries in their guest registers. The Court therefore must resort to arguing that warrantless inspections are not "necessary" because other alternatives exist.

The Court suggests that police could obtain an administrative subpoena to search a guest register and, if a motel moves to quash, the police could "guar[d] the registry pending a hearing" on the motion. This proposal is equal parts 1984 and Alice in Wonderland. It protects motels from government inspection of their registers by authorizing government agents to seize the registers (if "guarding" entails forbidding the register to be moved) or to upset guests by a prolonged police presence at the motel. The Court also notes that police can obtain an *ex parte* warrant before conducting a register inspection. Presumably such warrants could issue without probable cause of wrongdoing by a particular motel; otherwise, this would be no alternative at all. Even so, under this regime police would have to obtain an *ex parte* warrant before *every* inspection. That is because law enforcement would have no way of knowing ahead of time which motels would refuse consent to a search upon request; and if they wait to obtain a warrant until consent is refused, motels will have the opportunity to falsify their guest registers while the police jump through the procedural hoops required to obtain a warrant. It is quite plausible that the costs of this always-get-a-warrant "alternative" would be prohibitive for a police force in one of America's largest cities, juggling numerous law-enforcement priorities, and confronting more than 2,000 motels within its jurisdiction.

But all that discussion is in any case irrelevant. The administrative search need only be reasonable. It is not the burden of Los Angeles to show that there are no less restrictive means of achieving the City's purposes.

The Court reaches its wrongheaded conclusion not simply by misapplying our precedent, but by mistaking our precedent for the Fourth Amendment itself. Rather than bother with the text of that Amendment, the Court relies exclusively on our administrative-search cases. But the Constitution predates 1967, and it remains the supreme law of the land today. Because I believe that the limited warrantless searches authorized by Los Angeles's ordinance are reasonable under the circumstances, I respectfully dissent.

Justice ALITO with whom Justice THOMAS joins, dissenting.

After today, the city of Los Angeles can never, under any circumstances, enforce its 116–year–old requirement that hotels make their registers available to police officers. That is because the Court holds that §41.49(3)(a) of the Los Angeles Municipal Code (2015) is *facially* unconstitutional. Before entering a judgment with such serious safety and federalism implications, the Court must conclude that every application of this law is unconstitutional—*i.e.*, that "'no set of circumstances exists under which the [law] would be valid.'" I have doubts about the Court's approach to administrative searches and closely regulated industries. But even if the Court were 100% correct, it still should uphold §41.49(3)(a) because many other applications of this law are constitutional. Here are five examples.

Example One. The police have probable cause to believe that a register contains evidence of a crime. They go to a judge and get a search warrant. The hotel operator, however, refuses to surrender the register, but instead stashes it away. Officers could tear the hotel apart looking for it. Or they could simply order the operator to produce it. The Fourth Amendment does not create a right to defy a warrant. Hence §41.49(3)(a) could be constitutionally applied in this scenario. Indeed, the Court concedes that it is proper to apply a California obstruction of justice law in such a case. How could applying a city law with a similar effect be different? And a specific law gives more notice than a general law.

Example Two. A murderer has kidnapped a woman with the intent to rape and kill her and there is reason to believe he is holed up in a certain motel. The Fourth Amendment's reasonableness standard accounts for exigent circumstances.

When the police arrive, the motel operator folds her arms and says the register is locked in a safe. Invoking §41.49(3)(a), the police order the operator to turn over the register. She refuses. The Fourth Amendment does not protect her from arrest.

Example Three. A neighborhood of "pay by the hour" motels is a notorious gathering spot for child-sex traffickers. Police officers drive through the neighborhood late one night and see unusual amounts of activity at a particular motel. The officers stop and ask the motel operator for the names of those who paid with cash to rent rooms for less than three hours. The operator refuses to provide the information. Requesting to see the register—and arresting the operator for failing to provide it—would be reasonable under the "totality of the circumstances."

Example Four. A motel is operated by a dishonest employee. He has been charging more for rooms than he records, all the while pocketing the difference. The owner finds out and eagerly consents to a police inspection of the register. But when officers arrive and ask to see the register, the operator hides it. The Fourth Amendment does not allow the operator's refusal to defeat the owner's consent.

Example Five. A "mom and pop" motel always keeps its old-fashioned guest register open on the front desk. Anyone who wants to can walk up and leaf through it. (Such motels are not as common as they used to be, but Los Angeles is a big place.) The motel has no reasonable expectation of privacy in the register, and no one doubts that police officers—like anyone else—can enter into the lobby. But when an officer starts looking at the register, as others do, the motel operator at the desk snatches it away and will not give it back. Arresting that person would not violate the Fourth Amendment.

These are just five examples. There are many more. The Court rushes past examples like these by suggesting that §41.49(3)(a) does no "work" in such scenarios. That is not true. Under threat of legal sanction, this law orders hotel operators to do things they do not want to do.

There are serious arguments that the Fourth Amendment's application to warrantless searches and seizures is inherently inconsistent with facial challenges. But assuming such facial challenges ever make sense conceptually, this particular one fails under basic principles of facial invalidation. The Court's contrary holding is befuddling. I respectfully dissent.

G. Stop and Frisk

4. What Is Sufficient for Reasonable Suspicion? (casebook p. 338)

b. *Reasonable Suspicion Based on Informants' Tips* (casebook p. 342)

What if police pull over a car based on an anonymous tip that the driver was driving erratically? That is the issue in *Navarette v. California*.

2. Searches and Seizures

Navarette v. California
134 S. Ct. 1683 (2014)

Justice THOMAS delivered the opinion of the Court.

After a 911 caller reported that a vehicle had run her off the road, a police officer located the vehicle she identified during the call and executed a traffic stop. We hold that the stop complied with the Fourth Amendment because, under the totality of the circumstances, the officer had reasonable suspicion that the driver was intoxicated.

I

On August 23, 2008, a Mendocino County 911 dispatch team for the California Highway Patrol (CHP) received a call from another CHP dispatcher in neighboring Humboldt County. The Humboldt County dispatcher relayed a tip from a 911 caller, which the Mendocino County team recorded as follows: "'Showing southbound Highway 1 at mile marker 88, Silver Ford 150 pickup. Plate of 8-David-94925. Ran the reporting party off the roadway and was last seen approximately five [minutes] ago.'" The Mendocino County team then broadcast that information to CHP officers at 3:47 p.m.

A CHP officer heading northbound toward the reported vehicle responded to the broadcast. At 4:00 p.m., the officer passed the truck near mile marker 69. At about 4:05 p.m., after making a U-turn, he pulled the truck over. A second officer, who had separately responded to the broadcast, also arrived on the scene. As the two officers approached the truck, they smelled marijuana. A search of the truck bed revealed 30 pounds of marijuana. The officers arrested the driver, petitioner Lorenzo Prado Navarette, and the passenger, petitioner José Prado Navarette.

II

The Fourth Amendment permits brief investigative stops—such as the traffic stop in this case—when a law enforcement officer has "a particularized and objective basis for suspecting the particular person stopped of criminal activity." The "reasonable suspicion" necessary to justify such a stop "is dependent upon both the content of information possessed by police and its degree of reliability." The standard takes into account "the totality of the circumstances—the whole picture." Although a mere "hunch" does not create reasonable suspicion, the level of suspicion the standard requires is "considerably less than proof of wrongdoing by a preponderance of the evidence," and "obviously less" than is necessary for probable cause.

These principles apply with full force to investigative stops based on information from anonymous tips. We have firmly rejected the argument "that reasonable cause for a[n investigative stop] can only be based on the officer's personal observation, rather than on information supplied by another person." Of course, "an anonymous tip *alone* seldom demonstrates the informant's basis of knowledge or veracity." That is because "ordinary citizens generally do not provide extensive recitations of the basis of their everyday observations," and an anonymous tipster's veracity is "'by hypothesis largely unknown, and unknowable.'" But under appropriate circumstances, an anonymous tip can demonstrate "sufficient indicia of reliability to provide reasonable suspicion to make [an] investigatory stop."

Our decisions in *Alabama v. White* (1990), and *Florida v. J. L.* (2000), are useful guides. In *White*, an anonymous tipster told the police that a woman would drive from a particular apartment building to a particular motel in a brown Plymouth station wagon with a broken right tail light. The tipster further asserted that the woman would be transporting cocaine. After confirming the innocent details, officers stopped the station wagon as it neared the motel and found cocaine in the vehicle. We held that the officers' corroboration of certain details made the anonymous tip sufficiently reliable to create reasonable suspicion of criminal activity. By accurately predicting future behavior, the tipster demonstrated "a special familiarity with respondent's affairs," which in turn implied that the tipster had "access to reliable information about that individual's illegal activities."

In *J. L.*, by contrast, we determined that no reasonable suspicion arose from a bare-bones tip that a young black male in a plaid shirt standing at a bus stop was carrying a gun. The tipster did not explain how he knew about the gun, nor did he suggest that he had any special familiarity with the young man's affairs. As a result, police had no basis for believing "that the tipster ha[d] knowledge of concealed criminal activity." Furthermore, the tip included no predictions of future behavior that could be corroborated to assess the tipster's credibility. We accordingly concluded that the tip was insufficiently reliable to justify a stop and frisk.

The initial question in this case is whether the 911 call was sufficiently reliable to credit the allegation that petitioners' truck "ran the [caller] off the roadway." Even assuming for present purposes that the 911 call was anonymous, we conclude that the call bore adequate indicia of reliability for the officer to credit the caller's account. The officer was therefore justified in proceeding from the premise that the truck had, in fact, caused the caller's car to be dangerously diverted from the highway.

By reporting that she had been run off the road by a specific vehicle — a silver Ford F-150 pickup, license plate 8D94925 — the caller necessarily claimed eyewitness knowledge of the alleged dangerous driving. That basis of knowledge lends significant support to the tip's reliability. A driver's claim that another vehicle ran her off the road, however, necessarily implies that the informant knows the other car was driven dangerously.

There is also reason to think that the 911 caller in this case was telling the truth. Police confirmed the truck's location near mile marker 69 (roughly 19 highway miles south of the location reported in the 911 call) at 4:00 p.m. (roughly 18 minutes after the 911 call). That timeline of events suggests that the caller reported the incident soon after she was run off the road. That sort of contemporaneous report has long been treated as especially reliable. In evidence law, we generally credit the proposition that statements about an event and made soon after perceiving that event are especially trustworthy because "substantial contemporaneity of event and statement negate the likelihood of deliberate or conscious misrepresentation."

As this case illustrates, 911 calls can be recorded, which provides victims with an opportunity to identify the false tipster's voice and subject him to prosecution. The 911 system also permits law enforcement to verify important information about the caller. None of this is to suggest that tips in 911 calls are *per se* reliable. Given the foregoing technological and regulatory developments, however, a reasonable officer could conclude that a false tipster would think twice before using such a system. The caller's use of the 911 system is therefore one of the relevant circumstances that, taken together, justified the officer's reliance on the information reported in the 911 call.

Even a reliable tip will justify an investigative stop only if it creates reasonable suspicion that "criminal activity may be afoot." We must therefore determine whether the 911 caller's report of being run off the roadway created reasonable suspicion of an ongoing crime such as drunk driving as opposed to an isolated episode of past recklessness. We conclude that the behavior alleged by the 911 caller, "viewed from the standpoint of an objectively reasonable police officer, amount[s] to reasonable suspicion" of drunk driving. The stop was therefore proper.

Reasonable suspicion depends on "the factual and practical considerations of everyday life on which reasonable and prudent men, not legal technicians, act." Under that commonsense approach, we can appropriately recognize certain driving behaviors as sound indicia of drunk driving. Indeed, the accumulated experience of thousands of officers suggests that these sorts of erratic behaviors are strongly correlated with drunk driving. Of course, not all traffic infractions imply intoxication. Unconfirmed reports of driving without a seatbelt or slightly over the speed limit, for example, are so tenuously connected to drunk driving that a stop on those grounds alone would be constitutionally suspect. But a reliable tip alleging the dangerous behaviors discussed above generally would justify a traffic stop on suspicion of drunk driving.

The 911 caller in this case reported more than a minor traffic infraction and more than a conclusory allegation of drunk or reckless driving. Instead, she alleged a specific and dangerous result of the driver's conduct: running another car off the highway. That conduct bears too great a resemblance to paradigmatic manifestations of drunk driving to be dismissed as an isolated example of recklessness. Running another vehicle off the road suggests lane-positioning problems, decreased vigilance, impaired judgment, or some combination of those recognized drunk driving cues. And the experience of many officers suggests that a driver who almost strikes a vehicle or another object—the exact scenario that ordinarily causes "running [another vehicle] off the roadway"—is likely intoxicated. As a result, we cannot say that the officer acted unreasonably under these circumstances in stopping a driver whose alleged conduct was a significant indicator of drunk driving.

Petitioners' attempts to second-guess the officer's reasonable suspicion of drunk driving are unavailing. It is true that the reported behavior might also be explained by, for example, a driver responding to "an unruly child or other distraction." But we have consistently recognized that reasonable suspicion "need not rule out the possibility of innocent conduct."

Nor did the absence of additional suspicious conduct, after the vehicle was first spotted by an officer, dispel the reasonable suspicion of drunk driving. It is hardly surprising that the appearance of a marked police car would inspire more careful driving for a time. Extended observation of an allegedly drunk driver might eventually dispel a reasonable suspicion of intoxication, but the 5-minute period in this case hardly sufficed in that regard. Of course, an officer who already has such a reasonable suspicion need not surveil a vehicle at length in order to personally observe suspicious driving. This would be a particularly inappropriate context to depart from that settled rule, because allowing a drunk driver a second chance for dangerous conduct could have disastrous consequences.

III

Like *White*, this is a "close case." Under the totality of the circumstances, we find the indicia of reliability in this case sufficient to provide the officer with reasonable suspicion that the driver of the reported vehicle had run another vehicle off the road. That made it reasonable under the circumstances for the officer to execute a traffic stop. We accordingly affirm.

Justice SCALIA, with whom Justice GINSBURG, Justice SOTOMAYOR, and Justice KAGAN join, dissenting.

Today's opinion does not explicitly adopt a departure from our normal Fourth Amendment requirement that anonymous tips must be corroborated; it purports to adhere to our prior cases. Be not deceived.

Law enforcement agencies follow closely our judgments on matters such as this, and they will identify at once our new rule: So long as the caller identifies where the car is, anonymous claims of a single instance of possibly careless or reckless driving, called in to 911, will support a traffic stop. This is not my concept, and I am sure would not be the Framers', of a people secure from unreasonable searches and seizures.

I

The California Highway Patrol in this case knew nothing about the tipster on whose word—and that alone—they seized Lorenzo and José Prado Navarette. They did not know her name. They did not know her phone number or address.

2.   Searches and Seizures

They did not even know where she called from (she may have dialed in from a neighboring county).

The tipster said the truck had "[run her] off the roadway," but the police had no reason to credit that charge and many reasons to doubt it, beginning with the peculiar fact that the accusation was anonymous. "[E]liminating accountability . . . is ordinarily the very purpose of anonymity." The unnamed tipster "can lie with impunity." Anonymity is especially suspicious with respect to the call that is the subject of the present case. When does a victim complain to the police about an arguably criminal act (running the victim off the road) without giving his identity, so that he can accuse and testify when the culprit is caught?

The question before us, the Court agrees, is whether the "content of information possessed by police and its degree of reliability," gave the officers reasonable suspicion that the driver of the truck (Lorenzo) was committing an ongoing crime. When the only source of the government's information is an informant's tip, we ask whether the tip bears sufficient "indicia of reliability," to establish "a particularized and objective basis for suspecting the particular person stopped of criminal activity."

Here the Court makes a big deal of the fact that the tipster was dead right about the fact that a silver Ford F-150 truck (license plate 8D94925) was traveling south on Highway 1 somewhere near mile marker 88. But everyone in the world who saw the car would have that knowledge, and anyone who wanted the car stopped would have to provide that information.

The Court says, that "[b]y reporting that she had been run off the road by a specific vehicle . . . the caller necessarily claimed eyewitness knowledge." So what? The issue is not how she claimed to know, but whether what she claimed to know was true. The claim to "eyewitness knowledge" of being run off the road supports *not at all* its veracity; nor does the amazing, mystifying prediction (so far short of what existed in *White*) that the petitioners' truck *would be heading south on Highway 1*.

The Court finds "reason to think" that the informant "was telling the truth" in the fact that police observation confirmed that the truck had been driving near the spot at which, and at the approximate time at which, the tipster alleged she had been run off the road. So, the Court says, we can fairly suppose that the accusation was true.

No, we cannot. [T]he Court says that another "indicator of veracity" is the anonymous tipster's mere "use of the 911 emergency system," Because, you see, recent "technological and regulatory developments" suggest that the identities of unnamed 911 callers are increasingly less likely to remain unknown. Indeed, the systems are able to identify "the caller's geographic location with increasing specificity." *Amici* disagree with this, see Brief for National Association of Criminal Defense Lawyers and the present case surely suggests that *amici* are right—since we know neither the identity of the tipster nor even the county from which the call was made. But assuming the Court is right about the ease of identifying 911 callers, it proves absolutely nothing in the present case unless the anonymous caller was *aware* of that fact. "It is the tipster's *belief* in anonymity, not its *reality*, that will control his behavior." There is no reason to believe that your average anonymous 911 tipster is aware that 911 callers are readily identifiable.

II

All that has been said up to now assumes that the anonymous caller made, at least in effect, an accusation of drunken driving. But in fact she did not. She said that the petitioners' truck "'[r]an [me] off the roadway.'" That neither asserts that the driver was drunk nor even raises the *likelihood* that the driver was drunk. The most it conveys is that the truck did some apparently nontypical thing that forced the tipster off the roadway, whether partly or fully, temporarily or permanently. Who really knows what (if anything) happened? The truck might have swerved to avoid an animal, a pothole, or a jaywalking pedestrian.

But let us assume the worst of the many possibilities: that it was a careless, reckless, or even intentional maneuver that forced the tipster off the road. Lorenzo might have been distracted by his use of a hands-free cell phone, or distracted by an intense sports argument with Jose, Or, indeed, he might have intentionally forced the tipster off the road because of some personal animus, or hostility to her "Make Love, Not War" bumper sticker. I fail to see how reasonable suspicion of a *discrete instance* of irregular or hazardous driving generates a reasonable suspicion of *ongoing intoxicated driving*. What proportion of the hundreds of thousands — perhaps millions — of careless, reckless, or intentional traffic violations committed each day is attributable to drunken drivers? I say 0.1 percent. I have no basis for that except my own guesswork. But unless the Court has some basis in reality to believe that the proportion is many orders of magnitude above that — say 1 in 10 or at least 1 in 20 — it has no grounds for its unsupported assertion that the tipster's report in this case gave rise to a *reasonable suspicion* of drunken driving.

Bear in mind that that is the only basis for the stop that has been asserted in this litigation. The stop required suspicion of an ongoing crime, not merely suspicion of having run someone off the road earlier. And driving while being a careless or reckless person, unlike driving while being a drunk person, is not an ongoing crime. In other words, in order to stop the petitioners the officers here not only had to assume without basis the accuracy of the anonymous accusation but also had to posit an unlikely reason (drunkenness) for the accused behavior.

In sum, at the moment the police spotted the truck, it was more than merely "*possib[le]*" that the petitioners were not committing an ongoing traffic crime. It was overwhelmingly likely that they were not.

III

It gets worse. Not only, it turns out, did the police have no good reason *at first* to believe that Lorenzo was driving drunk, they had very good reason *at last* to know that he was not. The Court concludes that the tip, plus confirmation of the truck's location, produced reasonable suspicion that the truck not only had been *but still was* barreling dangerously and drunkenly down Highway 1. In fact, alas, it was not, and the officers knew it. They followed the truck for five minutes, presumably to see if it was being operated recklessly. And *that* was good police work. While the anonymous tip was not enough to support a stop for drunken driving under *Terry v. Ohio* (1968), it was surely enough to counsel observation of the truck to see if it was driven by a drunken driver. But the pesky little detail left out of the Court's reasonable-suspicion equation is that, for the five minutes that the truck was being followed (five minutes is a *long* time), Lorenzo's driving was irreproachable. Had the officers witnessed the petitioners violate a single traffic law, they would have had cause to stop the truck, and this case would not be before us. And not only was the driving *irreproachable*, but the State offers no evidence to suggest that the petitioners even did anything *suspicious*, such as suddenly slowing down, pulling off to the side of the road, or turning somewhere to see whether they were being followed. Consequently, the tip's suggestion of ongoing drunken driving (if it could be deemed to suggest that) not only went uncorroborated; it was affirmatively undermined.

Similarly, here, the crime supposedly suggested by the tip was ongoing intoxicated driving, the hallmarks of which are many, readily identifiable, and difficult to conceal. That the officers witnessed nary a minor traffic violation nor any other "sound indici[um] of drunk driving," strongly suggests that the suspected crime was *not* occurring after all. The tip's implication of continuing criminality, already weak, grew even weaker.

Resisting this line of reasoning, the Court curiously asserts that, since drunk drivers who see marked squad cars in their rearview mirrors may evade detection simply by driving "more careful[ly]," the "absence of additional suspicious conduct" is "hardly surprising" and thus largely irrelevant. Whether a drunk driver drives drunkenly, the Court seems to think, is up to him. That is not how I understand the influence of alcohol. I subscribe to the more traditional view that the dangers of intoxicated driving are the intoxicant's impairing effects on the body—effects that no mere act of the will can resist. Consistent with this view, I take it as a fundamental premise of our intoxicated-driving laws that a driver soused enough to swerve once can be expected to swerve again—and soon. If he does not, and if the only evidence of his first episode of irregular driving is a mere inference from an uncorroborated, vague, and nameless tip, then the Fourth Amendment requires that he be left alone.

The Court's opinion serves up a freedom-destroying cocktail consisting of two parts patent falsity: (1) that anonymous 911 reports of traffic violations are reliable so long as they correctly identify a car and its location, and (2) that a single instance of careless or reckless driving necessarily supports a reasonable suspicion of drunkenness. All the malevolent 911 caller need do is assert a traffic violation, and the targeted car will be stopped, forcibly if necessary, by the police. If the driver turns out not to be drunk (which will almost always be the case), the caller need fear no consequences, even if 911 knows his identity. After all, he never alleged drunkenness, but merely called in a traffic violation—and on that point his word is as good as his victim's.

Drunken driving is a serious matter, but so is the loss of our freedom to come and go as we please without police interference. To prevent and detect murder we do not allow searches without probable cause or targeted *Terry* stops without reasonable suspicion. We should not do so for drunken driving either. After today's opinion all of us on the road, and not just drug dealers, are at risk of having our freedom of movement curtailed on suspicion of drunkenness, based upon a phone tip, true or false, of a single instance of careless driving. I respectfully dissent.

Chapter 3

THE EXCLUSIONARY RULE

C. When Does the Exclusionary Rule Apply? (casebook p. 387)

If the police illegally stop an individual and then learn that the there is an outstanding warrant, must evidence gained from a search incident to the arrest be excluded?

Utah v. Strieff
136 S. Ct. 2056 (2016)

Justice THOMAS delivered the opinion of the Court.

To enforce the Fourth Amendment's prohibition against "unreasonable searches and seizures," this Court has at times required courts to exclude evidence obtained by unconstitutional police conduct. But the Court has also held that, even when there is a Fourth Amendment violation, this exclusionary rule does not apply when the costs of exclusion outweigh its deterrent benefits. In some cases, for example, the link between the unconstitutional conduct and the discovery of the evidence is too attenuated to justify suppression. The question in this case is whether this attenuation doctrine applies when an officer makes an unconstitutional investigatory stop; learns during that stop that the suspect is subject to a valid arrest warrant; and proceeds to arrest the suspect and seize incriminating evidence during a search incident to that arrest. We hold that the evidence the officer seized as part of the search incident to arrest is admissible because the officer's discovery of the arrest warrant attenuated the connection between the unlawful stop and the evidence seized incident to arrest.

I

This case began with an anonymous tip. In December 2006, someone called the South Salt Lake City police's drug-tip line to report "narcotics activity" at a particular residence. Narcotics detective Douglas Fackrell investigated the tip. Over the course of about a week, Officer Fackrell conducted intermittent surveillance of the home. He observed visitors who left a few minutes after arriving at the house. These visits were sufficiently frequent to raise his suspicion that the occupants were dealing drugs.

One of those visitors was respondent Edward Strieff. Officer Fackrell observed Strieff exit the house and walk toward a nearby convenience store. In the store's parking lot, Officer Fackrell detained Strieff, identified himself, and asked Strieff what he was doing at the residence.

As part of the stop, Officer Fackrell requested Strieff's identification, and Strieff produced his Utah identification card. Officer Fackrell relayed Strieff's information to a police dispatcher, who reported that Strieff had an outstanding arrest warrant for a traffic violation. Officer Fackrell then arrested Strieff pursuant to that warrant. When Officer Fackrell searched Strieff incident to the arrest, he discovered a baggie of methamphetamine and drug paraphernalia.

The State charged Strieff with unlawful possession of methamphetamine and drug paraphernalia. Strieff moved to suppress the evidence, arguing that the evidence was inadmissible because it was derived from an unlawful investigatory stop. At the suppression hearing, the prosecutor conceded that Officer Fackrell lacked reasonable suspicion for the stop but argued that the evidence should not be suppressed because the existence of a valid arrest warrant attenuated the connection between the unlawful stop and the discovery of the contraband.

II

In the 20th century, however, the exclusionary rule—the rule that often requires trial courts to exclude unlawfully seized evidence in a criminal trial—became the principal judicial remedy to deter Fourth Amendment violations.

Under the Court's precedents, the exclusionary rule encompasses both the "primary evidence obtained as a direct result of an illegal search or seizure" and, relevant here, "evidence later discovered and found to be derivative of an illegality," the so-called "'fruit of the poisonous tree.'" But the significant costs of this rule have led us to deem it "applicable only . . . where its deterrence benefits outweigh its substantial social costs." "Suppression of evidence . . . has always been our last resort, not our first impulse."

We have accordingly recognized several exceptions to the rule. Three of these exceptions involve the causal relationship between the unconstitutional act and the discovery of evidence. First, the independent source doctrine allows trial courts to admit evidence obtained in an unlawful search if officers independently acquired it from a separate, independent source. Second, the inevitable discovery doctrine allows for the admission of evidence that would have been discovered even without the unconstitutional source. Third, and at issue here, is the attenuation doctrine: Evidence is admissible when the connection between unconstitutional police conduct and the evidence is remote or has been interrupted by some intervening circumstance, so that "the interest protected by the constitutional guarantee that has been violated would not be served by suppression of the evidence obtained."

Turning to the application of the attenuation doctrine to this case, we first address a threshold question: whether this doctrine applies at all to a case like this, where the intervening circumstance that the State relies on is the discovery of a valid, pre-existing, and untainted arrest warrant. The three factors articulated in

3. The Exclusionary Rule

Brown v. Illinois (1975), guide our analysis. First, we look to the "temporal proximity" between the unconstitutional conduct and the discovery of evidence to determine how closely the discovery of evidence followed the unconstitutional search. Second, we consider "the presence of intervening circumstances." Third, and "particularly" significant, we examine "the purpose and flagrancy of the official misconduct." In evaluating these factors, we assume without deciding (because the State conceded the point) that Officer Fackrell lacked reasonable suspicion to initially stop Strieff.

The first factor, temporal proximity between the initially unlawful stop and the search, favors suppressing the evidence. Our precedents have declined to find that this factor favors attenuation unless "substantial time" elapses between an unlawful act and when the evidence is obtained. Here, however, Officer Fackrell discovered drug contraband on Strieff's person only minutes after the illegal stop.

In contrast, the second factor, the presence of intervening circumstances, strongly favors the State. In this case, the warrant was valid, it predated Officer Fackrell's investigation, and it was entirely unconnected with the stop. And once Officer Fackrell discovered the warrant, he had an obligation to arrest Strieff. "A warrant is a judicial mandate to an officer to conduct a search or make an arrest, and the officer has a sworn duty to carry out its provisions." *United States v. Leon* (1984). Officer Fackrell's arrest of Strieff thus was a ministerial act that was independently compelled by the pre-existing warrant. And once Officer Fackrell was authorized to arrest Strieff, it was undisputedly lawful to search Strieff as an incident of his arrest to protect Officer Fackrell's safety.

Finally, the third factor, "the purpose and flagrancy of the official misconduct," also strongly favors the State. The exclusionary rule exists to deter police misconduct. The third factor of the attenuation doctrine reflects that rationale by favoring exclusion only when the police misconduct is most in need of deterrence—that is, when it is purposeful or flagrant.

Officer Fackrell was at most negligent. In stopping Strieff, Officer Fackrell made two good-faith mistakes. First, he had not observed what time Strieff entered the suspected drug house, so he did not know how long Strieff had been there. Officer Fackrell thus lacked a sufficient basis to conclude that Strieff was a short-term visitor who may have been consummating a drug transaction. Second, because he lacked confirmation that Strieff was a short-term visitor, Officer Fackrell should have asked Strieff whether he would speak with him, instead of demanding that Strieff do so. Officer Fackrell's stated purpose was to "find out what was going on [in] the house." Nothing prevented him from approaching Strieff simply to ask. But these errors in judgment hardly rise to a purposeful or flagrant violation of Strieff's Fourth Amendment rights.

While Officer Fackrell's decision to initiate the stop was mistaken, his conduct thereafter was lawful. The officer's decision to run the warrant check was a "negligibly burdensome precautio[n]" for officer safety. And Officer Fackrell's actual search of Strieff was a lawful search incident to arrest. Moreover, there is no indication that this unlawful stop was part of any systemic or recurrent police misconduct. To the contrary, all the evidence suggests that the stop was an isolated instance of negligence that occurred in connection with a bona fide investigation of a suspected drug house. Officer Fackrell saw Strieff leave a suspected drug house. And his suspicion about the house was based on an anonymous tip and his personal observations.

Applying these factors, we hold that the evidence discovered on Strieff's person was admissible because the unlawful stop was sufficiently attenuated by the pre-existing arrest warrant. Although the illegal stop was close in time to Strieff's arrest, that consideration is outweighed by two factors supporting the State. The outstanding arrest warrant for Strieff's arrest is a critical intervening circumstance that is wholly independent of the illegal stop. The discovery of that warrant broke the causal chain between the unconstitutional stop and the discovery of evidence by compelling Officer Fackrell to arrest Strieff. And, it is especially significant that there is no evidence that Officer Fackrell's illegal stop reflected flagrantly unlawful police misconduct.

We hold that the evidence Officer Fackrell seized as part of his search incident to arrest is admissible because his discovery of the arrest warrant attenuated the connection between the unlawful stop and the evidence seized from Strieff incident to arrest. The judgment of the Utah Supreme Court, accordingly, is reversed.

Justice SOTOMAYOR, with whom Justice GINSBURG joins as to Parts I, II, and III, dissenting.

The Court today holds that the discovery of a warrant for an unpaid parking ticket will forgive a police officer's violation of your Fourth Amendment rights. Do not be soothed by the opinion's technical language: This case allows the police to stop you on the street, demand your identification, and check it for outstanding traffic warrants—even if you are doing nothing wrong. If the officer discovers a warrant for a fine you forgot to pay, courts will now excuse his illegal stop and will admit into evidence anything he happens to find by searching you after arresting you on the warrant. Because the Fourth Amendment should prohibit, not permit, such misconduct, I dissent.

I

Minutes after Edward Strieff walked out of a South Salt Lake City home, an officer stopped him, questioned him, and took his identification to run it through a police database. The officer did not suspect that Strieff had done anything wrong. Strieff just happened to be the first person to leave a house that the officer thought might contain "drug activity."

As the State of Utah concedes, this stop was illegal. The Fourth Amendment protects people from "unreasonable searches and seizures." An officer breaches that protection when he detains a pedestrian to check his license without any evidence that the person is engaged in a crime. The officer deepens the breach when he prolongs the detention just to fish further for evidence of wrongdoing. In his search for lawbreaking, the officer in this case himself broke the law.

II

It is tempting in a case like this, where illegal conduct by an officer uncovers illegal conduct by a civilian, to forgive the officer. After all, his instincts, although unconstitutional, were correct. But a basic principle lies at the heart of the Fourth Amendment: Two wrongs don't make a right. When "lawless police conduct" uncovers evidence of lawless civilian conduct, this Court has long required later criminal trials to exclude the illegally obtained evidence.

This "exclusionary rule" removes an incentive for officers to search us without proper justification. It also keeps courts from being "made party to lawless invasions of the constitutional rights of citizens by permitting unhindered governmental use of the fruits of such invasions." When courts admit only lawfully obtained evidence, they encourage "those who formulate law enforcement polices, and the officers who implement them, to incorporate Fourth Amendment ideals into their value system." But when courts admit illegally obtained evidence as well, they reward "manifest neglect if not an open defiance of the prohibitions of the Constitution."

These factors confirm that the officer in this case discovered Strieff's drugs by exploiting his own illegal conduct. The officer did not ask Strieff to volunteer his name only to find out, days later, that Strieff had a warrant against him. The officer illegally stopped Strieff and immediately ran a warrant check. The officer's discovery of a warrant was not some intervening surprise that he could not have anticipated. Utah lists over 180,000 misdemeanor warrants in its database, and at the time of the arrest, Salt Lake County had a "backlog of outstanding warrants" so large that it faced the "potential for civil liability." The officer's violation was also calculated to procure evidence. His sole reason for stopping Strieff, he acknowledged, was investigative—he wanted to discover whether drug activity was going on in the house Strieff had just exited.

The warrant check, in other words, was not an "intervening circumstance" separating the stop from the search for drugs. It was part and parcel of the officer's illegal "expedition for evidence in the hope that something might turn up." Under our precedents, because the officer found Strieff's drugs by exploiting his own constitutional violation, the drugs should be excluded.

III

The Court sees things differently. To the Court, the fact that a warrant gives an officer cause to arrest a person severs the connection between illegal policing and the resulting discovery of evidence. This is a remarkable proposition: The mere existence of a warrant not only gives an officer legal cause to arrest and search a person, it also forgives an officer who, with no knowledge of the warrant at all, unlawfully stops that person on a whim or hunch.

The majority misses the point when it calls the warrant check here a " 'negligibly burdensome precautio[n]' " taken for the officer's "safety." Remember, the officer stopped Strieff without suspecting him of committing any crime. By his own account, the officer did not fear Strieff. The majority also posits that the officer could not have exploited his illegal conduct because he did not violate the Fourth Amendment on purpose. Rather, he made "good-faith mistakes." Never mind that the officer's sole purpose was to fish for evidence. The majority casts his unconstitutional actions as "negligent" and therefore incapable of being deterred by the exclusionary rule.

But the Fourth Amendment does not tolerate an officer's unreasonable searches and seizures just because he did not know any better. Even officers prone to negligence can learn from courts that exclude illegally obtained evidence. Indeed, they are perhaps the most in need of the education, whether by the judge's opinion, the prosecutor's future guidance, or an updated manual on criminal procedure. If the officers are in doubt about what the law requires, exclusion gives them an "incentive to err on the side of constitutional behavior."

Most striking about the Court's opinion is its insistence that the event here was "isolated," with "no indication that this unlawful stop was part of any systemic or recurrent police misconduct." Respectfully, nothing about this case is isolated.

Outstanding warrants are surprisingly common. When a person with a traffic ticket misses a fine payment or court appearance, a court will issue a warrant. When a person on probation drinks alcohol or breaks curfew, a court will issue a warrant. The States and Federal Government maintain databases with over 7.8 million outstanding warrants, the vast majority of which appear to be for minor offenses. Even these sources may not track the "staggering" numbers of warrants, "'drawers and drawers'" full, that many cities issue for traffic violations and ordinance infractions. The Department of Justice recently reported that in the town of Ferguson, Missouri, with a population of 21,000, 16,000 people had outstanding warrants against them. In Newark, New Jersey, officers stopped 52,235 pedestrians within a 4–year period and ran warrant checks on 39,308 of them. The Justice Department analyzed these warrant-checked stops and reported that "approximately 93% of the stops would have been considered unsupported by articulated reasonable suspicion."

I do not doubt that most officers act in "good faith" and do not set out to break the law. That does not mean these stops are "isolated instance[s] of negligence," however. Many are the product of institutionalized training procedures. The New York City Police Department long trained officers to, in the words of a District Judge, "stop and question first, develop reasonable suspicion later."

The majority does not suggest what makes this case "isolated" from these and countless other examples. Nor does it offer guidance for how a defendant can prove that his arrest was the result of "widespread" misconduct. Surely it should not take a federal investigation of Salt Lake County before the Court would protect someone in Strieff's position.

IV

Writing only for myself, and drawing on my professional experiences, I would add that unlawful "stops" have severe consequences much greater than the inconvenience suggested by the name. This Court has given officers an array of instruments to probe and examine you. When we condone officers' use of these devices without adequate cause, we give them reason to target pedestrians in an arbitrary manner. We also risk treating members of our communities as second-class citizens.

Although many Americans have been stopped for speeding or jaywalking, few may realize how degrading a stop can be when the officer is looking for more. This Court has allowed an officer to stop you for whatever reason he wants—so long as he can point to a pretextual justification after the fact. *Whren v. United States* (1996). The indignity of the stop is not limited to an officer telling you that you look like a criminal. The officer may next ask for your "consent" to inspect your bag or purse without telling you that you can decline. Regardless of your answer, he may order you to stand "helpless, perhaps facing a wall with [your] hands raised." If the officer thinks you might be dangerous, he may then "frisk" you for weapons. This involves more than just a pat down. As onlookers pass by, the officer may " 'feel with sensitive fingers every portion of [your] body. A thorough search [may] be made of [your] arms and armpits, waistline and back, the groin and area about the testicles, and entire surface of the legs down to the feet.' "

The officer's control over you does not end with the stop. If the officer chooses, he may handcuff you and take you to jail for doing nothing more than speeding, jaywalking, or "driving [your] pickup truck . . . with [your] 3-year-old son and 5-year-old daughter . . . without [your] seatbelt fastened." *Atwater v. Lago Vista* (2001). At the jail, he can fingerprint you, swab DNA from the inside of your mouth, and force you to "shower with a delousing agent" while you "lift [your] tongue, hold out [your] arms, turn around, and lift [your] genitals." *Florence v. Board of Chosen Freeholders of County of Burlington* (2012); *Maryland v. King* (2013). Even if you are innocent, you will now join the 65 million Americans with an arrest record and experience the "civil death" of discrimination by employers, landlords, and whoever else conducts a background check. And, of course, if you fail to pay bail or appear for court, a judge will issue a warrant to render you "arrestable on sight" in the future.

This case involves a *suspicionless* stop, one in which the officer initiated this chain of events without justification. As the Justice Department notes, many innocent people are subjected to the humiliations of these unconstitutional searches. The white defendant in this case shows that anyone's dignity can be violated in this manner. But it is no secret that people of color are disproportionate victims of this type of scrutiny. See M. Alexander, The New Jim Crow 95-136

(2010). For generations, black and brown parents have given their children "the talk"—instructing them never to run down the street; always keep your hands where they can be seen; do not even think of talking back to a stranger—all out of fear of how an officer with a gun will react to them. See, e.g.,W.E.B. Du Bois, The Souls of Black Folk (1903); J. Baldwin, The Fire Next Time (1963); T. Coates, Between the World and Me (2015).

By legitimizing the conduct that produces this double consciousness, this case tells everyone, white and black, guilty and innocent, that an officer can verify your legal status at any time. It says that your body is subject to invasion while courts excuse the violation of your rights. It implies that you are not a citizen of a democracy but the subject of a carceral state, just waiting to be cataloged.

We must not pretend that the countless people who are routinely targeted by police are "isolated." They are the canaries in the coal mine whose deaths, civil and literal, warn us that no one can breathe in this atmosphere. See L. Guinier & G. Torres, The Miner's Canary 274-283 (2002). They are the ones who recognize that unlawful police stops corrode all our civil liberties and threaten all our lives. Until their voices matter too, our justice system will continue to be anything but.

Justice KAGAN, with whom Justice GINSBURG joins, dissenting.

If a police officer stops a person on the street without reasonable suspicion, that seizure violates the Fourth Amendment. And if the officer pats down the unlawfully detained individual and finds drugs in his pocket, the State may not use the contraband as evidence in a criminal prosecution. That much is beyond dispute. The question here is whether the prohibition on admitting evidence dissolves if the officer discovers, after making the stop but before finding the drugs, that the person has an outstanding arrest warrant. Because that added wrinkle makes no difference under the Constitution, I respectfully dissent.

Since *Brown v. Illinois* (1975), three factors have guided that analysis. First, the closer the "temporal proximity" between the unlawful act and the discovery of evidence, the greater the deterrent value of suppression. Second, the more "purpose[ful]" or "flagran[t]" the police illegality, the clearer the necessity, and better the chance, of preventing similar misbehavior. And third, the presence (or absence) of "intervening circumstances" makes a difference: The stronger the causal chain between the misconduct and the evidence, the more exclusion will curb future constitutional violations. Here, as shown below, each of those considerations points toward suppression: Nothing in Fackrell's discovery of an outstanding warrant so attenuated the connection between his wrongful behavior and his detection of drugs as to diminish the exclusionary rule's deterrent benefits.

Start where the majority does: The temporal proximity factor, it forthrightly admits, "favors suppressing the evidence." After all, Fackrell's discovery of drugs came just minutes after the unconstitutional stop. And in prior decisions, this Court has made clear that only the lapse of "substantial time" between the two could favor admission. So the State, by all accounts, takes strike one.

3. The Exclusionary Rule

Move on to the purposefulness of Fackrell's conduct, where the majority is less willing to see a problem for what it is. The majority chalks up Fackrell's Fourth Amendment violation to a couple of innocent "mistakes." But far from a Barney Fife-type mishap, Fackrell's seizure of Strieff was a calculated decision, taken with so little justification that the State has never tried to defend its legality. In *Brown*, the Court held those facts to support suppression—and they do here as well. Swing and a miss for strike two.

Finally, consider whether any intervening circumstance "br[oke] the causal chain" between the stop and the evidence. Fackrell's discovery of an arrest warrant—the only event the majority thinks intervened—was an eminently foreseeable consequence of stopping Strieff. As Fackrell testified, checking for outstanding warrants during a stop is the "normal" practice of South Salt Lake City police. In other words, the department's standard detention procedures—stop, ask for identification, run a check—are partly designed to find outstanding warrants. And find them they will, given the staggering number of such warrants on the books.

To take just a few examples: The State of California has 2.5 million outstanding arrest warrants (a number corresponding to about 9% of its adult population); Pennsylvania (with a population of about 12.8 million) contributes 1.4 million more; and New York City (population 8.4 million) adds another 1.2 million. So outstanding warrants do not appear as bolts from the blue. They are the run-of-the-mill results of police stops—what officers look for when they run a routine check of a person's identification and what they know will turn up with fair regularity. In short, they are nothing like what intervening circumstances are supposed to be. Strike three.

The majority's misapplication of *Brown*'s three-part inquiry creates unfortunate incentives for the police—indeed, practically invites them to do what Fackrell did here. Consider an officer who, like Fackrell, wishes to stop someone for investigative reasons, but does not have what a court would view as reasonable suspicion. If the officer believes that any evidence he discovers will be inadmissible, he is likely to think the unlawful stop not worth making—precisely the deterrence the exclusionary rule is meant to achieve. But when he is told of today's decision? Now the officer knows that the stop may well yield admissible evidence: So long as the target is one of the many millions of people in this country with an outstanding arrest warrant, anything the officer finds in a search is fair game for use in a criminal prosecution. The officer's incentive to violate the Constitution thus increases: From here on, he sees potential advantage in stopping individuals without reasonable suspicion—exactly the temptation the exclusionary rule is supposed to remove. Because the majority thus places Fourth Amendment protections at risk, I respectfully dissent.

Chapter 4

POLICE INTERROGATION AND THE PRIVILEGE AGAINST SELF-INCRIMINATION

B. Fifth Amendment Limits on In-Custodial Interrogation

5. Waiver of *Miranda* Rights

a. *What Is Sufficient to Constitute a Waiver?* (casebook p. 550)

In *Berguis v. Thompkins* (casebook p. 553), the Court held that the right to remain silent must be expressly invoked. *Berguis v. Thompkins* was after a person was arrested and *Miranda* warnings were given. What about *before* a person is taken into custody, arrested, and given *Miranda* warnings?

Salinas v. Texas
133 S. Ct. 2174 (2013)

Justice ALITO announced the judgment of the Court and delivered an opinion in which THE CHIEF JUSTICE and Justice KENNEDY join.

Without being placed in custody or receiving *Miranda* warnings, petitioner voluntarily answered the questions of a police officer who was investigating a murder. But petitioner balked when the officer asked whether a ballistics test would show that the shell casings found at the crime scene would match petitioner's shotgun. Petitioner was subsequently charged with murder, and at trial prosecutors argued that his reaction to the officer's question suggested that he was guilty. Petitioner claims that this argument violated the Fifth Amendment, which guarantees that "[n]o person . . . shall be compelled in any criminal case to be a witness against himself."

Petitioner's Fifth Amendment claim fails because he did not expressly invoke the privilege against self-incrimination in response to the officer's question. It has long been settled that the privilege "generally is not self-executing" and that a witness who desires its protection "'must claim it.'" Although "no ritualistic formula is necessary in order to invoke the privilege," a witness does not do so by simply standing mute.

4. Police Interrogation and the Privilege Against Self-Incrimination

I

On the morning of December 18, 1992, two brothers were shot and killed in their Houston home. There were no witnesses to the murders, but a neighbor who heard gunshots saw someone run out of the house and speed away in a dark-colored car. Police recovered six shotgun shell casings at the scene. The investigation led police to petitioner, who had been a guest at a party the victims hosted the night before they were killed. Police visited petitioner at his home, where they saw a dark blue car in the driveway. He agreed to hand over his shotgun for ballistics testing and to accompany police to the station for questioning.

Petitioner's interview with the police lasted approximately one hour. All agree that the interview was noncustodial, and the parties litigated this case on the assumption that he was not read *Miranda* warnings. For most of the interview, petitioner answered the officer's questions. But when asked whether his shotgun "would match the shells recovered at the scene of the murder," petitioner declined to answer. Instead, petitioner "[l]ooked down at the floor, shuffled his feet, bit his bottom lip, cl[e]nched his hands in his lap, [and] began to tighten up." After a few moments of silence, the officer asked additional questions, which petitioner answered.

Petitioner did not testify at trial. Over his objection, prosecutors used his reaction to the officer's question during the 1993 interview as evidence of his guilt. The jury found petitioner guilty, and he received a 20-year sentence.

We granted certiorari, to resolve a division of authority in the lower courts over whether the prosecution may use a defendant's assertion of the privilege against self-incrimination during a noncustodial police interview as part of its case in chief. But because petitioner did not invoke the privilege during his interview, we find it unnecessary to reach that question.

II

The privilege against self-incrimination "is an exception to the general principle that the Government has the right to everyone's testimony." To prevent the privilege from shielding information not properly within its scope, we have long held that a witness who " 'desires the protection of the privilege . . . must claim it' " at the time he relies on it.

That requirement ensures that the Government is put on notice when a witness intends to rely on the privilege so that it may either argue that the testimony sought could not be self-incriminating, or cure any potential self-incrimination through a grant of immunity, The express invocation requirement also gives courts tasked with evaluating a Fifth Amendment claim a contemporaneous record establishing the witness' reasons for refusing to answer. In these ways, insisting that witnesses expressly invoke the privilege "assures that the Government obtains all the information to which it is entitled."

4. Police Interrogation and the Privilege Against Self-Incrimination

We have previously recognized two exceptions to the requirement that witnesses invoke the privilege, but neither applies here. First, we held in *Griffin v. California* (1965), that a criminal defendant need not take the stand and assert the privilege at his own trial. That exception reflects the fact that a criminal defendant has an "absolute right not to testify." Because petitioner had no comparable unqualified right during his interview with police, his silence falls outside the *Griffin* exception.

Second, we have held that a witness' failure to invoke the privilege must be excused where governmental coercion makes his forfeiture of the privilege involuntary. Thus, in *Miranda*, we said that a suspect who is subjected to the "inherently compelling pressures" of an unwarned custodial interrogation need not invoke the privilege. Due to the uniquely coercive nature of custodial interrogation, a suspect in custody cannot be said to have voluntarily forgone the privilege "unless [he] fails to claim [it] after being suitably warned."

Petitioner cannot benefit from that principle because it is undisputed that his interview with police was voluntary. As petitioner himself acknowledges, he agreed to accompany the officers to the station and "was free to leave at any time during the interview." That places petitioner's situation outside the scope of *Miranda* and other cases in which we have held that various forms of governmental coercion prevented defendants from voluntarily invoking the privilege. The critical question is whether, under the "circumstances" of this case, petitioner was deprived of the ability to voluntarily invoke the Fifth Amendment. He was not. We have before us no allegation that petitioner's failure to assert the privilege was involuntary, and it would have been a simple matter for him to say that he was not answering the officer's question on Fifth Amendment grounds. Because he failed to do so, the prosecution's use of his noncustodial silence did not violate the Fifth Amendment.

B

Petitioner urges us to adopt a third exception to the invocation requirement for cases in which a witness stands mute and thereby declines to give an answer that officials suspect would be incriminating. Our cases all but foreclose such an exception, which would needlessly burden the Government's interests in obtaining testimony and prosecuting criminal activity. We therefore decline petitioner's invitation to craft a new exception to the "general rule" that a witness must assert the privilege to subsequently benefit from it.

Our cases establish that a defendant normally does not invoke the privilege by remaining silent. We have also repeatedly held that the express invocation requirement applies even when an official has reason to suspect that the answer to his question would incriminate the witness.

Petitioner's proposed exception would also be very difficult to reconcile with *Berghuis v. Thompkins* (2010). There, we held in the closely related context of post-*Miranda* silence that a defendant failed to invoke the privilege when he refused to respond to police questioning for 2 hours and 45 minutes. If the extended custodial silence in that case did not invoke the privilege, then surely the momentary silence in this case did not do so either.

At oral argument, counsel for petitioner suggested that it would be unfair to require a suspect unschooled in the particulars of legal doctrine to do anything more than remain silent in order to invoke his "right to remain silent." But popular misconceptions notwithstanding, the Fifth Amendment guarantees that no one may be "compelled in any criminal case to be a witness against himself"; it does not establish an unqualified "right to remain silent." A witness' constitutional right to refuse to answer questions depends on his reasons for doing so, and courts need to know those reasons to evaluate the merits of a Fifth Amendment claim.

C

Finally, we are not persuaded by petitioner's arguments that applying the usual express invocation requirement where a witness is silent during a noncustodial police interview will prove unworkable in practice. We also reject petitioner's argument that an express invocation requirement will encourage police officers to " 'unfairly "tric[k]" ' " suspects into cooperating. Petitioner worries that officers could unduly pressure suspects into talking by telling them that their silence could be used in a future prosecution. But as petitioner himself concedes, police officers "have done nothing wrong" when they "accurately stat[e] the law." So long as police do not deprive a witness of the ability to voluntarily invoke the privilege, there is no Fifth Amendment violation.

Before petitioner could rely on the privilege against self-incrimination, he was required to invoke it. Because he failed to do so, the judgment of the Texas Court of Criminal Appeals is affirmed.

Justice THOMAS, with whom Justice SCALIA joins, concurring in the judgment.

We granted certiorari to decide whether the Fifth Amendment privilege against compulsory self-incrimination prohibits a prosecutor from using a defendant's pre-custodial silence as evidence of his guilt. The plurality avoids reaching that question and instead concludes that Salinas' Fifth Amendment claim fails because he did not expressly invoke the privilege. I think there is a simpler way to resolve this case. In my view, Salinas' claim would fail even if he had invoked the privilege because the prosecutor's comments regarding his precustodial silence did not compel him to give self-incriminating testimony.

In *Griffin v. California* (1965), this Court held that the Fifth Amendment prohibits a prosecutor or judge from commenting on a defendant's failure to testify. The Court reasoned that such comments, and any adverse inferences drawn from them, are a "penalty" imposed on the defendant's exercise of his Fifth Amendment privilege. Salinas argues that we should extend *Griffin*'s no-adverse-inference rule to a defendant's silence during a precustodial interview. I have previously explained that the Court's decision in *Griffin* "lacks foundation in the Constitution's text, history, or logic" and should not be extended. I adhere to that view today.

4. Police Interrogation and the Privilege Against Self-Incrimination

Griffin is impossible to square with the text of the Fifth Amendment, which provides that "[n]o person . . . shall be compelled in any criminal case to be a witness against himself." A defendant is not "compelled . . . to be a witness against himself" simply because a jury has been told that it may draw an adverse inference from his silence.

Nor does the history of the Fifth Amendment support *Griffin*. At the time of the founding, English and American courts strongly encouraged defendants to give unsworn statements and drew adverse inferences when they failed to do so. Given *Griffin*'s indefensible foundation, I would not extend it to a defendant's silence during a precustodial interview. I agree with the plurality that Salinas' Fifth Amendment claim fails and, therefore, concur in the judgment.

Justice BREYER, with whom Justice GINSBURG, Justice SOTOMAYOR, and Justice KAGAN join, dissenting.

In my view the Fifth Amendment here prohibits the prosecution from commenting on the petitioner's silence in response to police questioning. And I dissent from the Court's contrary conclusion.

The question before us is whether the Fifth Amendment prohibits the prosecutor from eliciting and commenting upon the evidence about Salinas' silence. The plurality believes that the Amendment does not bar the evidence and comments because Salinas "did not expressly invoke the privilege against self-incrimination" when he fell silent during the questioning at the police station. But, in my view, that conclusion is inconsistent with this Court's case law and its underlying practical rationale.

The Fifth Amendment prohibits prosecutors from commenting on an individual's silence where that silence amounts to an effort to avoid becoming "a witness against himself." This Court has specified that "a rule of evidence" permitting "commen[t] . . . by counsel" in a criminal case upon a defendant's failure to testify "violates the Fifth Amendment." And, since "it is impermissible to penalize an individual for exercising his Fifth Amendment privilege when he is under police custodial interrogation," the "prosecution may not . . . use at trial *the fact that he stood mute* or claimed his privilege in the face of accusation."

Particularly in the context of police interrogation, a contrary rule would undermine the basic protection that the Fifth Amendment provides. To permit a prosecutor to comment on a defendant's constitutionally protected silence would put that defendant in an impossible predicament. He must either answer the question or remain silent. If he answers the question, he may well reveal, for example, prejudicial facts, disreputable associates, or suspicious circumstances — even if he is innocent. If he remains silent, the prosecutor may well use that silence to suggest a consciousness of guilt. And if the defendant then takes the witness stand in order to explain either his speech or his silence, the prosecution may introduce, say for impeachment purposes, a prior conviction that the law would otherwise make inadmissible. Thus, where the Fifth Amendment is at issue, to allow comment on silence directly or indirectly can compel an individual to act as "a witness against himself"—very much what the Fifth Amendment forbids. And that is similarly so whether the questioned individual, as part of his decision to remain silent, invokes the Fifth Amendment explicitly or implicitly, through words, through deeds, or through reference to surrounding circumstances.

It is consequently not surprising that this Court, more than half a century ago, explained that "no ritualistic formula is necessary in order to invoke the privilege." Thus, a prosecutor may not comment on a defendant's failure to testify at trial—even if neither the defendant nor anyone else ever mentions a Fifth Amendment right not to do so. Circumstances, not a defendant's statement, tie the defendant's silence to the right. Similarly, a prosecutor may not comment on the fact that a defendant in custody, *after* receiving *Miranda* warnings, "stood mute"—regardless of whether he "claimed his privilege" in so many words. Again, it is not any explicit statement but, instead, the defendant's deeds (silence) and circumstances (receipt of the warnings) that tie together silence and constitutional right.

Applying these principles to the present case, I would hold that Salinas need not have expressly invoked the Fifth Amendment. The context was that of a criminal investigation. Police told Salinas that and made clear that he was a suspect. His interrogation took place at the police station. Salinas was not represented by counsel. The relevant question—about whether the shotgun from Salinas' home would incriminate him—amounted to a switch in subject matter. And it was obvious that the new question sought to ferret out whether Salinas was guilty of murder.

These circumstances give rise to a reasonable inference that Salinas' silence derived from an exercise of his Fifth Amendment rights. This Court has recognized repeatedly that many, indeed most, Americans are aware that they have a constitutional right not to incriminate themselves by answering questions posed by the police during an interrogation conducted in order to figure out the perpetrator of a crime. The nature of the surroundings, the switch of topic, the particular question—all suggested that the right we have and generally *know* we have was at issue at the critical moment here. Salinas, not being represented by counsel, would not likely have used the precise words "Fifth Amendment" to invoke his rights because he would not likely have been aware of technical legal requirements, such as a need to identify the Fifth Amendment by name.

At the same time, the need to categorize Salinas' silence as based on the Fifth Amendment is supported here by the presence, in full force, of the predicament I discussed earlier, namely that of not forcing Salinas to choose between incrimination through speech and incrimination through silence.

I recognize that other cases may arise where facts and circumstances surrounding an individual's silence present a closer question. The critical question—whether those circumstances give rise to a fair inference that the silence rests on the Fifth Amendment—will not always prove easy to administer. But that consideration does not support the plurality's rule-based approach here, for the administrative problems accompanying the plurality's approach are even worse.

4. Police Interrogation and the Privilege Against Self-Incrimination

Far better, in my view, to pose the relevant question directly: Can one fairly infer from an individual's silence and surrounding circumstances an exercise of the Fifth Amendment's privilege? The need for simplicity, the constitutional importance of applying the Fifth Amendment to those who seek its protection, and this Court's case law all suggest that this is the right question to ask here. And the answer to that question in the circumstances of today's case is clearly: yes.

For these reasons, I believe that the Fifth Amendment prohibits a prosecutor from commenting on Salinas's silence.

Chapter 9

PLEA BARGAINING AND GUILTY PLEAS

C. Guilty Pleas (casebook p. 845)

In *Chaidez v. United* States, 133 S. Ct. 1102 (2013), the Supreme Court held that *Padilla v. Kentucky*, 129 S. Ct. 1317 (2010), does not apply retroactively to cases already final on direct review.

Chapter 10

SPEEDY TRIAL RIGHTS

C. Due Process and Speedy Trial Rights

2. Post-Charging Delay and Speedy Trial Rights

b. *Constitutional Protections* (casebook p. 882)

Although the Supreme Court ultimately dismissed *Boyer v. Louisiana* 133 S. Ct. 1702 (2013), as improvidently granted, four Justices argued that a State's failure to adequately fund its defense lawyers counts against the prosecution in a determination under *Barker v. Wingo*, 407 U.S. 514 (1972), of whether there was a Speedy Trial right violation.

d. *Speedy Trial Rights and Sentencing (casebook p. 882)*

The Supreme Court held in *Betterman v. Montana*, 136 S. Ct. 1609 (2016), that the Sixth Amendment right to speedy trial does not apply to sentencing proceedings. Instead, defendants can raise due process challenges if there are undue delays in sentencing.

Betterman v. Montana
136 S. Ct. 1609 (2016)

Justice GINSBURG delivered the opinion of the Court.

The Sixth Amendment to the U.S. Constitution provides that "[i]n all criminal prosecutions, the accused shall enjoy the right to a speedy and public trial, by an impartial jury. . . . " Does the Sixth Amendment's speedy trial guarantee apply to the sentencing phase of a criminal prosecution? That is the sole question this case presents. We hold that the guarantee protects the accused from arrest or indictment through trial, but does not apply once a defendant has been found guilty at trial or has pleaded guilty to criminal charges. For inordinate delay in sentencing, although the Speedy Trial Clause does not govern, a defendant may have other recourse, including, in appropriate circumstances, tailored relief under the Due Process Clauses of the Fifth and Fourteenth Amendments.

I

Ordered to appear in court on domestic assault charges, Brandon Betterman failed to show up and was therefore charged with bail jumping. After pleading guilty to the bail-jumping charge, he was jailed for over 14 months awaiting sentence on that conviction. The holdup, in large part, was due to institutional delay: the presentence report took nearly five months to complete; the trial court took several months to deny two presentence motions; and the court was slow in setting a sentencing hearing. Betterman was eventually sentenced to seven years' imprisonment, with four of those years suspended. Arguing that the 14-month gap between conviction and sentencing violated his speedy trial right, Betterman appealed.

We granted certiorari to resolve a split among courts over whether the Speedy Trial Clause applies to such delay. Holding that the Clause does not apply to delayed sentencing, we affirm the Montana Supreme Court's judgment.

II

Criminal proceedings generally unfold in three discrete phases. First, the State investigates to determine whether to arrest and charge a suspect. Once charged, the suspect stands accused but is presumed innocent until conviction upon trial or guilty plea. After conviction, the court imposes sentence. There are checks against delay throughout this progression, each geared to its particular phase.

In the first stage—before arrest or indictment, when the suspect remains at liberty—statutes of limitations provide the primary protection against delay, with the Due Process Clause as a safeguard against fundamentally unfair prosecutorial conduct.

The Sixth Amendment's Speedy Trial Clause homes in on the second period: from arrest or indictment through conviction. The constitutional right, our precedent holds, does not attach until this phase begins, that is, when a defendant is arrested or formally accused. Today we hold that the right detaches upon conviction, when this second stage ends.

Prior to conviction, the accused is shielded by the presumption of innocence. The Speedy Trial Clause implements that presumption by "preventing undue and oppressive incarceration prior to trial, minimizing anxiety and concern accompanying public accusation, and limiting the possibilities that long delay will impair the ability of an accused to defend himself."

Our reading comports with the historical understanding. At the founding, "accused" described a status preceding "convicted." And "trial" meant a discrete episode after which judgment (i.e., sentencing) would follow. This Court's precedent aligns with the text and history of the Speedy Trial Clause. Detaining the accused pretrial, we have said, disadvantages him, and the imposition is "especially unfortunate" as to those "ultimately found to be innocent."

10. Speedy Trial Rights

The sole remedy for a violation of the speedy trial right—dismissal of the charges, see *Strunk v. United States* (1973)—fits the preconviction focus of the Clause. It would be an unjustified windfall, in most cases, to remedy sentencing delay by vacating validly obtained convictions. Betterman concedes that a dismissal remedy ordinarily would not be in order once a defendant has been convicted.

The manner in which legislatures have implemented the speedy trial guarantee matches our reading of the Clause. Congress passed the Speedy Trial Act of 1974, 18 U.S.C. §3161 et seq., "to give effect to the sixth amendment right." With certain exceptions, the Act directs—on pain of dismissal of the charges, §3162(a)—that no more than 30 days pass between arrest and indictment, §3161(b), and that no more than 70 days pass between indictment and trial, §3161(c)(1). The Act says nothing, however, about the period between conviction and sentencing.

Betterman asks us to take account of the prevalence of guilty pleas and the resulting scarcity of trials in today's justice system. The sentencing hearing has largely replaced the trial as the forum for dispute resolution, Betterman urges. Therefore, he maintains, the concerns supporting the right to a speedy trial now recommend a speedy sentencing hearing. The modern reality, however, does not bear on the presumption-of-innocence protection at the heart of the Speedy Trial Clause. And factual disputes, if any there be, at sentencing, do not go to the question of guilt; they are geared, instead, to ascertaining the proper sentence within boundaries set by statutory minimums and maximums.

Moreover, central feature of contemporary sentencing in both federal and state courts is preparation by the probation office, and review by the parties and the court, of a presentence investigation report. This aspect of the system requires some amount of wholly reasonable presentencing delay.

As we have explained, at the third phase of the criminal-justice process, i.e., between conviction and sentencing,the Constitution's presumption-of-innocence-protective speedy trial right is not engaged. That does not mean, however, that defendants lack any protection against undue delay at this stage. The primary safeguard comes from statutes and rules. The federal rule on point directs the court to "impose sentence without unnecessary delay." Fed. Rule Crim. Proc. 32(b)(1). Further, as at the prearrest stage, due process serves as a backstop against exorbitant delay. After conviction, a defendant's due process right to liberty, while diminished, is still present. He retains an interest in a sentencing proceeding that is fundamentally fair. But because Betterman advanced no due process claim here, we express no opinion on how he might fare under that more pliable standard.

Justice SOTOMAYOR, concurring.

I agree with the Court that petitioner cannot bring a claim under the Speedy Trial Clause for a delay between his guilty plea and his sentencing. As the majority notes, however, a defendant may have "other recourse" for such a delay, "including, in appropriate circumstances, tailored relief under the Due Process Clauses of the Fifth and Fourteenth Amendments." I write separately to emphasize that the question is an open one.

[I]t seems to me that the *Barker* factors capture many of the concerns posed in the sentencing delay context and that because the *Barker* test is flexible, it will allow courts to take account of any differences between trial and sentencing delays.

Chapter 11

RIGHT TO COUNSEL

D. Standard for "Effective Assistance" of Counsel

5. Right to Retain Experts (casebook p. 913)

In *Hinton v. Alabama*, 134 S. Ct. 1081 (2014) (per curiam), the Court held that failure by defense counsel to request additional funds to hire a competent expert may constitute ineffective assistance of counsel.

Chapter 12

TRIAL RIGHTS

D. Trial Rights: Due Process, Right of Confrontation, and Privilege Against Self-Incrimination

1. Right of Confrontation

b. *Right to Confront Witnesses* (casebook p. 1026)

In *Ohio v. Clark*, 135 S. Ct. 2173 (2015), the Court reaffirmed its approach in *Davis v. Washington* (2006) and *Michigan v. Bryant* (2010). Statements are not testimonial, even if made to individuals like teachers who have a duty to report such communications, so long as the primary purpose of the statements was to deal with an ongoing emergency. Accordingly, the Confrontation Clause does not bar a teacher from testifying regarding a child's statement about suspected child abuse.

Ohio v. Clark
135 S. Ct. 2173 (2015)

Justice ALITO delivered the opinion of the Court.

Darius Clark sent his girlfriend hundreds of miles away to engage in prostitution and agreed to care for her two young children while she was out of town. A day later, teachers discovered red marks on her 3-year-old son, and the boy identified Clark as his abuser. The question in this case is whether the Sixth Amendment's Confrontation Clause prohibited prosecutors from introducing those statements when the child was not available to be cross-examined. Because neither the child nor his teachers had the primary purpose of assisting in Clark's prosecution, the child's statements do not implicate the Confrontation Clause and therefore were admissible at trial.

I

Darius Clark, who went by the nickname "Dee," lived in Cleveland, Ohio, with his girlfriend, T. T., and her two children: L.P., a 3-year-old boy, and A. T., an 18-month-old girl. Clark was also T. T.'s pimp, and he would regularly send her on trips to Washington, D. C., to work as a prostitute. In March 2010, T. T. went on one such trip, and she left the children in Clark's care.

The next day, Clark took L.P. to preschool. In the lunchroom, one of L.P.'s teachers, Ramona Whitley, observed that L.P.'s left eye appeared bloodshot. She asked him "'[w]hat happened,'" and he initially said nothing. Eventually, however, he told the teacher that he "'fell.'" Ibid. When they moved into the brighter lights of a classroom, Whitley noticed "'[r]ed marks, like whips of some sort,'" on L.P.'s face. Ibid. She notified the lead teacher, Debra Jones, who asked L.P., "'Who did this? What happened to you?'" According to Jones, L.P. "'seemed kind of bewildered'" and "'said something like, Dee, Dee.'" Jones asked L.P. whether Dee is "big or little," to which L.P. responded that "Dee is big." Jones then brought L.P. to her supervisor, who lifted the boy's shirt, revealing more injuries. Whitley called a child abuse hotline to alert authorities about the suspected abuse.

When Clark later arrived at the school, he denied responsibility for the injuries and quickly left with L.P. The next day, a social worker found the children at Clark's mother's house and took them to a hospital, where a physician discovered additional injuries suggesting child abuse. L.P. had a black eye, belt marks on his back and stomach, and bruises all over his body. A. T. had two black eyes, a swollen hand, and a large burn on her cheek, and two pigtails had been ripped out at the roots of her hair.

A grand jury indicted Clark on five counts of felonious assault (four related to A. T. and one related to L.P.), two counts of endangering children (one for each child), and two counts of domestic violence (one for each child). At trial, the State introduced L.P.'s statements to his teachers as evidence of Clark's guilt, but L.P. did not testify. Under Ohio law, children younger than 10 years old are incompetent to testify if they "appear incapable of receiving just impressions of the facts and transactions respecting which they are examined, or of relating them truly." After conducting a hearing, the trial court concluded that L.P. was not competent to testify. But under Ohio Rule of Evidence 807, which allows the admission of reliable hearsay by child abuse victims, the court ruled that L.P.'s statements to his teachers bore sufficient guarantees of trustworthiness to be admitted as evidence.

Clark moved to exclude testimony about L.P.'s out-of-court statements under the Confrontation Clause. The trial court denied the motion, ruling that L.P.'s responses were not testimonial statements covered by the Sixth Amendment. The jury found Clark guilty on all counts except for one assault count related to A. T., and it sentenced him to 28 years' imprisonment. Clark appealed his conviction, and a state appellate court reversed on the ground that the introduction of L.P.'s out-of-court statements violated the Confrontation Clause.

In a 4-to-3 decision, the Supreme Court of Ohio affirmed. It held that, under this Court's Confrontation Clause decisions, L.P.'s statements qualified as testimonial because the primary purpose of the teachers' questioning "was not to deal with an existing emergency but rather to gather evidence potentially relevant to a subsequent criminal prosecution." The court noted that Ohio has a "mandatory reporting" law that requires certain professionals, including preschool teachers, to report suspected child abuse to government authorities. In the court's view, the teachers acted as agents of the State under the mandatory reporting law and "sought facts concerning past criminal activity to identify the person responsible, eliciting statements that 'are functionally identical to live, in-court testimony, doing precisely what a witness does on direct examination.'" We granted certiorari and we now reverse.

II

A

The Sixth Amendment's Confrontation Clause, which is binding on the States through the Fourteenth Amendment, provides: "In all criminal prosecutions, the accused shall enjoy the right . . . to be confronted with the witnesses against him." In *Ohio v. Roberts* (1980), we interpreted the Clause to permit the admission of out-of-court statements by an unavailable witness, so long as the statements bore "adequate 'indicia of reliability.'" Such indicia are present, we held, if "the evidence falls within a firmly rooted hearsay exception" or bears "particularized guarantees of trustworthiness."

In *Crawford v. Washington* (2004), we adopted a different approach. We explained that "witnesses," under the Confrontation Clause, are those "who bear testimony," and we defined "testimony" as "a solemn declaration or affirmation made for the purpose of establishing or proving some fact." The Sixth Amendment, we concluded, prohibits the introduction of testimonial statements by a nontestifying witness, unless the witness is "unavailable to testify, and the defendant had had a prior opportunity for cross-examination." Applying that definition to the facts in Crawford, we held that statements by a witness during police questioning at the station house were testimonial and thus could not be admitted. But our decision in Crawford did not offer an exhaustive definition of "testimonial" statements. Instead, Crawford stated that the label "applies at a minimum to prior testimony at a preliminary hearing, before a grand jury, or at a former trial; and to police interrogations."

Our more recent cases have labored to flesh out what it means for a statement to be "testimonial." In *Davis v. Washington and Hammon v. Indiana* (2006), which we decided together, we dealt with statements given to law enforcement officers by the victims of domestic abuse. The victim in Davis made statements to a 911 emergency operator during and shortly after her boyfriend's violent attack. In *Hammon*, the victim, after being isolated from her abusive husband, made statements to police that were memorialized in a "'battery affidavit.'"

We held that the statements in *Hammon* were testimonial, while the statements in *Davis* were not. Announcing what has come to be known as the "primary purpose" test, we explained: "Statements are nontestimonial when made in the course of police interrogation under circumstances objectively indicating that the primary purpose of the interrogation is to enable police assistance to meet an ongoing emergency. They are testimonial when the circumstances objectively indicate that there is no such ongoing emergency, and that the primary purpose of the interrogation is to establish or prove past events potentially relevant to later criminal prosecution." Because the cases involved statements to law enforcement officers, we reserved the question whether similar statements to individuals other than law enforcement officers would raise similar issues under the Confrontation Clause.

In *Michigan v. Bryant* (2011), we further expounded on the primary purpose test. The inquiry, we emphasized, must consider "all of the relevant circumstances." And we reiterated our view in *Davis* that, when "the primary purpose of an interrogation is to respond to an 'ongoing emergency,' its purpose is not to create a record for trial and thus is not within the scope of the [Confrontation] Clause." At the same time, we noted that "there may be other circumstances, aside from ongoing emergencies, when a statement is not procured with a primary purpose of creating an out-of-court substitute for trial testimony." "[T]he existence vel non of an ongoing emergency is not the touchstone of the testimonial inquiry." Instead, "whether an ongoing emergency exists is simply one factor . . . that informs the ultimate inquiry regarding the 'primary purpose' of an interrogation."

One additional factor is "the informality of the situation and the interrogation." A "formal station-house interrogation," like the questioning in Crawford, is more likely to provoke testimonial statements, while less formal questioning is less likely to reflect a primary purpose aimed at obtaining testimonial evidence against the accused. In the end, the question is whether, in light of all the circumstances, viewed objectively, the "primary purpose" of the conversation was to "creat[e] an out-of-court substitute for trial testimony."

B

In this case, we consider statements made to preschool teachers, not the police. We are therefore presented with the question we have repeatedly reserved: whether statements to persons other than law enforcement officers are subject to the Confrontation Clause. Because at least some statements to individuals who are not law enforcement officers could conceivably raise confrontation concerns, we decline to adopt a categorical rule excluding them from the Sixth Amendment's reach. Nevertheless, such statements are much less likely to be testimonial than statements to law enforcement officers. And considering all the relevant circumstances here, L.P.'s statements clearly were not made with the primary purpose of creating evidence for Clark's prosecution. Thus, their introduction at trial did not violate the Confrontation Clause.

L.P.'s statements occurred in the context of an ongoing emergency involving suspected child abuse. When L.P.'s teachers noticed his injuries, they rightly became worried that the 3-year-old was the victim of serious violence. Because the teachers needed to know whether it was safe to release L.P. to his guardian at the end of the day, they needed to determine who might be abusing the child. Thus, the immediate concern was to protect a vulnerable child who needed help. Our holding in *Bryant* is instructive. As in *Bryant*, the emergency in this case was ongoing, and the circumstances were not entirely clear. L.P.'s teachers were not sure who had abused him or how best to secure his safety. Nor were they sure whether any other children might be at risk. As a result, their questions and L.P.'s answers were primarily aimed at identifying and ending the threat. Though not as harried, the conversation here was also similar to the 911 call in *Davis*. The teachers' questions were meant to identify the abuser in order to protect the victim from future attacks. Whether the teachers thought that this would be done by apprehending the abuser or by some other means is irrelevant. And the circumstances in this case were unlike the interrogation in *Hammon*, where the police knew the identity of the assailant and questioned the victim after shielding her from potential harm.

There is no indication that the primary purpose of the conversation was to gather evidence for Clark's prosecution. On the contrary, it is clear that the first objective was to protect L.P. At no point did the teachers inform L.P. that his answers would be used to arrest or punish his abuser. L.P. never hinted that he intended his statements to be used by the police or prosecutors. And the conversation between L.P. and his teachers was informal and spontaneous. The teachers asked L.P. about his injuries immediately upon discovering them, in the informal setting of a preschool lunchroom and classroom, and they did so precisely as any concerned citizen would talk to a child who might be the victim of abuse. This was nothing like the formalized station-house questioning in Crawford or the police interrogation and battery affidavit in Hammon.

L.P.'s age fortifies our conclusion that the statements in question were not testimonial. Statements by very young children will rarely, if ever, implicate the Confrontation Clause. Few preschool students understand the details of our criminal justice system. Rather, "[r]esearch on children's understanding of the legal system finds that" young children "have little understanding of prosecution." Thus, it is extremely unlikely that a 3-year-old child in L.P.'s position would intend his statements to be a substitute for trial testimony. On the contrary, a young child in these circumstances would simply want the abuse to end, would want to protect other victims, or would have no discernible purpose at all.

As a historical matter, moreover, there is strong evidence that statements made in circumstances similar to those facing L.P. and his teachers were admissible at common law. Neither Crawford nor any of the cases that it has produced has mounted evidence that the adoption of the Confrontation Clause was understood to require the exclusion of evidence that was regularly admitted in criminal cases at the time of the founding. Certainly, the statements in this case are nothing like the notorious use of ex parte examination in Sir Walter Raleigh's trial for treason, which we have frequently identified as "the principal evil at which the Confrontation Clause was directed."

Finally, although we decline to adopt a rule that statements to individuals who are not law enforcement officers are categorically outside the Sixth Amendment, the fact that L.P. was speaking to his teachers remains highly relevant. Courts must evaluate challenged statements in context, and part of that context is the questioner's identity. Statements made to someone who is not principally charged with uncovering and prosecuting criminal behavior are significantly less likely to be testimonial than statements given to law enforcement officers. It is common sense that the relationship between a student and his teacher is very different from that between a citizen and the police. We do not ignore that reality. In light of these circumstances, the Sixth Amendment did not prohibit the State from introducing L.P.'s statements at trial.

III

Clark's efforts to avoid this conclusion are all off-base. He emphasizes Ohio's mandatory reporting obligations, in an attempt to equate L.P.'s teachers with the police and their caring questions with official interrogations. But the comparison is inapt. The teachers' pressing concern was to protect L.P. and remove him from harm's way. Like all good teachers, they undoubtedly would have acted with the same purpose whether or not they had a state-law duty to report abuse. And mandatory reporting statutes alone cannot convert a conversation between a concerned teacher and her student into a law enforcement mission aimed primarily at gathering evidence for a prosecution.

IV

We reverse the judgment of the Supreme Court of Ohio and remand the case for further proceedings not inconsistent with this opinion.

Justice SCALIA, with whom Justice GINSBURG joins, concurring in the judgment.

I agree with the Court's holding, and with its refusal to decide two questions quite unnecessary to that holding: what effect Ohio's mandatory-reporting law has in transforming a private party into a state actor for Confrontation Clause purposes, and whether a more permissive Confrontation Clause test—one less likely to hold the statements testimonial—should apply to interrogations by private actors. The statements here would not be testimonial under the usual test applicable to informal police interrogation.

I write separately, however, to protest the Court's shoveling of fresh dirt upon the Sixth Amendment right of confrontation so recently rescued from the grave in *Crawford v. Washington* (2004). For several decades before that case, we had been allowing hearsay statements to be admitted against a criminal defendant if they bore "'indicia of reliability.'" *Ohio v. Roberts* (1980). Prosecutors, past and present, love that flabby test. Crawford sought to bring our application of the Confrontation Clause back to its original meaning, which was to exclude unconfronted statements made by witnesses—i.e., statements that were testimonial.

Crawford remains the law. But when else has the categorical overruling, the thorough repudiation, of an earlier line of cases been described as nothing more than "adopt[ing] a different approach," as though Crawford is only a matter of twiddle-dum twiddle-dee preference, and the old, pre-Crawford "approach" remains available?

12. Trial Rights

The Confrontation Clause categorically entitles a defendant to be confronted with the witnesses against him; and the primary-purpose test sorts out, among the many people who interact with the police informally, who is acting as a witness and who is not. Those who fall into the former category bear testimony, and are therefore acting as "witnesses," subject to the right of confrontation. There are no other mysterious requirements that the Court declines to name.

Justice THOMAS, concurring in the judgment.

I agree with the Court that Ohio mandatory reporters are not agents of law enforcement, that statements made to private persons or by very young children will rarely implicate the Confrontation Clause, and that the admission of the statements at issue here did not implicate that constitutional provision. I nonetheless cannot join the majority's analysis. In the decade since we first sought to return to the original meaning of the Confrontation Clause, we have carefully reserved consideration of that Clause's application to statements made to private persons for a case in which it was squarely presented.

This is that case; yet the majority does not offer clear guidance on the subject, declaring only that "the primary purpose test is a necessary, but not always sufficient, condition" for a statement to fall within the scope of the Confrontation Clause. The primary purpose test, however, is just as much "an exercise in fiction . . . disconnected from history" for statements made to private persons as it is for statements made to agents of law enforcement, if not more so.

Instead, I would use the same test for statements to private persons that I have employed for statements to agents of law enforcement, assessing whether those statements bear sufficient indicia of solemnity to qualify as testimonial. I have identified several categories of extrajudicial statements that bear sufficient indicia of solemnity to fall within the original meaning of testimony.

Here, L.P.'s statements do not bear sufficient indicia of solemnity to qualify as testimonial. They were neither contained in formalized testimonial materials nor obtained as the result of a formalized dialogue initiated by police. Instead, they were elicited during questioning by L.P.'s teachers at his preschool. Nor is there any indication that L.P.'s statements were offered at trial to evade confrontation. To the contrary, the record suggests that the prosecution would have produced L.P. to testify had he been deemed competent to do so. The admission of L.P.'s extrajudicial statements thus does not implicate the Confrontation Clause.

Chapter 13

SENTENCING

D. The Death Penalty

3. Recent Limits on the Scope of the Death Penalty

a. Prohibition of the Death Penalty for Mentally Retarded Defendants (casebook p. 1124)

In *Hall v. Florida*, 134 S. Ct. 1986 (2014), the Court clarified that the standard to be used to determine whether the execution of a mentally disabled defendant would violate the Eighth Amendment is not determined by an IQ test score alone. Rather, courts are to consider a range of evidence related to the defendant's mental disability.

Hall v. Florida
134 S. Ct. 1986 (2014)

Justice KENNEDY delivered the opinion of the Court.

This Court has held that the Eighth and Fourteenth Amendments to the Constitution forbid the execution of persons with intellectual disability. *Atkins v. Virginia* (2002). Florida law defines intellectual disability to require an IQ test score of 70 or less. If, from test scores, a prisoner is deemed to have an IQ above 70, all further exploration of intellectual disability is foreclosed. This rigid rule, the Court now holds, creates an unacceptable risk that persons with intellectual disability will be executed, and thus is unconstitutional.

I

On February 21, 1978, Freddie Lee Hall, petitioner here, and his accomplice, Mark Ruffin, kidnaped, beat, raped, and murdered Karol Hurst, a pregnant, 21-year-old newlywed. Afterward, Hall and Ruffin drove to a convenience store they planned to rob. In the parking lot of the store, they killed Lonnie Coburn, a sheriff's deputy who attempted to apprehend them. Hall received the death penalty for both murders, although his sentence for the Coburn murder was later reduced on account of insufficient evidence of premeditation.

Hall argues that he cannot be executed because of his intellectual disability. Previous opinions of this Court have employed the term "mental retardation."

This opinion uses the term "intellectual disability" to describe the identical phenomenon.

When Hall was first sentenced, this Court had not yet ruled that the Eighth Amendment prohibits States from imposing the death penalty on persons with intellectual disability. See *Penry v. Lynaugh* (1989). And at the time, Florida law did not consider intellectual disability as a statutory mitigating factor.

After this Court held that capital defendants must be permitted to present nonstatutory mitigating evidence in death penalty proceedings, Hall was resentenced. Hall then presented substantial and unchallenged evidence of intellectual disability. School records indicated that his teachers identified him on numerous occasions as "[m]entally retarded." Hall had been prosecuted for a different, earlier crime. His lawyer in that matter later testified that the lawyer "[c]ouldn't really understand anything [Hall] said." And, with respect to the murder trial given him in this case, Hall's counsel recalled that Hall could not assist in his own defense because he had "'a mental . . . level much lower than his age,'" at best comparable to the lawyer's 4-year-old daughter. A number of medical clinicians testified that, in their professional opinion, Hall was "significantly retarded," was "mentally retarded," and had levels of understanding "typically [seen] with toddlers."

As explained below in more detail, an individual's ability or lack of ability to adapt or adjust to the requirements of daily life, and success or lack of success in doing so, is central to the framework followed by psychiatrists and other professionals in diagnosing intellectual disability. Hall's siblings testified that there was something "very wrong" with him as a child. Hall was "slow with speech and . . . slow to learn." He "walked and talked long after his other brothers and sisters," and had "great difficulty forming his words."

Hall's upbringing appeared to make his deficits in adaptive functioning all the more severe. Hall was raised—in the words of the sentencing judge—"under the most horrible family circumstances imaginable." Although "[t]eachers and siblings alike immediately recognized [Hall] to be significantly mentally retarded . . . [t]his retardation did not garner any sympathy from his mother, but rather caused much scorn to befall him." Hall was "[c]onstantly beaten because he was 'slow' or because he made simple mistakes." His mother "would strap [Hall] to his bed at night, with a rope thrown over a rafter. In the morning, she would awaken Hall by hoisting him up and whipping him with a belt, rope, or cord." Hall was beaten "ten or fifteen times a week sometimes." His mother tied him "in a 'croaker' sack, swung it over a fire, and beat him," "buried him in the sand up to his neck to 'strengthen his legs,'" and "held a gun on Hall . . . while she poked [him] with sticks."

The jury, notwithstanding this testimony, voted to sentence Hall to death, and the sentencing court adopted the jury's recommendation. The court found that there was "substantial evidence in the record" to support the finding that "Freddie Lee Hall has been mentally retarded his entire life." Yet the court also "suspect[ed] that the defense experts [were] guilty of some professional overkill," because "[n]othing of which the experts testified could explain how a psychotic, mentally-retarded, brain-damaged, learning-disabled, speech-impaired person could formulate a plan whereby a car was stolen and a convenience store was robbed." The sentencing court went on to state that, even assuming the expert testimony to be accurate, "the learning disabilities, mental retardation, and other mental difficulties . . . cannot be used to justify, excuse or extenuate the moral culpability of the defendant in this cause." Hall was again sentenced to death.

In 2002, this Court ruled that the Eighth Amendment prohibited the execution of persons with intellectual disability. On November 30, 2004, Hall filed a motion claiming that he had intellectual disability and could not be executed. More than five years later, Florida held a hearing to consider Hall's motion. Hall again presented evidence of intellectual disability, including an IQ test score of 71. (Hall had received nine IQ evaluations in 40 years, with scores ranging from 60 to 80, but the sentencing court excluded the two scores below 70 for evidentiary reasons, leaving only scores between 71 and 80.) In response, Florida argued that Hall could not be found intellectually disabled because Florida law requires that, as a threshold matter, Hall show an IQ test score of 70 or below before presenting any additional evidence of his intellectual disability.

II

The Eighth Amendment provides that "[e]xcessive bail shall not be required, nor excessive fines imposed, nor cruel and unusual punishments inflicted." The Fourteenth Amendment applies those restrictions to the States. "By protecting even those convicted of heinous crimes, the Eighth Amendment reaffirms the duty of the government to respect the dignity of all persons."

To enforce the Constitution's protection of human dignity, this Court looks to the "evolving standards of decency that mark the progress of a maturing society." The Eighth Amendment's protection of dignity reflects the Nation we have been, the Nation we are, and the Nation we aspire to be.

The Eighth Amendment prohibits certain punishments as a categorical matter. No natural-born citizen may be denaturalized. No person may be sentenced to death for a crime committed as a juvenile. *Roper* (2005). And, as relevant for this case, persons with intellectual disability may not be executed. *Atkins*.

No legitimate penological purpose is served by executing a person with intellectual disability. To do so contravenes the Eighth Amendment, for to impose the harshest of punishments on an intellectually disabled person violates his or her inherent dignity as a human being. "[P]unishment is justified under one or more of three principal rationales: rehabilitation, deterrence, and retribution." Rehabilitation, it is evident, is not an applicable rationale for the death penalty. As for deterrence, those with intellectual disability are, by reason of their condition, likely unable to make the calculated judgments that are the premise for the deterrence rationale. They have a "diminished ability" to "process information, to learn from experience, to engage in logical reasoning, or to control impulses . . . [which] make[s] it less likely that they can process the information of the possibility of execution as a penalty and, as a result, control their conduct based upon that information." Retributive values are also ill-served by executing those with intellectual disability. The diminished capacity of the intellectually disabled lessens moral culpability and hence the retributive value of the punishment.

A further reason for not imposing the death penalty on a person who is intellectually disabled is to protect the integrity of the trial process. These persons face "a special risk of wrongful execution" because they are more likely to give false confessions, are often poor witnesses, and are less able to give meaningful assistance to their counsel. This is not to say that under current law persons with intellectual disability who "meet the law's requirements for criminal responsibility" may not be tried and punished. They may not, however, receive the law's most severe sentence.

The question this case presents is how intellectual disability must be defined in order to implement these principles and the holding of *Atkins*. To determine if Florida's cutoff rule is valid, it is proper to consider the psychiatric and professional studies that elaborate on the purpose and meaning of IQ scores to determine how the scores relate to the holding of *Atkins*. This in turn leads to a better understanding of how the legislative policies of various States, and the holdings of state courts, implement the *Atkins* rule. That understanding informs our determination whether there is a consensus that instructs how to decide the specific issue presented here. And, in conclusion, this Court must express its own independent determination reached in light of the instruction found in those sources and authorities.

III

A

On its face, the Florida statute could be consistent with the views of the medical community. Florida's statute defines intellectual disability for purposes of an *Atkins* proceeding as "significantly subaverage general intellectual functioning existing concurrently with deficits in adaptive behavior and manifested during the period from conception to age 18." The statute further defines "significantly subaverage general intellectual functioning" as "performance that is two or more standard deviations from the mean score on a standardized intelligence test."

Nothing in the statute precludes Florida from taking into account the IQ test's standard error of measurement, and as discussed below there is evidence that Florida's Legislature intended to include the measurement error in the calculation. But the Florida Supreme Court has interpreted the provisions more narrowly. It has held that a person whose test score is above 70, including a score within the margin for measurement error, does not have an intellectual disability and is barred from presenting other evidence that would show his faculties are limited. That strict IQ test score cutoff of 70 is the issue in this case.

Pursuant to this mandatory cutoff, sentencing courts cannot consider even substantial and weighty evidence of intellectual disability as measured and made manifest by the defendant's failure or inability to adapt to his social and cultural environment, including medical histories, behavioral records, school tests and reports, and testimony regarding past behavior and family circumstances. This is so even though the medical community accepts that all of this evidence can be probative of intellectual disability, including for individuals who have an IQ test score above 70.

Florida's rule disregards established medical practice in two interrelated ways. It takes an IQ score as final and conclusive evidence of a defendant's intellectual capacity, when experts in the field would consider other evidence. It also relies on a purportedly scientific measurement of the defendant's abilities, his IQ score, while refusing to recognize that the score is, on its own terms, imprecise.

The professionals who design, administer, and interpret IQ tests have agreed, for years now, that IQ test scores should be read not as a single fixed number but as a range. Each IQ test has a "standard error of measurement," often referred to by the abbreviation "SEM." An individual's IQ test score on any given exam may fluctuate for a variety of reasons. These include the test-taker's health; practice from earlier tests; the environment or location of the test; the examiner's demeanor; the subjective judgment involved in scoring certain questions on the exam; and simple lucky guessing.

The SEM reflects the reality that an individual's intellectual functioning cannot be reduced to a single numerical score. Even when a person has taken multiple tests, each separate score must be assessed using the SEM, and the analysis of multiple IQ scores jointly is a complicated endeavor. Despite these professional explanations, Florida law used the test score as a fixed number, thus barring further consideration of other evidence bearing on the question of intellectual disability.

B

A significant majority of States implement the protections of *Atkins* by taking the SEM into account, thus acknowledging the error inherent in using a test score without necessary adjustment. Only the Kentucky and Virginia Legislatures have adopted a fixed score cutoff identical to Florida's. Alabama also may use a strict IQ score cutoff at 70, although not as a result of legislative action.

In addition to these States, Arizona, Delaware, Kansas, North Carolina, and Washington have statutes which could be interpreted to provide a bright-line cutoff leading to the same result that Florida mandates in its cases. That these state laws might be interpreted to require a bright-line cutoff does not mean that they will be so interpreted, however.

Thus, at most nine States mandate a strict IQ score cutoff at 70. Of these, four States (Delaware, Kansas, North Carolina, and Washington) appear not to have considered the issue in their courts. On the other side of the ledger stand the 18 States that have abolished the death penalty, either in full or for new offenses, and Oregon, which has suspended the death penalty and executed only two individuals in the past 40 years.

Since *Atkins*, five States have abolished the death penalty through legislation. (Connecticut, Maryland, New Jersey, New Mexico). In addition, the New York Court of Appeals invalidated New York's death penalty under the State Constitution in 2004.

In addition to these States, at least five others have passed legislation allowing a defendant to present additional evidence of intellectual disability even when an IQ test score is above 70. (California, Idaho, Louisiana, Nevada and Utah.) The U.S. Code likewise does not set a strict IQ cutoff.

In summary, every state legislature to have considered the issue after *Atkins*— save Virginia's—and whose law has been interpreted by its courts has taken a position contrary to that of Florida. Indeed, the Florida Legislature, which passed the relevant legislation prior to *Atkins*, might well have believed that its law would not create a fixed cutoff at 70.

The rejection of the strict 70 cutoff in the vast majority of States and the "consistency in the trend" toward recognizing the SEM provide strong evidence of consensus that our society does not regard this strict cutoff as proper or humane.

C

Atkins itself acknowledges the inherent error in IQ testing:

> "Not all people who claim to be mentally retarded will be so impaired as to fall within the range of mentally retarded offenders about whom there is a national consensus. As was our approach in *Ford v. Wainwright* with regard to insanity, 'we leave to the State[s] the task of developing appropriate ways to enforce the constitutional restriction upon [their] execution of sentences.'"

As discussed above, the States play a critical role in advancing protections and providing the Court with information that contributes to an understanding of how intellectual disability should be measured and assessed. But *Atkins* did not give the States unfettered discretion to define the full scope of the constitutional protection.

D

The actions of the States and the precedents of this Court "give us essential instruction," but the inquiry must go further. "[T]he Constitution contemplates that in the end our own judgment will be brought to bear on the question of the acceptability of the death penalty under the Eighth Amendment." That exercise of independent judgment is the Court's judicial duty. In this Court's independent judgment, the Florida statute, as interpreted by its courts, is unconstitutional.

It is the Court's duty to interpret the Constitution, but it need not do so in isolation. The legal determination of intellectual disability is distinct from a medical diagnosis, but it is informed by the medical community's diagnostic framework.

By failing to take into account the SEM and setting a strict cutoff at 70, Florida "goes against the unanimous professional consensus." Neither Florida nor its *amici* point to a single medical professional who supports this cutoff.

Intellectual disability is a condition, not a number. Courts must recognize, as does the medical community, that the test is imprecise. This is not to say that an IQ test score is unhelpful. It is of considerable significance, as the medical community recognizes. But in using these scores to assess a defendant's eligibility for the death penalty, a State must afford these test scores the same studied skepticism that those who design and use the tests do, and understand that an IQ test score represents a range rather than a fixed number. A State that ignores the inherent imprecision of these tests risks executing a person who suffers from intellectual disability.

Justice ALITO, with whom THE CHIEF JUSTICE, Justice SCALIA, and Justice THOMAS join, dissenting.

The Court's approach in this case marks a new and most unwise turn in our Eighth Amendment case law. In *Atkins* and other cases, the Court held that the prohibition of cruel and unusual punishment embodies the "evolving standards of decency that mark the progress of a maturing society," and the Court explained that "those evolving standards should be informed by objective factors to the maximum possible extent."

In . . . prior cases, when the Court referred to the evolving standards of a maturing "society," the Court meant the standards of *American society as a whole*. Now, however, the Court strikes down a state law based on the evolving standards of *professional societies*, most notably the American Psychiatric Association (APA). This approach cannot be reconciled with the framework prescribed by our Eighth Amendment cases.

While *Atkins* identified a consensus against the execution of the intellectually disabled, the Court observed that there was "serious disagreement" among the States with respect to the best method for "determining which offenders are in fact retarded." The Court therefore "le[ft] to the States the task of developing appropriate ways" to identify these defendants.

Consistent with the role that *Atkins* left for the States, Florida follows the procedure now at issue. On the Court's count, "at most nine States mandate a strict IQ score cutoff at 70"; 22 States allow defendants to present "additional evidence" when an individual's test score is between 70 and 75; and 19 States have abolished the death penalty or have long suspended its operation.

Not only are the States divided on the question whether the SEM should play a role in determining whether a capital defendant is intellectually disabled, but the States that require consideration of the SEM do not agree on the role that the SEM should play.

In light of all this, the resolution of this case should be straightforward: Just as there was no methodological consensus among the States at the time of *Atkins*, there is no such consensus today. And in the absence of such a consensus, we have no basis for holding that Florida's method contravenes our society's standards of decency.

The Court's reliance on the views of professional associations will also lead to serious practical problems. I will briefly note a few. First, because the views of professional associations often change, tying Eighth Amendment law to these views will lead to instability and continue to fuel protracted litigation. Second, the Court's approach implicitly calls upon the Judiciary either to follow every new change in the thinking of these professional organizations or to judge the validity of each new change. Third, the Court's approach requires the Judiciary to determine which professional organizations are entitled to special deference. And what if professional organizations disagree? The Court provides no guidance for deciding which organizations' views should govern. Fourth, the Court binds Eighth Amendment law to definitions of intellectual disability that are promulgated for use in making a variety of decisions that are quite different from the decision whether the imposition of a death sentence in a particular case would serve a valid penological end.

Because I find no consensus among the States, I would not independently assess the method that Florida has adopted for determining intellectual disability. But even if it were appropriate for us to look beyond the evidence of societal standards, I could not conclude that Florida's method is unconstitutional.

We have been presented with no solid evidence that the longstanding reliance on multiple IQ test scores as a measure of intellectual functioning is so unreasonable or outside the ordinary as to be unconstitutional.

d.   *Method of Execution* (casebook p. 1145)

In *Glossip v. Gross*, 135 S. Ct. 2726 (2015), the Court rejected a challenge to the use of midazolam in Oklahoma's three-drug execution protocol. While the key issue was whether the use of the drug met the standards set in *Baze* for execution by lethal injection, the Court discussed two requirements for defendants challenging their execution. They must show: (1) the method being used creates an unacceptable risk of severe pain; and (2) there is a known and available alternative method of execution. In his dissent, Justice Breyer called for full briefing for a complete reexamination of the constitutionality of the death penalty.

Glossip v. Gross
135 S. Ct. 2726 (2015)

Justice ALITO delivered the opinion of the Court.

Prisoners sentenced to death in the State of Oklahoma filed an action in federal court contending that the method of execution now used by the State violates the Eighth Amendment because it creates an unacceptable risk of severe pain. They argue that midazolam, the first drug employed in the State's current three-drug protocol, fails to render a person insensate to pain. After holding an evidentiary hearing, the District Court denied four prisoners' application for a preliminary injunction, finding that they had failed to prove that midazolam is ineffective. The Court of Appeals for the Tenth Circuit affirmed and accepted the District Court's finding of fact regarding midazolam's efficacy.

For two independent reasons, we also affirm. First, the prisoners failed to identify a known and available alternative method of execution that entails a lesser risk of pain, a requirement of all Eighth Amendment method-of-execution claims. Second, the District Court did not commit clear error when it found that the prisoners failed to establish that Oklahoma's use of a massive dose of midazolam in its execution protocol entails a substantial risk of severe pain.

I

A

The death penalty was an accepted punishment at the time of the adoption of the Constitution and the Bill of Rights. In that era, death sentences were usually carried out by hanging. Hanging remained the standard method of execution through much of the 19th century, but that began to change in the century's later years. In the 1880's, the Legislature of the State of New York appointed a commission to find "'the most humane and practical method known to modern science of carrying into effect the sentence of death in capital cases.'" The commission recommended electrocution, and in 1888, the Legislature enacted a law providing for this method of execution. In subsequent years, other States followed New York's lead in the "'belief that electrocution is less painful and more humane than hanging.'"

In 1921, the Nevada Legislature adopted another new method of execution, lethal gas, after concluding that this was "the most humane manner known to modern science." The Nevada Supreme Court rejected the argument that the use of lethal gas was unconstitutional, and other States followed Nevada's lead. Nevertheless, hanging and the firing squad were retained in some States, and electrocution remained the predominant method of execution until the 9-year hiatus in executions that ended with our judgment in *Gregg v. Georgia* (1976).

After *Gregg* reaffirmed that the death penalty does not violate the Constitution, some States once again sought a more humane way to carry out death sentences. They eventually adopted lethal injection, which today is "by far the most prevalent method of execution in the United States."

While methods of execution have changed over the years, "[t]his Court has never invalidated a State's chosen procedure for carrying out a sentence of death as the infliction of cruel and unusual punishment." In *Wilkerson v. Utah* (1879), the Court upheld a sentence of death by firing squad. In *In re Kemmler* (1890), the Court rejected a challenge to the use of the electric chair. And the Court did not retreat from that holding even when presented with a case in which a State's initial attempt to execute a prisoner by electrocution was unsuccessful. Most recently, in *Baze v. Rees* (2008), seven Justices agreed that the three-drug protocol just discussed does not violate the Eighth Amendment.

Our decisions in this area have been animated in part by the recognition that because it is settled that capital punishment is constitutional, "[i]t necessarily follows that there must be a [constitutional] means of carrying it out." Holding that the Eighth Amendment demands the elimination of essentially all risk of pain would effectively outlaw the death penalty altogether.

B

Baze cleared any legal obstacle to use of the most common three-drug protocol that had enabled States to carry out the death penalty in a quick and painless fashion. But a practical obstacle soon emerged, as anti-death-penalty advocates pressured pharmaceutical companies to refuse to supply the drugs used to carry out death sentences. The sole American manufacturer of sodium thiopental, the first drug used in the standard three-drug protocol, was persuaded to cease production of the drug. After suspending domestic production in 2009, the company planned to resume production in Italy. Activists then pressured both the company and the Italian Government to stop the sale of sodium thiopental for use in lethal injections in this country. That effort proved successful, and in January 2011, the company announced that it would exit the sodium thiopental market entirely.

After other efforts to procure sodium thiopental proved unsuccessful, States sought an alternative, and they eventually replaced sodium thiopental with pentobarbital, another barbiturate. In December 2010, Oklahoma became the first State to execute an inmate using pentobarbital. That execution occurred without incident, and States gradually shifted to pentobarbital as their supplies of sodium thiopental ran out. Before long, however, pentobarbital also became unavailable. Oklahoma eventually became unable to acquire the drug through any means. C

Unable to acquire either sodium thiopental or pentobarbital, some States have turned to midazolam, a sedative in the benzodiazepine family of drugs. Oklahoma has already used this three-drug protocol twice: to execute Clayton Lockett in April 2014 and Charles Warner in January 2015.

The Lockett execution caused Oklahoma to implement new safety precautions as part of its lethal injection protocol. When Oklahoma executed Lockett, its protocol called for the administration of 100 milligrams of midazolam, as compared to the 500 milligrams that are currently required. On the morning of his execution, Lockett cut himself twice at "'the bend of the elbow.'" That evening, the execution team spent nearly an hour making at least one dozen attempts to establish intravenous (IV) access to Lockett's cardiovascular system, including at his arms and elsewhere on his body. The team eventually believed that it had established intravenous access through Lockett's right femoral vein, and it covered the injection access point with a sheet, in part to preserve Lockett's dignity during the execution. After the team administered the midazolam and a physician determined that Lockett was unconscious, the team next administered the paralytic agent and most of the potassium chloride. Lockett began to move and speak, at which point the physician lifted the sheet and determined that the IV had "infiltrated," which means that "the IV fluid, rather than entering Lockett's blood stream, had leaked into the tissue surrounding the IV access point." The execution team stopped administering the remaining potassium chloride and terminated the execution about 33 minutes after the midazolam was first injected. About 10 minutes later, Lockett was pronounced dead.

An investigation into the Lockett execution concluded that "the viability of the IV access point was the single greatest factor that contributed to the difficulty in administering the execution drugs." The investigation recommended several changes to Oklahoma's execution protocol.

II

A

In June 2014, after Oklahoma switched from pentobarbital to midazolam and executed Lockett. Oklahoma death row inmates filed an action under 42 U. S. C. §1983 challenging the State's new lethal injection protocol. The complaint alleged that Oklahoma's use of midazolam violates the Eighth Amendment's prohibition of cruel and unusual punishment.

In November 2014, four of those plaintiffs—Richard Glossip, Benjamin Cole, John Grant, and Warner—filed a motion for a preliminary injunction. All four men had been convicted of murder and sentenced to death by Oklahoma juries. Glossip hired Justin Sneed to kill his employer, Barry Van Treese. Sneed entered a room where Van Treese was sleeping and beat him to death with a baseball bat. Cole murdered his 9-month-old daughter after she would not stop crying. Cole bent her body backwards until he snapped her spine in half. After the child died, Cole played video games. Grant, while serving terms of imprisonment totaling 130 years, killed Gay Carter, a prison food service supervisor, by pulling her into a mop closet and stabbing her numerous times with a shank. Warner anally raped and murdered an 11-month-old girl. The child's injuries included two skull fractures, internal brain injuries, two fractures to her jaw, a lacerated liver, and a bruised spleen and lungs.

The Oklahoma Court of Criminal Appeals affirmed the murder conviction and death sentence of each offender. Having exhausted the avenues for challenging their convictions and sentences, they moved for a preliminary injunction against Oklahoma's lethal injection protocol.

B

In December 2014, after discovery, the District Court held a 3-day evidentiary hearing on the preliminary injunction motion. The District Court heard testimony from 17 witnesses and reviewed numerous exhibits. Dr. David Lubarsky, an anesthesiologist, and Dr. Larry Sasich, a doctor of pharmacy, provided expert testimony about midazolam for petitioners, and Dr. Roswell Evans, a doctor of pharmacy, provided expert testimony for respondents.

After reviewing the evidence, the District Court issued an oral ruling denying the motion for a preliminary injunction. The District Court then held that petitioners failed to establish a likelihood of success on the merits of their claim that the use of midazolam violates the Eighth Amendment. The court provided two independent reasons for this conclusion. First, the court held that petitioners failed to identify a known and available method of execution that presented a substantially less severe risk of pain than the method that the State proposed to use. Second, the court found that petitioners failed to prove that Oklahoma's protocol "presents a risk that is 'sure or very likely to cause serious illness and needless suffering,' amounting to 'an objectively intolerable risk of harm.'" The court emphasized that the Oklahoma protocol featured numerous safeguards, including the establishment of two IV access sites, confirmation of the viability of those sites, and monitoring of the offender's level of consciousness throughout the procedure.

The District Court supported its decision with findings of fact about midazolam. It found that a 500-milligram dose of midazolam "would make it a virtual certainty that any individual will be at a sufficient level of unconsciousness to resist the noxious stimuli which could occur from the application of the second and third drugs." Indeed, it found that a 500-milligram dose alone would likely cause death by respiratory arrest within 30 minutes or an hour.

The Court of Appeals for the Tenth Circuit affirmed. The Court of Appeals explained that our decision in *Baze* requires a plaintiff challenging a lethal injection protocol to demonstrate that the risk of severe pain presented by an execution protocol is substantial "'when compared to the known and available alternatives.'" And it agreed with the District Court that petitioners had not identified any such alternative.

III

The Eighth Amendment, made applicable to the States through the Fourteenth Amendment, prohibits the infliction of "cruel and unusual punishments." The controlling opinion in *Baze* first concluded that prisoners cannot successfully challenge a method of execution unless they establish that the method presents a risk that is "'sure or very likely to cause serious illness and needless suffering,' and give rise to 'sufficiently imminent dangers.'" To prevail on such a claim, "there must be a 'substantial risk of serious harm,' an 'objectively intolerable risk of harm' that prevents prison officials from pleading that they were 'subjectively blameless for purposes of the Eighth Amendment.'" The controlling opinion also stated that prisoners "cannot successfully challenge a State's method of execution merely by showing a slightly or marginally safer alternative." Instead, prisoners must identify an alternative that is "feasible, readily implemented, and in fact significantly reduce[s] a substantial risk of severe pain."

The challenge in *Baze* failed both because the Kentucky inmates did not show that the risks they identified were substantial and imminent, and because they did not establish the existence of a known and available alternative method of execution that would entail a significantly less severe risk. Petitioners' arguments here fail for similar reasons.

IV

Our first ground for affirmance is based on petitioners' failure to satisfy their burden of establishing that any risk of harm was substantial when compared to a known and available alternative method of execution. In their amended complaint, petitioners proffered that the State could use sodium thiopental as part of a single-drug protocol. They have since suggested that it might also be constitutional for Oklahoma to use pentobarbital. But the District Court found that both sodium thiopental and pentobarbital are now unavailable to Oklahoma's Department of Corrections.

Petitioners do not seriously contest this factual finding, and they have not identified any available drug or drugs that could be used in place of those that Oklahoma is now unable to obtain. Nor have they shown a risk of pain so great that other acceptable, available methods must be used. Instead, they argue that they need not identify a known and available method of execution that presents less risk. But this argument is inconsistent with the controlling opinion in *Baze*, which imposed a requirement that the Court now follows.

V

We also affirm for a second reason: The District Court did not commit clear error when it found that midazolam is highly likely to render a person unable to feel pain during an execution. We emphasize four points at the outset of our analysis.

First, we review the District Court's factual findings under the deferential "clear error" standard. This standard does not entitle us to overturn a finding "simply because [we are] convinced that [we] would have decided the case differently."

Second, petitioners bear the burden of persuasion on this issue. Although petitioners expend great effort attacking peripheral aspects of Dr. Evans' testimony, they make little attempt to prove what is critical, i.e., that the evidence they presented to the District Court establishes that the use of midazolam is sure or very likely to result in needless suffering.

Third, numerous courts have concluded that the use of midazolam as the first drug in a three-drug protocol is likely to render an inmate insensate to pain that might result from administration of the paralytic agent and potassium chloride. Our review is even more deferential where, as here, multiple trial courts have reached the same finding, and multiple appellate courts have affirmed those findings.

Fourth, challenges to lethal injection protocols test the boundaries of the authority and competency of federal courts. Although we must invalidate a lethal injection protocol if it violates the Eighth Amendment, federal courts should not "embroil [themselves] in ongoing scientific controversies beyond their expertise." Accordingly, an inmate challenging a protocol bears the burden to show, based on evidence presented to the court, that there is a substantial risk of severe pain.

A

Petitioners attack the District Court's findings of fact on two main grounds. First, they argue that even if midazolam is powerful enough to induce unconsciousness, it is too weak to maintain unconsciousness and insensitivity to pain once the second and third drugs are administered. Second, while conceding that the 500-milligram dose of midazolam is much higher than the normal therapeutic dose, they contend that this fact is irrelevant because midazolam has a "ceiling effect" — that is, at a certain point, an increase in the dose administered will not have any greater effect on the inmate. Neither argument succeeds.

The District Court found that midazolam is capable of placing a person "at a sufficient level of unconsciousness to resist the noxious stimuli which could occur from the application of the second and third drugs." This conclusion was not clearly erroneous. Respondents' expert, Dr. Evans, testified that the proper administration of a 500-milligram dose of midazolam would make it "a virtual certainty" that any individual would be "at a sufficient level of unconsciousness to resist the noxious stimuli which could occur from application of the 2nd and 3rd drugs" used in the Oklahoma protocol. And petitioners' experts acknowledged that they had no contrary scientific proof.

Oklahoma has also adopted important safeguards to ensure that midazolam is properly administered. The District Court emphasized three requirements in particular: The execution team must secure both a primary and backup IV access site, it must confirm the viability of the IV sites, and it must continuously monitor the offender's level of consciousness. The District Court did not commit clear error in concluding that these safeguards help to minimize any risk that might occur in the event that midazolam does not operate as intended.

B

Petitioners assert that midazolam's "ceiling effect" undermines the District Court's finding about the effectiveness of the huge dose administered in the Oklahoma protocol. Petitioners argue that midazolam has a "ceiling" above which any increase in dosage produces no effect. As a result, they maintain, it is wrong to assume that a 500-milligram dose has a much greater effect than a therapeutic dose of about 5 milligrams.

Petitioners provided little probative evidence on this point, and the speculative evidence that they did present to the District Court does not come close to establishing that its factual findings were clearly erroneous. Dr. Sasich stated in his expert report that the literature "indicates" that midazolam has a ceiling effect, but he conceded that he "was unable to determine the midazolam dose for a ceiling effect on unconsciousness because there is no literature in which such testing has been done." Dr. Lubarsky's report was similar and the testimony of petitioners' experts at the hearing was no more compelling.

C

Petitioners' remaining arguments about midazolam all lack merit. First, we are not persuaded by petitioners' argument that Dr. Evans' testimony should have been rejected because of some of the sources listed in his report. Second, petitioners argue that Dr. Evans' expert report contained a mathematical error, but we find this argument insignificant. Third, petitioners argue that there is no consensus among the States regarding midazolam's efficacy because only four States (Oklahoma, Arizona, Florida, and Ohio) have used midazolam as part of an execution. But while the near-universal use of the particular protocol at issue in Baze supported our conclusion that this protocol did not violate the Eighth Amendment, we did not say that the converse was true, i.e., that other protocols or methods of execution are of doubtful constitutionality. That argument, if accepted, would hamper the adoption of new and potentially more humane methods of execution and would prevent States from adapting to changes in the availability of suitable drugs.

Fourth, petitioners argue that difficulties with Oklahoma's execution of Lockett and Arizona's July 2014 execution of Joseph Wood establish that midazolam is sure or very likely to cause serious pain. We are not persuaded. Aside from the Lockett execution, 12 other executions have been conducted using the three-drug protocol at issue here, and those appear to have been conducted without any significant problems.

Finally, we find it appropriate to respond to the principal dissent's groundless suggestion that our decision is tantamount to allowing prisoners to be "drawn and quartered, slowly tortured to death, or actually burned at the stake." That is simply not true, and the principal dissent's resort to this outlandish rhetoric reveals the weakness of its legal arguments.

Justice SCALIA, with whom Justice THOMAS joins, concurring.

I join the opinion of the Court, and write to respond to Justice Breyer's plea for judicial abolition of the death penalty.

Welcome to Groundhog Day. The scene is familiar: Petitioners, sentenced to die for the crimes they committed (including, in the case of one petitioner since put to death, raping and murdering an 11-month-old baby), come before this Court asking us to nullify their sentences as "cruel and unusual" under the Eighth Amendment. They rely on this provision because it is the only provision they can rely on. They were charged by a sovereign State with murder. They were afforded counsel and tried before a jury of their peers—tried twice, once to determine whether they were guilty and once to determine whether death was the appropriate sentence. They were duly convicted and sentenced. They were granted the right to appeal and to seek postconviction relief, first in state and then in federal court. And now, acknowledging that their convictions are unassailable, they ask us for clemency, as though clemency were ours to give.

The response is also familiar: A vocal minority of the Court, waving over their heads a ream of the most recent abolitionist studies (a superabundant genre) as though they have discovered the lost folios of Shakespeare, insist that now, at long last, the death penalty must be abolished for good. Mind you, not once in the history of the American Republic has this Court ever suggested the death penalty is categorically impermissible. The reason is obvious: It is impossible to hold unconstitutional that which the Constitution explicitly contemplates. The Fifth Amendment provides that "[n]o person shall be held to answer for a capital . . . crime, unless on a presentment or indictment of a Grand Jury," and that no person shall be "deprived of life . . . without due process of law." Nevertheless, today Justice Breyer takes on the role of the abolitionists in this long-running drama, arguing that the text of the Constitution and two centuries of history must yield to his "20 years of experience on this Court," and inviting full briefing on the continued permissibility of capital punishment.

Historically, the Eighth Amendment was understood to bar only those punishments that added "'terror, pain, or disgrace'" to an otherwise permissible capital sentence. Rather than bother with this troubling detail, Justice Breyer elects to contort the constitutional text. Redefining "cruel" to mean "unreliable," "arbitrary," or causing "excessive delays," and "unusual" to include a "decline in use," he proceeds to offer up a white paper devoid of any meaningful legal argument.

Even accepting Justice Breyer's rewriting of the Eighth Amendment, his argument is full of internal contradictions and (it must be said) gobbledy-gook. He says that the death penalty is cruel because it is unreliable; but it is convictions, not punishments, that are unreliable.

Justice Breyer next says that the death penalty is cruel because it is arbitrary. To prove this point, he points to a study of 205 cases that "measured the 'egregiousness' of the murderer's conduct" with "a system of metrics," and then "compared the egregiousness of the conduct of the 9 defendants sentenced to death with the egregiousness of the conduct of defendants in the remaining 196 cases [who were not sentenced to death]." If only Aristotle, Aquinas, and Hume knew that moral philosophy could be so neatly distilled into a pocket-sized, vade mecum "system of metrics." Of course it cannot: Egregiousness is a moral judgment susceptible of few hard-and-fast rules.

Justice Breyer's third reason that the death penalty is cruel is that it entails delay, thereby (1) subjecting inmates to long periods on death row and (2) undermining the penological justifications of the death penalty. The first point is nonsense. Life without parole is an even lengthier period than the wait on death row; and if the objection is that death row is a more confining environment, the solution should be modifying the environment rather than abolishing the death penalty. Justice Breyer further asserts that "whatever interest in retribution might be served by the death penalty as currently administered, that interest can be served almost as well by a sentence of life in prison without parole." My goodness. If he thinks the death penalty not much more harsh (and hence not much more retributive), why is he so keen to get rid of it? With all due respect, whether the death penalty and life imprisonment constitute more-or-less equivalent retribution is a question far above the judiciary's pay grade.

And finally, Justice Breyer speculates that it does not "seem likely" that the death penalty has a "significant" deterrent effect. It seems very likely to me, and there are statistical studies that say so. The suggestion that the incremental deterrent effect of capital punishment does not seem "significant" reflects, it seems to me, a let-them-eat-cake obliviousness to the needs of others. Let the People decide how much incremental deterrence is appropriate.

Justice THOMAS, with whom Justice SCALIA joins, concurring.

I agree with the Court that petitioners' Eighth Amendment claim fails. I write separately to respond to Justice Breyer's dissent questioning the constitutionality of the death penalty generally. Justice Breyer's assertion that the death penalty in this country has fallen short of the aspiration that capital punishment be reserved for the "worst of the worst" —a notion itself based on an implicit proportionality principle that has long been discredited, merits further comment.

There is a reason the choice between life and death, within legal limits, is left to the jurors and judges who sit through the trial, and not to legal elites (or law students). That reason is memorialized not once, but twice, in our Constitution: Article III guarantees that "[t]he Trial of all Crimes, except in cases of Impeachment, shall be by Jury" and that "such Trial shall be held in the State where the said Crimes shall have been committed." Art. III, §2, cl. 3. And the Sixth Amendment promises that "[i]n all criminal prosecutions, the accused shall enjoy the right to a . . . trial, by an impartial jury of the State and district wherein the crime shall have been committed." Those provisions ensure that capital defendants are given the option to be sentenced by a jury of their peers who, collectively, are better situated to make the moral judgment between life and death than are the products of contemporary American law schools.

We owe victims more than this sort of pseudoscientific assessment of their lives. It is bad enough to tell a mother that her child's murder is not "worthy" of society's ultimate expression of moral condemnation. But to do so based on cardboard stereotypes or cold mathematical calculations is beyond my comprehension.

A small sample of the applications for a stay of execution that have come before the Court this Term alone proves my point. Mark Christeson was due to be executed in October 2014 for his role in the murder of Susan Brouk and her young children, Adrian and Kyle. After raping Ms. Brouk at gunpoint, he and his accomplice drove the family to a remote pond, where Christeson cut Ms. Brouk's throat with a bone knife. Although bleeding profusely, she stayed alive long enough to tell her children she loved them and to watch as Christeson murdered them—her son, by cutting his throat twice and drowning him; her daughter, by pressing down on her throat until she suffocated. Christeson and his accomplice then threw Ms. Brouk—alive but barely breathing—into the pond to drown on top of her dead children. Ibid. This Court granted him a stay of execution.

Some of our most "egregious" cases have been those in which we have granted relief based on an unfounded Eighth Amendment claim. For example, we have granted relief in a number of egregious cases based on this Court's decision in Atkins v. Virginia (2002), exempting certain "mentally retarded" offenders from the death penalty. Last Term, the Court granted relief to a man who kidnaped, beat, raped, and murdered a 21-year-old pregnant newlywed, Karol Hurst, also murdering her unborn child, and then, on the same day, murdered a sheriff's deputy acting in the line of duty. Hall v. Florida (2014).

The Court has also misinterpreted the Eighth Amendment to grant relief in egregious cases involving rape. In Kennedy v. Louisiana (2008), the Court granted relief to a man who had been sentenced to death for raping his 8-year-old step-daughter. The rape was so violent that it "separated her cervix from the back of her vagina, causing her rectum to protrude into the vaginal structure," and tore her "entire perineum . . . from the posterior fourchette to the anus." And in Coker v. Georgia (1977), the Court granted relief to a petitioner who had escaped from prison, broken into the home of a young married couple and their newborn, forced the wife to bind her husband, gagged her husband with her underwear, raped her (even after being told that she was recovering from a recent childbirth), and then kidnaped her after threatening her husband. In each case, the Court crafted an Eighth Amendment right to be free from execution for the crime of rape.

Whatever one's views on the permissibility or wisdom of the death penalty, I doubt anyone would disagree that each of these crimes was egregious enough to merit the severest condemnation that society has to offer. The only constitutional problem with the fact that these criminals were spared that condemnation, while others were not, is that their amnesty came in the form of unfounded claims. Arbitrariness has nothing to do with it. To the extent that we are ill at ease with these disparate outcomes, it seems to me that the best solution is for the Court to stop making up Eighth Amendment claims in its ceaseless quest to end the death penalty through undemocratic means.

Justice BREYER, with whom Justice GINSBURG joins, dissenting.

For the reasons stated in Justice Sotomayor's opinion, I dissent from the Court's holding. But rather than try to patch up the death penalty's legal wounds one at a time, I would ask for full briefing on a more basic question: whether the death penalty violates the Constitution.

The relevant legal standard is the standard set forth in the Eighth Amendment. The Constitution there forbids the "inflict[ion]" of "cruel and unusual punishments." The Court has recognized that a "claim that punishment is excessive is judged not by the standards that prevailed in 1685 when Lord Jeffreys presided over the 'Bloody Assizes' or when the Bill of Rights was adopted, but rather by those that currently prevail." Indeed, the Constitution prohibits various gruesome punishments that were common in Blackstone's day.

Nearly 40 years ago, this Court upheld the death penalty under statutes that, in the Court's view, contained safeguards sufficient to ensure that the penalty would be applied reliably and not arbitrarily. The circumstances and the evidence of the death penalty's application have changed radically since then. Given those changes, I believe that it is now time to reopen the question.

In 1976, the Court thought that the constitutional infirmities in the death penalty could be healed; the Court in effect delegated significant responsibility to the States to develop procedures that would protect against those constitutional problems. Almost 40 years of studies, surveys, and experience strongly indicate, however, that this effort has failed. Today's administration of the death penalty involves three fundamental constitutional defects: (1) serious unreliability, (2) arbitrariness in application, and (3) unconscionably long delays that undermine the death penalty's penological purpose. Perhaps as a result, most places within the United States have abandoned its use.

I

"Cruel"—Lack of Reliability

This Court has specified that the finality of death creates a "qualitative difference" between the death penalty and other punishments (including life in prison). That "qualitative difference" creates "a corresponding difference in the need for reliability in the determination that death is the appropriate punishment in a specific case." There is increasing evidence, however, that the death penalty as now applied lacks that requisite reliability.

For one thing, despite the difficulty of investigating the circumstances surrounding an execution for a crime that took place long ago, researchers have found convincing evidence that, in the past three decades, innocent people have been executed.

For another, the evidence that the death penalty has been wrongly imposed (whether or not it was carried out), is striking. Last year, in 2014, six death row inmates were exonerated based on actual innocence. All had been imprisoned for more than 30 years (and one for almost 40 years) at the time of their exonerations.

The stories of three of the men exonerated within the last year are illustrative. DNA evidence showed that Henry Lee McCollum did not commit the rape and murder for which he had been sentenced to death. Last Term, this Court ordered that Anthony Ray Hinton, who had been convicted of murder, receive further hearings in state court; he was exonerated earlier this year because the forensic evidence used against him was flawed.

Furthermore, exonerations occur far more frequently where capital convictions, rather than ordinary criminal convictions, are at issue. Researchers have calculated that courts (or State Governors) are 130 times more likely to exonerate a defendant where a death sentence is at issue. They are nine times more likely to exonerate where a capital murder, rather than a noncapital murder, is at issue. [R]esearchers estimate that about 4% of those sentenced to death are actually innocent,

Finally, if we expand our definition of "exoneration" (which we limited to errors suggesting the defendant was actually innocent) and thereby also categorize as "erroneous" instances in which courts failed to follow legally required procedures, the numbers soar. Between 1973 and 1995, courts identified prejudicial errors in 68% of the capital cases before them.

This research and these figures are likely controversial. Full briefing would allow us to scrutinize them with more care. But, at a minimum, they suggest a serious problem of reliability. They suggest that there are too many instances in which courts sentence defendants to death without complying with the necessary procedures; and they suggest that, in a significant number of cases, the death sentence is imposed on a person who did not commit the crime.

II

"Cruel"—Arbitrariness

The arbitrary imposition of punishment is the antithesis of the rule of law.

Despite the Gregg Court's hope for fair administration of the death penalty, 40 years of further experience make it increasingly clear that the death penalty is imposed arbitrarily, i.e., without the "reasonable consistency" legally necessary to reconcile its use with the Constitution's commands.

Thorough studies of death penalty sentences support this conclusion. A recent study, for example, examined all death penalty sentences imposed between 1973 and 2007 in Connecticut, a State that abolished the death penalty in 2012. The study reviewed treatment of all homicide defendants. It found 205 instances in which Connecticut law made the defendant eligible for a death sentence. Courts imposed a death sentence in 12 of these 205 cases, of which 9 were sustained on appeal. The study then measured the "egregiousness" of the murderer's conduct in those 9 cases, developing a system of metrics designed to do so. It then compared the egregiousness of the conduct of the 9 defendants sentenced to death with the egregiousness of the conduct of defendants in the remaining 196 cases (those in which the defendant, though found guilty of a death-eligible offense, was ultimately not sentenced to death). Application of the studies' metrics made clear that only 1 of those 9 defendants was indeed the "worst of the worst" (or was, at least, within the 15% considered most "egregious"). The remaining eight were not. Their behavior was no worse than the behavior of at least 33 and as many as 170 other defendants (out of a total pool of 205) who had not been sentenced to death.

Such studies indicate that the factors that most clearly ought to affect application of the death penalty—namely, comparative egregiousness of the crime—often do not. Other studies show that circumstances that ought not to affect application of the death penalty, such as race, gender, or geography, often do.

13. Sentencing

Numerous studies, for example, have concluded that individuals accused of murdering white victims, as opposed to black or other minority victims, are more likely to receive the death penalty. Fewer, but still many, studies have found that the gender of the defendant or the gender of the victim makes a not-otherwise-warranted difference.

Geography also plays an important role in determining who is sentenced to death. And that is not simply because some States permit the death penalty while others do not. Rather within a death penalty State, the imposition of the death penalty heavily depends on the county in which a defendant is tried. Between 2004 and 2009, for example, just 29 counties (fewer than 1% of counties in the country) accounted for approximately half of all death sentences imposed nationwide.

What accounts for this county-by-county disparity? Some studies indicate that the disparity reflects the decisionmaking authority, the legal discretion, and ultimately the power of the local prosecutor. Others suggest that the availability of resources for defense counsel (or the lack thereof) helps explain geographical differences. Still others indicate that the racial composition of and distribution within a county plays an important role. Finally, some studies suggest that political pressures, including pressures on judges who must stand for election, can make a difference. Thus, whether one looks at research indicating that irrelevant or improper factors—such as race, gender, local geography, and resources—do significantly determine who receives the death penalty, or whether one looks at research indicating that proper factors—such as "egregiousness"—do not determine who receives the death penalty, the legal conclusion must be the same: The research strongly suggests that the death penalty is imposed arbitrarily.

Justice Thomas catalogues the tragic details of various capital cases, (concurring opinion), but this misses my point. Every murder is tragic, but unless we return to the mandatory death penalty struck down in Woodson, the constitutionality of capital punishment rests on its limited application to the worst of the worst.

III

"Cruel"—Excessive Delays

The problems of reliability and unfairness almost inevitably lead to a third independent constitutional problem: excessively long periods of time that individuals typically spend on death row, alive but under sentence of death.

[U]nless we abandon the procedural requirements that assure fairness and reliability, we are forced to confront the problem of increasingly lengthy delays in capital cases. Ultimately, though these legal causes may help to explain, they do not mitigate the harms caused by delay itself.

Consider first the statistics. In 2014, 35 individuals were executed. Those executions occurred, on average, nearly 18 years after a court initially pronounced its sentence of death. The length of the average delay has increased dramatically over the years. Nearly half of the 3,000 inmates now on death row have been there for more than 15 years. And, at present execution rates, it would take more than 75 years to carry out those 3,000 death sentences; thus, the average person on death row would spend an additional 37.5 years there before being executed.

These lengthy delays create two special constitutional difficulties. First, a lengthy delay in and of itself is especially cruel because it "subjects death row inmates to decades of especially severe, dehumanizing conditions of confinement." Second, lengthy delay undermines the death penalty's penological rationale. One might ask, why can Congress or the States not deal directly with the delay problem? Why can they not take steps to shorten the time between sentence and execution, and thereby mitigate the problems just raised? The answer is that shortening delay is much more difficult than one might think. And that is in part because efforts to do so risk causing procedural harms that also undermine the death penalty's constitutionality.

A death penalty system that seeks procedural fairness and reliability brings with it delays that severely aggravate the cruelty of capital punishment and significantly undermine the rationale for imposing a sentence of death in the first place. But a death penalty system that minimizes delays would undermine the legal system's efforts to secure reliability and procedural fairness.

IV

"Unusual"—Decline in Use of the Death Penalty

The Eighth Amendment forbids punishments that are cruel and unusual. Last year, in 2014, only seven States carried out an execution. Perhaps more importantly, in the last two decades, the imposition and implementation of the death penalty have increasingly become unusual. I can illustrate the significant decline in the use of the death penalty in several ways.

An appropriate starting point concerns the trajectory of the number of annual death sentences nationwide, from the 1970's to present day. In 1977—just after the Supreme Court made clear that, by modifying their legislation, States could reinstate the death penalty—137 people were sentenced to death. Many States having revised their death penalty laws to meet Furman's requirements, the number of death sentences then increased. Between 1986 and 1999, 286 persons on average were sentenced to death each year. But, approximately 15 years ago, the numbers began to decline, and they have declined rapidly ever since. In 1999, 279 persons were sentenced to death. Last year, just 73 persons were sentenced to death.

Next, one can consider state-level data. Often when deciding whether a punishment practice is, constitutionally speaking, "unusual," this Court has looked to the number of States engaging in that practice. In this respect, the number of active death penalty States has fallen dramatically. In 1972, when the Court decided Furman, the death penalty was lawful in 41 States. Nine States had abolished it. As of today, 19 States have abolished the death penalty (along with the District of Columbia), although some did so prospectively only.

Accordingly, 30 States have either formally abolished the death penalty or have not conducted an execution in more than eight years. Indeed, last year, only seven States conducted an execution. In other words, in 43 States, no one was executed. Moreover, we have said that it "'is not so much the number of these States that is significant, but the consistency of the direction of change.'" These circumstances perhaps reflect the fact that a majority of Americans, when asked to choose between the death penalty and life in prison without parole, now choose the latter.

I rely primarily upon domestic, not foreign events, in pointing to changes and circumstances that tend to justify the claim that the death penalty, constitutionally speaking, is "unusual." I note, however, that many nations—indeed, 95 of the 193 members of the United Nations—have formally abolished the death penalty and an additional 42 have abolished it in practice. V

I recognize a strong counterargument that favors constitutionality. We are a court. Why should we not leave the matter up to the people acting democratically through legislatures? The Constitution foresees a country that will make most important decisions democratically. Most nations that have abandoned the death penalty have done so through legislation, not judicial decision. And legislators, unlike judges, are free to take account of matters such as monetary costs, which I do not claim are relevant here.

The answer is that the matters I have discussed, such as lack of reliability, the arbitrary application of a serious and irreversible punishment, individual suffering caused by long delays, and lack of penological purpose are quintessentially judicial matters. They concern the infliction—indeed the unfair, cruel, and unusual infliction—of a serious punishment upon an individual. I recognize that in 1972 this Court, in a sense, turned to Congress and the state legislatures in its search for standards that would increase the fairness and reliability of imposing a death penalty. The legislatures responded. But, in the last four decades, considerable evidence has accumulated that those responses have not worked.

Thus we are left with a judicial responsibility. The Eighth Amendment sets forth the relevant law, and we must interpret that law. For the reasons I have set forth in this opinion, I believe it highly likely that the death penalty violates the Eighth Amendment. At the very least, the Court should call for full briefing on the basic question.

Justice SOTOMAYOR, with whom Justice GINSBURG, Justice BREYER, and Justice KAGAN join, dissenting.

Petitioners, three inmates on Oklahoma's death row, challenge the constitutionality of the State's lethal injection protocol. The State plans to execute petitioners using three drugs: midazolam, rocuronium bromide, and potassium chloride. The latter two drugs are intended to paralyze the inmate and stop his heart. But they do so in a torturous manner, causing burning, searing pain. It is thus critical that the first drug, midazolam, do what it is supposed to do, which is to render and keep the inmate unconscious. Petitioners claim that midazolam cannot be expected to perform that function, and they have presented ample evidence showing that the State's planned use of this drug poses substantial, constitutionally intolerable risks.

Nevertheless, the Court today turns aside petitioners' plea that they at least be allowed a stay of execution while they seek to prove midazolam's inadequacy. The Court achieves this result in two ways: first, by deferring to the District Court's decision to credit the scientifically unsupported and implausible testimony of a single expert witness; and second, by faulting petitioners for failing to satisfy the wholly novel requirement of proving the availability of an alternative means for their own executions. On both counts the Court errs. As a result, it leaves petitioners exposed to what may well be the chemical equivalent of being burned at the stake.

I

A

The Eighth Amendment succinctly prohibits the infliction of "cruel and unusual punishments." Seven years ago, in *Baze v. Rees* (2008), the Court addressed the application of this mandate to Kentucky's lethal injection protocol. In *Baze*, it was undisputed that absent a "proper dose of sodium thiopental," there would be a "substantial, constitutionally unacceptable risk of suffocation from the administration of pancuronium bromide and pain from the injection of potassium chloride." That is because, if given to a conscious inmate, pancuronium bromide would leave him or her asphyxiated and unable to demonstrate "any outward sign of distress," while potassium chloride would cause "excruciating pain." But the Baze petitioners conceded that if administered as intended, Kentucky's method of execution would nevertheless "result in a humane death," as the "proper administration" of sodium thiopental "eliminates any meaningful risk that a prisoner would experience pain from the subsequent injections of pancuronium and potassium chloride." Based on that premise, the Court ultimately rejected the challenge to Kentucky's protocol, with the plurality opinion concluding that the State's procedures for administering these three drugs ensured there was no "objectively intolerable risk" of severe pain.

B

For many years, Oklahoma performed executions using the same three drugs at issue in *Baze*. After *Baze* was decided, however, the primary producer of sodium thiopental refused to continue permitting the drug to be used in executions. Like a number of other States, Oklahoma opted to substitute pentobarbital, another barbiturate, in its place. But in March 2014, shortly before two scheduled executions, Oklahoma found itself unable to secure this drug. The State rescheduled the executions for the following month to give it time to locate an alternative anesthetic. In less than a week, a group of officials from the Oklahoma Department of Corrections and the Attorney General's office selected midazolam to serve as a replacement for pentobarbital.

Soon thereafter, Oklahoma used midazolam for the first time in its execution of Clayton Lockett. That execution did not go smoothly. Ten minutes after an intravenous (IV) line was set in Lockett's groin area and 100 milligrams of midazolam were administered, an attending physician declared Lockett unconscious. When the paralytic and potassium chloride were administered, however, Lockett awoke. Various witnesses reported that Lockett began to writhe against his restraints, saying, "[t]his s*** is f***ing with my mind," "something is wrong," and "[t]he drugs aren't working." State officials ordered the blinds lowered, then halted the execution. But 10 minutes later—approximately 40 minutes after the execution began—Lockett was pronounced dead.

C

In June 2014, inmates on Oklahoma's death row filed a 42 U. S. C. §1983 suit against respondent prison officials challenging the constitutionality of Oklahoma's method of execution. They contended, among other things, that the State's intended use of midazolam would violate the Eighth Amendment because, unlike sodium thiopental or pentobarbital, the drug "is incapable of producing a state of unawareness that will be reliably maintained after either of the other two pain-producing drugs . . . is injected." The District Court held a 3-day evidentiary hearing, at which petitioners relied principally on the testimony of two experts: Dr. David Lubarsky, an anesthesiologist, and Dr. Larry Sasich, a doctor of pharmacy. The State, in turn, based its case on the testimony of Dr. Roswell Evans, also a doctor of pharmacy.

To a great extent, the experts' testimony overlapped. All three experts agreed that . . . midazolam is subject to a ceiling effect, which means that there is a point at which increasing the dose of the drug does not result in any greater effect. The experts' opinions diverged, however, on the crucial questions of how this ceiling effect operates, and whether it will prevent midazolam from keeping a condemned inmate unconscious when the second and third lethal injection drugs are administered.

D

The District Court denied petitioners' motion for a preliminary injunction. It began by making a series of factual findings regarding the characteristics of midazolam and its use in Oklahoma's execution protocol. Most relevant here, the District Court found that "[t]he proper administration of 500 milligrams of midazolam . . . would make it a virtual certainty that an individual will be at a sufficient level of unconsciousness to resist the noxious stimuli which could occur from the application of the second and third drugs." [T]he district court concluded:

"Dr. Evans testified persuasively . . . that whatever the ceiling effect of midazolam may be with respect to anesthesia, which takes effect at the spinal cord level, there is no ceiling effect with respect to the ability of a 500 milligram dose of midazolam to effectively paralyze the brain, a phenomenon which is not anesthesia but does have the effect of shutting down respiration and eliminating the individual's awareness of pain."

II

I begin with the second of the Court's two holdings: that the District Court properly found that petitioners did not demonstrate a likelihood of showing that Oklahoma's execution protocol poses an unconstitutional risk of pain. In reaching this conclusion, the Court sweeps aside substantial evidence showing that, while midazolam may be able to induce unconsciousness, it cannot be utilized to maintain unconsciousness in the face of agonizing stimuli.

A.

Like the Court, I would review for clear error the District Court's finding that 500 milligrams of midazolam will render someone sufficiently unconscious "'to resist the noxious stimuli which could occur from the application of the second and third drugs.'" Unlike the Court, however, I would do so without abdicating our duty to examine critically the factual predicates for the District Court's finding—namely, Dr. Evans' testimony that midazolam has a "ceiling effect" only "at the spinal cord level," and that a "500 milligram dose of midazolam" can therefore "effectively paralyze the brain." [J]ust because a purported expert says something does not make it so. Especially when important constitutional rights are at stake, federal district courts must carefully evaluate the premises and evidence on which scientific conclusions are based, and appellate courts must ensure that the courts below have in fact carefully considered all the evidence presented. Here, given the numerous flaws in Dr. Evans' testimony, there can be little doubt that the District Court clearly erred in relying on it.

To begin, Dr. Evans identified no scientific literature to support his opinion regarding midazolam's properties at higher-than-normal doses. Dr. Evans' testimony seems to have been based on the Web site www.drugs.com. Most importantly, nothing from drugs.com—or, for that matter, any other source in the record—corroborated Dr. Evans' key testimony that midazolam's ceiling effect is limited to the spinal cord and does not pertain to the brain.

[Other] scientific sources also appear to demonstrate that Dr. Evans' spinal-cord theory—i.e., that midazolam's ceiling effect is limited to the spinal cord—was premised on a basic misunderstanding of midazolam's mechanism of action.

In sum, then, Dr. Evans' conclusions were entirely unsupported by any study or third-party source, contradicted by the extrinsic evidence proffered by petitioners, inconsistent with the scientific understanding of midazolam's properties, and apparently premised on basic logical errors.

B.

[T]o prevail on their claim, petitioners need only establish an intolerable risk of pain, not a certainty. Here, the State is attempting to use midazolam to produce an effect the drug has never previously been demonstrated to produce, and despite studies indicating that at some point increasing the dose will not actually increase the drug's effect.

13. Sentencing

Finally, none of the State's "safeguards" for administering these drugs would seem to mitigate the substantial risk that midazolam will not work, as the Court contends. Protections ensuring that officials have properly secured a viable IV site will not enable midazolam to have an effect that it is chemically incapable of having. Nor is there any indication that the State's monitoring of the inmate's consciousness will be able to anticipate whether the inmate will remain unconscious while the second and third drugs are administered. No one questions whether midazolam can induce unconsciousness. The problem, as Lockett's execution vividly illustrates, is that an unconscious inmate may be awakened by the pain and respiratory distress caused by administration of the second and third drugs. At that point, even if it were possible to determine whether the inmate is conscious—dubious, given the use of a paralytic—it is already too late.

III

The Court's conclusion that petitioners' challenge also fails because they identified no available alternative means by which the State may kill them is legally indefensible.

This Court has long recognized that certain methods of execution are categorically off-limits. Although Wilkerson approved the particular method at issue—the firing squad—it made clear that "public dissection," "burning alive," and other "punishments of torture . . . in the same line of unnecessary cruelty, are forbidden by [the Eighth A]mendment to the Constitution."

In the more than a century since, the Members of this Court have often had cause to debate the full scope of the Eighth Amendment's prohibition of cruel and unusual punishment. But there has been little dispute that it at the very least precludes the imposition of "barbarous physical punishments."

The Court today, however, would convert this categorical prohibition into a conditional one. A method of execution that is intolerably painful—even to the point of being the chemical equivalent of burning alive—will, the Court holds, be unconstitutional if, and only if, there is a "known and available alternative" method of execution. It deems Baze to foreclose any argument to the contrary.

Baze held no such thing. Because the position that a plaintiff challenging a method of execution under the Eighth Amendment must prove the availability of an alternative means of execution did not "represent the views of a majority of the Court," it was not the holding of the plurality.

In reengineering Baze to support its newfound rule, the Court appears to rely on a flawed syllogism. If the death penalty is constitutional, the Court reasons, then there must be a means of accomplishing it, and thus some available method of execution must be constitutional. But even accepting that the death penalty is, in the abstract, consistent with evolving standards of decency, the Court's conclusion does not follow. If all available means of conducting an execution constitute cruel and unusual punishment, then conducting the execution will constitute cruel and usual punishment. Nothing compels a State to perform an execution.

153

It does not get a constitutional free pass simply because it desires to deliver the ultimate penalty; its ends do not justify any and all means. If a State wishes to carry out an execution, it must do so subject to the constraints that our Constitution imposes on it, including the obligation to ensure that its chosen method is not cruel and unusual. Certainly the condemned has no duty to devise or pick a constitutional instrument of his or her own death.

Chapter 14

DOUBLE JEOPARDY

C. No Retrial Following Conviction or Acquittal. Exceptions to the Double Jeopardy Rule

1. No Retrial After Acquittal (casebook p. 1161)

As the Court discussed in *Evans v. Michigan*, 133 S. Ct. 1069 (2013), a retrial is not permitted even if a judge grants an acquittal because he incorrectly assumed there were additional unproved elements of the charged offense.

Evans v. Michigan
133 S. Ct. 1069 (2013)

Justice SOTOMAYOR delivered the opinion of the Court.

When the State of Michigan rested its case at petitioner Lamar Evans' arson trial, the court entered a directed verdict of acquittal, based upon its view that the State had not provided sufficient evidence of a particular element of the offense. It turns out that the unproven "element" was not actually a required element at all. We must decide whether an erroneous acquittal such as this nevertheless constitutes an acquittal for double jeopardy purposes, which would mean that Evans could not be retried. This Court has previously held that a judicial acquittal premised upon a "misconstruction" of a criminal statute is an "acquittal on the merits . . . [that] bars retrial." *Arizona v. Rumsey* (1984). Seeing no meaningful constitutional distinction between a trial court's "misconstruction" of a statute and its erroneous addition of a statutory element, we hold that a midtrial acquittal in these circumstances is an acquittal for double jeopardy purposes as well.

The State charged Evans with burning "other real property," a violation of Mich. Comp. Laws §750.73 (1981). The State's evidence at trial suggested that Evans had burned down an unoccupied house. At the close of the State's case, however, Evans moved for a directed verdict of acquittal. He pointed the court to the applicable Michigan Criminal Jury Instructions, which listed as the "Fourth" element of the offense "that the building was not a dwelling house." And the commentary to the Instructions emphasized, "an essential element is that the structure burned is not a dwelling house." Evans argued that Mich. Comp. Laws §750.72 criminalizes common-law arson, which requires that the structure burned be a dwelling, while the provision under which he was charged, §750.73, covers all other real property. Persuaded, the trial court granted the motion. The court explained that the "'testimony [of the homeowner] was this was a dwelling house,'" so the nondwelling requirement of §750.73 was not met.

On the State's appeal, the Michigan Court of Appeals reversed and remanded. Evans had conceded, and the court held, that under controlling precedent, burning "other real property" is a lesser included offense under Michigan law, and disproving the greater offense is not required. The court thus explained it was "undisputed that the trial court misperceived the elements of the offense with which [Evans] was charged and erred by directing a verdict."

We granted certiorari to resolve the disagreement among state and federal courts on the question whether retrial is barred when a trial court grants an acquittal because the prosecution had failed to prove an "element" of the offense that, in actuality, it did not have to prove.

In answering this question, we do not write on a clean slate. Quite the opposite. It has been half a century since we first recognized that the *Double Jeopardy Clause* bars retrial following a court-decreed acquittal, even if the acquittal is "based upon an egregiously erroneous foundation." *Fong Foo v. United States* (1962). A mistaken acquittal is an acquittal nonetheless, and we have long held that "[a] verdict of acquittal . . . could not be reviewed, on error or otherwise, without putting [a defendant] twice in jeopardy, and thereby violating the Constitution."

Our cases have applied *Fong Foo's* principle broadly. An acquittal is unreviewable whether a judge directs a jury to return a verdict of acquittal or forgoes that formality by entering a judgment of acquittal herself. And an acquittal precludes retrial even if it is premised upon an erroneous decision to exclude evidence; a mistaken understanding of what evidence would suffice to sustain a conviction; or a "misconstruction of the statute" defining the requirements to convict, In all these circumstances, "the fact that the acquittal may result from erroneous evidentiary rulings or erroneous interpretations of governing legal principles affects the accuracy of that determination, but it does not alter its essential character." *United States v. Scott* (1978).

Most relevant here, our cases have defined an acquittal to encompass any ruling that the prosecution's proof is insufficient to establish criminal liability for an offense. Thus an "acquittal" includes "a ruling by the court that the evidence is insufficient to convict," a "factual finding [that] necessarily establish[es] the criminal defendant's lack of criminal culpability," and any other "rulin[g] which relate[s] to the ultimate question of guilt or innocence." These sorts of substantive rulings stand apart from procedural rulings that may also terminate a case midtrial, which we generally refer to as dismissals or mistrials. Procedural dismissals include rulings on questions that "are unrelated to factual guilt or innocence," but "which serve other purposes," including "a legal judgment that a defendant, although criminally culpable, may not be punished" because of some problem like an error with the indictment.

Both procedural dismissals and substantive rulings result in an early end to trial, but we explained in *Scott* that the double jeopardy consequences of each differ. "[T]he law attaches particular significance to an acquittal," so a merits-related ruling concludes proceedings absolutely. This is because "[t]o permit a second trial after an acquittal, however mistaken the acquittal may have been, would present an unacceptably high risk that the Government, with its vastly superior resources, might wear down the defendant so that 'even though innocent he may be found guilty.'" And retrial following an acquittal would upset a defendant's expectation of repose.

The trial court granted Evans' motion under a rule that requires the court to "direct a verdict of acquittal on any charged offense as to which the evidence is insufficient to support conviction." This ruling was not a dismissal on a procedural ground "unrelated to factual guilt or innocence," like the question of "preindictment delay" in *Scott*, but rather a determination that the State had failed to prove its case. Under our precedents, then, Evans was acquitted.

There is no question the trial court's ruling was wrong; it was predicated upon a clear misunderstanding of what facts the State needed to prove under State law. But that is of no moment.

[T]he State and the United States object that this rule denies the prosecution a full and fair opportunity to present its evidence to the jury, while the defendant reaps a "windfall" from the trial court's unreviewable error. But sovereigns are hardly powerless to prevent this sort of situation. Nothing obligates a jurisdiction to afford its trial courts the power to grant a midtrial acquittal, and at least two States disallow the practice. Many jurisdictions, including the federal system, allow or encourage their courts to defer consideration of a motion to acquit until after the jury returns a verdict, which mitigates double jeopardy concerns. And for cases such as this, in which a trial court's interpretation of the relevant criminal statute is likely to prove dispositive, we see no reason why jurisdictions could not provide for mandatory continuances or expedited interlocutory appeals if they wished to prevent misguided acquittals from being entered. But having chosen to vest its courts with the power to grant midtrial acquittals, the State must bear the corresponding risk that some acquittals will be granted in error.

We hold that Evans' trial ended in an acquittal when the trial court ruled the State had failed to produce sufficient evidence of his guilt. The *Double Jeopardy Clause* thus bars retrial for his offense and should have barred the State's appeal. The judgment of the Supreme Court of Michigan is reversed.

Justice ALITO dissenting:

The Court holds that the *Double Jeopardy Clause* bars petitioner's retrial for arson because his attorney managed to convince a judge to terminate petitioner's first trial prior to verdict on the specious ground that the offense with which he was charged contains an imaginary "element" that the prosecution could not prove. The Court's decision makes no sense. It is not consistent with the original meaning of the *Double Jeopardy Clause*; it does not serve the purposes of the prohibition against double jeopardy; and contrary to the Court's reasoning, the trial judge's ruling was not an "acquittal," which our cases have "consistently" defined as a decision that "'actually represents a resolution, correct or not, of some or all of the factual *elements of the offense charged*.'" For no good reason, the Court deprives the State of Michigan of its right to have one fair opportunity to convict petitioner, and I therefore respectfully dissent.

I

The prohibition against double jeopardy "had its origin in the three common-law pleas of *autrefois acquit*, *autrefois convict*, and pardon," which "prevented the retrial of a person who had previously been acquitted, convicted, or pardoned for the same offense." As the Court has previously explained, "the common-law protection against double jeopardy historically applied only to charges on which a *jury* had rendered a *verdict*." As a result, the original understanding of the Clause, which is "hardly a matter of dispute," *Scott* does not compel the Court's conclusion that a defendant is acquitted for double jeopardy purposes whenever a *judge* issues a *preverdict* ruling that the prosecution has failed to prove a nonexistent "element" of the charged offense.

The *Double Jeopardy Clause* is largely based on "the deeply ingrained principle that the State with all its resources and power should not be allowed to make repeated attempts to convict an individual for an alleged offense, thereby subjecting him to embarrassment, expense and ordeal and compelling him to live in a continuing state of anxiety and insecurity, as well as enhancing the possibility that even though innocent he may be found guilty." *Yeager v. United States* (2009) Allowing retrial in the circumstances of the present case would not result in any such abuse. The prosecution would not be afforded a second opportunity to persuade the factfinder that its evidence satisfies the actual elements of the offense. Instead, because the trial judge's ruling in the first trial was not based on an actual element of the charged offense, retrial would simply give the prosecution one fair opportunity to prove its case.

The Court's decision also flies in the face of our established understanding of the meaning of an acquittal for double jeopardy purposes. The *Double Jeopardy Clause* provides that no person shall "be subject for the same *offence* to be twice put in jeopardy of life or limb." U.S. Const., Amdt. 5 (emphasis added). Thus, "[d]ouble-jeopardy analysis focuses on the individual 'offence' charged." And to determine what constitutes "the individual 'offence' charged," the Court homes in on the elements of the offense. See *United States v. Dixon* (1993). Consistent with the constitutional text's focus on the "offence"—and thus the elements—with which a defendant is charged, the Court's "double-jeopardy cases have consistently" defined an acquittal as a decision that "'actually represents a resolution, correct or not, of some or all of the factual elements of the offense charged.'"

Today, the Court effectively abandons the well-established definition of an acquittal. Instead, the Court proclaims that the dispositive question is whether a midtrial termination represented a "procedural dismissa[l]" or a "substantive rulin[g]." This reformulation of double jeopardy law is not faithful to our precedents—or to the *Double Jeopardy Clause* itself. The key question is not whether a ruling is "procedural" or "substantive" (whatever those terms mean in this context), but whether a ruling relates to the defendant's factual guilt or innocence with respect to the "offence," and thus the elements—with which he is charged.

When a judge evaluates the evidence and determines that the prosecution has not proved facts that are legally sufficient to satisfy the actual elements of the charged offense, the ruling, however labeled, represents an acquittal because it is founded on the defendant's factual innocence. But when a judge manufactures an additional "element" of an offense and then holds that there is insufficient evidence to prove that extra "element," the judge has not resolved the defendant's "factual guilt or innocence" as to any of the actual elements of the offense.

The Court may feel compelled to reach that result because it thinks that it would be unworkable to draw a distinction between a preverdict termination based on the trial judge's misconstruction of an element of an offense and a preverdict termination based on the judge's perception that a statute contains an "element" that is actually nonexistent. This practical concern is overblown. There may be cases in which this determination presents problems, but surely there are many cases in which the determination is quite easy. The present case is a perfect example, for here there is no real dispute that the trial judge's ruling was based on a nonexistent statutory "element."

I would hold that double jeopardy protection is not triggered by a judge's erroneous preverdict ruling that creates an "element" out of thin air and then holds that the element is not satisfied. I therefore respectfully dissent.

D. Exceptions to the Double Jeopardy Rule

2. Retrials After Mistrials

a. *Retrial After Mistrial for Hung Jury* (casebook p. 1164)

Even when a jury indicates that it would have likely have acquitted on a greater offense, but could not reach a verdict on a lesser offense, retrial is allowed on the greater offense so long as no formal verdict is issued before the mistrial is ordered.

Blueford v. Arkansas
132 S. Ct. 2044 (2012)

Chief Justice ROBERTS delivered the opinion of the Court.

The Double Jeopardy Clause protects against being tried twice for the same offense. The Clause does not, however, bar a second trial if the first ended in a mistrial. Before the jury concluded deliberations in this case, it reported that it was unanimous against guilt on charges of capital murder and first-degree murder, was deadlocked on manslaughter, and had not voted on negligent homicide. The court told the jury to continue to deliberate. The jury did so but still could not reach a verdict, and the court declared a mistrial. All agree that the defendant may be retried on charges of manslaughter and negligent homicide. The question is whether he may also be retried on charges of capital and first-degree murder.

I

One-year-old Matthew McFadden, Jr., suffered a severe head injury on November 28, 2007, while home with his mother's boyfriend, Alex Blueford. Despite treatment at a hospital, McFadden died a few days later.

The State of Arkansas charged Blueford with capital murder, but waived the death penalty. The State's theory at trial was that Blueford had injured McFadden intentionally, causing the boy's death "[u]nder circumstances manifesting extreme indifference to the value of human life." The defense, in contrast, portrayed the death as the result of Blueford accidentally knocking McFadden onto the ground.

The trial court instructed the jury that the charge of capital murder included three lesser offenses: first-degree murder, manslaughter, and negligent homicide. In addition to describing these offenses, the court addressed the order in which the jury was to consider them: "If you have a reasonable doubt of the defendant's guilt on the charge of capital murder, you will consider the charge of murder in the first degree. . . . If you have a reasonable doubt of the defendant's guilt on the charge of murder in the first degree, you will then consider the charge of manslaughter. . . . If you have a reasonable doubt of the defendant's guilt on the charge of manslaughter, you will then consider the charge of negligent homicide."

The prosecution commented on these instructions in its closing argument. It told the jury, for example, that "before you can consider a lesser included of capital murder, you must first, all 12, vote that this man is not guilty of capital murder." The prosecution explained that this was "not a situation where you just lay everything out here and say, well, we have four choices. Which one does it fit the most?" Rather, the prosecution emphasized, "unless all 12 of you agree that this man's actions were not consistent with capital murder, then and only then would you go down to murder in the first degree."

A few hours after beginning its deliberations, the jury sent the court a note asking "what happens if we cannot agree on a charge at all." The court called the jury back into the courtroom and issued a so-called "*Allen* instruction," emphasizing the importance of reaching a verdict. The jury then deliberated for a half hour more before sending out a second note, stating that it "cannot agree on any one charge in this case." When the court summoned the jury again, the jury foreperson reported that the jury was "hopelessly" deadlocked. The court asked the foreperson to disclose the jury's votes on each offense:

14. Double Jeopardy

"THE COURT: All right. If you have your numbers together, and I don't want names, but if you have your numbers I would like to know what your count was on capital murder.

"JUROR NUMBER ONE: That was unanimous against that. No.

"THE COURT: Okay, on murder in the first degree?

"JUROR NUMBER ONE: That was unanimous against that.

"THE COURT: Okay. Manslaughter?

"JUROR NUMBER ONE: Nine for, three against.

"THE COURT: Okay. And negligent homicide?

"JUROR NUMBER ONE: We did not vote on that, sir.

"THE COURT: Did not vote on that.

"JUROR NUMBER ONE: No, sir. We couldn't get past the manslaughter. Were we supposed to go past that? I thought we were supposed to go one at a time."

Following this exchange, the court gave another *Allen* instruction and sent the jurors back to the jury room. When the jury returned a half hour later, the foreperson stated that they had not reached a verdict. The court declared a mistrial and discharged the jury.

The State subsequently sought to retry Blueford. He moved to dismiss the capital and first-degree murder charges on double jeopardy grounds, citing the foreperson's report that the jurors had voted unanimously against guilt on those offenses. The trial court denied the motion, and the Supreme Court of Arkansas affirmed on interlocutory appeal. According to the State Supreme Court, the foreperson's report had no effect on the State's ability to retry Blueford, because the foreperson "was not making a formal announcement of acquittal" when she disclosed the jury's votes. This was not a case, the court observed, "where a formal verdict was announced or entered of record."

Blueford sought review in this Court, and we granted certiorari.

II

The Double Jeopardy Clause provides that no person shall "be subject for the same offence to be twice put in jeopardy of life or limb." U.S. Const., Amdt. 5. The Clause "guarantees that the State shall not be permitted to make repeated attempts to convict the accused, thereby subjecting him to embarrassment, expense and ordeal and compelling him to live in a continuing state of anxiety and insecurity, as well as enhancing the possibility that even though innocent he may be found guilty."

Blueford contends that the foreperson's report means that he cannot be tried again on charges of capital and first-degree murder. According to Blueford, the Double Jeopardy Clause prohibits a second trial on those charges, for two reasons.

A

Blueford's primary submission is that he cannot be retried for capital and first-degree murder because the jury actually acquitted him of those offenses. The

Arkansas Supreme Court noted—and Blueford acknowledges—that no formal judgment of acquittal was entered in his case. But none was necessary, Blueford maintains, because an acquittal is a matter of substance, not form.

We disagree. The foreperson's report was not a final resolution of anything. When the foreperson told the court how the jury had voted on each offense, the jury's deliberations had not yet concluded. The jurors in fact went back to the jury room to deliberate further, even after the foreperson had delivered her report. When they emerged a half hour later, the foreperson stated only that they were unable to reach a verdict. She gave no indication whether it was still the case that all 12 jurors believed Blueford was not guilty of capital or first-degree murder, that 9 of them believed he was guilty of manslaughter, or that a vote had not been taken on negligent homicide. The fact that deliberations continued after the report deprives that report of the finality necessary to constitute an acquittal on the murder offenses.

Blueford maintains, however, that any possibility that the jurors revisited the murder offenses was foreclosed by the instructions given to the jury. Those instructions, he contends, not only required the jury to consider the offenses in order, from greater to lesser, but also prevented it from transitioning from one offense to the next without unanimously—and definitively—resolving the greater offense in his favor. "A jury is presumed to follow its instructions." So, Blueford says, the foreperson's report that the jury was deadlocked on manslaughter necessarily establishes that the jury had acquitted Blueford of the greater offenses of capital and first-degree murder.

But even if we assume that the instructions required a unanimous vote before the jury could consider a lesser offense—as the State assumes for purposes of this case, nothing in the instructions prohibited the jury from reconsidering such a vote. It was therefore possible for Blueford's jury to revisit the offenses of capital and first-degree murder, notwithstanding its earlier votes. And because of that possibility, the foreperson's report prior to the end of deliberations lacked the finality necessary to amount to an acquittal on those offenses, quite apart from any requirement that a formal verdict be returned or judgment entered.

Blueford's argument assumes, however, that the votes reported by the foreperson did not change, even though the jury deliberated further after that report. That assumption is unjustified, because the reported votes were, for the reasons noted, not final.

B

Blueford maintains that even if the jury did not acquit him of capital and first-degree murder, a second trial on those offenses would nonetheless violate the Double Jeopardy Clause, because the trial court's declaration of a mistrial was improper. Blueford acknowledges that a trial can be discontinued without barring a subsequent one for the same offense when "particular circumstances manifest a necessity" to declare a mistrial. He also acknowledges that the trial court's reason for declaring a mistrial here—that the jury was unable to reach a verdict—has long been considered the "classic basis" establishing such a necessity. Blueford there-fore accepts that a second trial on manslaughter and negligent homicide would pose no double jeopardy problem. He contends, however, that there was no neces-sity for a mistrial on capital and first-degree murder, given the foreperson's report that the jury had voted unanimously against guilt on those charges. According to Blueford, the court at that time should have taken "some action," whether through partial verdict forms or other means, to allow the jury to give effect to those votes, and then considered a mistrial only as to the remaining charges.

We reject that suggestion. We have never required a trial court, before declar-ing a mistrial because of a hung jury, to consider any particular means of breaking the impasse—let alone to consider giving the jury new options for a verdict. As permitted under Arkansas law, the jury's options in this case were limited to two: either convict on one of the offenses, or acquit on all. The instructions explained those options in plain terms, and the verdict forms likewise contemplated no other outcome.

The jury in this case did not convict Blueford of any offense, but it did not acquit him of any either. When the jury was unable to return a verdict, the trial court properly declared a mistrial and discharged the jury. As a consequence, the Double Jeopardy Clause does not stand in the way of a second trial on the same offenses.

Justice SOTOMAYOR, with whom Justice GINSBURG and Justice KAGAN join, dissenting.

The Double Jeopardy Clause "unequivocally prohibits a second trial following an acquittal." To implement this rule, our cases have articulated two principles. First, an acquittal occurs if a jury's decision, "whatever its label, actu-ally represents a resolution, correct or not, of some or all of the factual elements of the offense charged." Second, a trial judge may not defeat a defendant's entitle-ment to "the verdict of a tribunal he might believe to be favorably disposed to his fate" by declaring a mistrial before deliberations end, absent a defendant's consent or a "'manifest necessity'" to do so.

Today's decision misapplies these longstanding principles. The Court holds that petitioner Alex Blueford was not acquitted of capital or first-degree murder, even though the forewoman of the Arkansas jury empaneled to try him announced in open court that the jury was "unanimous against" convicting Blueford of those crimes. Nor, the Court concludes, did the Double Jeopardy Clause oblige the trial judge to take any action to give effect to the jury's unambiguous decision before declaring a mistrial as to those offenses. The Court thus grants the State what the Constitution withholds: "the proverbial 'second bite at the apple.'"

I would . . . hold that the Double Jeopardy Clause requires a trial judge, in an acquittal-first jurisdiction, to honor a defendant's request for a partial verdict before declaring a mistrial on the ground of jury deadlock. Courts in acquittal-first jurisdictions have so held. Requiring a partial verdict in an acquittal-first jurisdiction ensures that the jurisdiction takes the bitter with the sweet.

Even if the Double Jeopardy Clause did not compel that broader rule, the facts of this case confirm that there was no necessity, let alone manifest necessity, for a mistrial. There was no reason for the judge not to have asked the jury, prior to discharge, whether it remained "unanimous against" conviction on capital and first-degree murder.

At its core, the Double Jeopardy Clause reflects the wisdom of the founding generation, familiar to "'every person acquainted with the history of governments,'" that "'state trials have been employed as a formidable engine in the hands of a dominant administration. . . . To prevent this mischief the ancient common law . . . provided that one acquittal or conviction should satisfy the law.'" The Double Jeopardy Clause was enacted "'[t]o perpetuate this wise rule, so favorable and necessary to the liberty of the citizen in a government like ours.'" This case demonstrates that the threat to individual freedom from reprosecutions that favor States and unfairly rescue them from weak cases has not waned with time. Only this Court's vigilance has.

I respectfully dissent.

Chapter 15

HABEAS CORPUS

B. The Issues That Must Be Addressed in Order for a Federal Court to Grant Habeas Corpus Relief

1. Is the Petition Time Barred? (casebook p. 1189)

McQuiggin v. Perkins
133 S. Ct. 1924 (2013)

Justice GINSBURG delivered the opinion of the Court.

This case concerns the "actual innocence" gateway to federal habeas review applied in *Schlup v. Delo* (1995), and further explained in *House v. Bell* (2006). In those cases, a convincing showing of actual innocence enabled habeas petitioners to overcome a procedural bar to consideration of the merits of their constitutional claims. Here, the question arises in the context of 28 U.S.C. §2244(d)(1), the statute of limitations on federal habeas petitions prescribed in the Antiterrorism and Effective Death Penalty Act of 1996. Specifically, if the petitioner does not file her federal habeas petition, at the latest, within one year of "the date on which the factual predicate of the claim or claims presented could have been discovered through the exercise of due diligence," §2244(d)(1)(D), can the time bar be overcome by a convincing showing that she committed no crime?

We hold that actual innocence, if proved, serves as a gateway through which a petitioner may pass whether the impediment is a procedural bar, as it was in *Schlup* and *House*, or, as in this case, expiration of the statute of limitations. We caution, however, that tenable actual-innocence gateway pleas are rare: "[A] petitioner does not meet the threshold requirement unless he persuades the district court that, in light of the new evidence, no juror, acting reasonably, would have voted to find him guilty beyond a reasonable doubt." And in making an assessment of the kind *Schlup* envisioned, "the timing of the [petition]" is a factor bearing on the "reliability of th[e] evidence" purporting to show actual innocence.

Our opinion clarifies that a federal habeas court, faced with an actual-innocence gateway claim, should count unjustifiable delay on a habeas petitioner's part, not as an absolute barrier to relief, but as a factor in determining whether actual innocence has been reliably shown.

I

On March 4, 1993, respondent Floyd Perkins attended a party in Flint, Michigan, in the company of his friend, Rodney Henderson, and an acquaintance, Damarr Jones. The three men left the party together. Henderson was later discovered on a wooded trail, murdered by stab wounds to his head.

Perkins was charged with the murder of Henderson. At trial, Jones was the key witness for the prosecution. He testified that Perkins alone committed the murder while Jones looked on.

Chauncey Vaughn, a friend of Perkins and Henderson, testified that, prior to the murder, Perkins had told him he would kill Henderson, and that Perkins later called Vaughn, confessing to his commission of the crime. A third witness, Torriano Player, also a friend of both Perkins and Henderson, testified that Perkins told him, had he known how Player felt about Henderson, he would not have killed Henderson.

Perkins, testifying in his own defense, offered a different account of the episode. He testified that he left Henderson and Jones to purchase cigarettes at a convenience store. When he exited the store, Perkins related, Jones and Henderson were gone. Perkins said that he then visited his girlfriend. About an hour later, Perkins recalled, he saw Jones standing under a streetlight with blood on his pants, shoes, and plaid coat.

The jury convicted Perkins of first-degree murder. He was sentenced to life in prison without the possibility of parole on October 27, 1993. The Michigan Court of Appeals affirmed Perkins' conviction and sentence, and the Michigan Supreme Court denied Perkins leave to appeal on January 31, 1997. Perkins' conviction became final on May 5, 1997.

Under the Antiterrorism and Effective Death Penalty Act of 1996 (AEDPA), 110 Stat. 1214, a state prisoner ordinarily has one year to file a federal petition for habeas corpus, starting from "the date on which the judgment became final by the conclusion of direct review or the expiration of the time for seeking such review." 28 U.S.C. §2244(d)(1)(A). If the petition alleges newly discovered evidence, however, the filing deadline is one year from "the date on which the factual predicate of the claim or claims presented could have been discovered through the exercise of due diligence." §2244(d)(1)(D).

Perkins filed his federal habeas corpus petition on June 13, 2008, more than 11 years after his conviction became final. Under Sixth Circuit precedent, the District Court stated, "a habeas petitioner who demonstrates a credible claim of actual innocence based on new evidence may, in exceptional circumstances, be entitled to equitable tolling of habeas limitations." But Perkins had not established exceptional circumstances, the District Court determined. In any event, the District Court observed, equitable tolling requires diligence and Perkins "ha[d] failed utterly to demonstrate the necessary diligence in exercising his rights." Alternatively, the District Court found that Perkins had failed to meet the strict standard by which pleas of actual innocence are measured: He had not shown that, taking account of all the evidence, "it is more likely than not that no reasonable juror would have convicted him," or even that the evidence was new.

Perkins appealed the District Court's judgment. Although recognizing that AEDPA's statute of limitations had expired and that Perkins had not diligently pursued his rights, the Sixth Circuit granted a certificate of appealability limited to a single question: Is reasonable diligence a precondition to relying on actual innocence as a gateway to adjudication of a federal habeas petition on the merits?

On consideration of the certified question, the Court of Appeals reversed the District Court's judgment. Adhering to Circuit precedent, the Sixth Circuit held that Perkins' gateway actual-innocence allegations allowed him to present his ineffective-assistance-of-counsel claim as if it were filed on time. On remand, the Court of Appeals instructed, "the [D]istrict [C]ourt [should] fully consider whether Perkins assert[ed] a credible claim of actual innocence."

II

In *Holland v. Florida* (2010), this Court addressed the circumstances in which a federal habeas petitioner could invoke the doctrine of "equitable tolling." *Holland* held that "a [habeas] petitioner is entitled to equitable tolling only if he shows (1) that he has been pursuing his rights diligently, and (2) that some extraordinary circumstance stood in his way and prevented timely filing." As the courts below comprehended, Perkins does not qualify for equitable tolling. In possession of all three affidavits by July 2002, he waited nearly six years to seek federal postconviction relief.

Perkins, however, asserts not an excuse for filing after the statute of limitations has run. Instead, he maintains that a plea of actual innocence can overcome AEDPA's one-year statute of limitations. He thus seeks an equitable *exception* to §2244(d)(1), not an extension of the time statutorily prescribed.

Decisions of this Court support Perkins' view of the significance of a convincing actual-innocence claim. We have not resolved whether a prisoner may be entitled to habeas relief based on a freestanding claim of actual innocence. *Herrera v. Collins*, 506 (1993). We have recognized, however, that a prisoner "otherwise subject to defenses of abusive or successive use of the writ [of habeas corpus] may have his federal constitutional claim considered on the merits if he makes a proper showing of actual innocence." In other words, a credible showing of actual innocence may allow a prisoner to pursue his constitutional claims (here, ineffective assistance of counsel) on the merits notwithstanding the existence of a procedural bar to relief. "This rule, or fundamental miscarriage of justice exception, is grounded in the 'equitable discretion' of habeas courts to see that federal constitutional errors do not result in the incarceration of innocent persons."

We have applied the miscarriage of justice exception to overcome various procedural defaults. These include "successive" petitions asserting previously rejected claims, "abusive" petitions asserting in a second petition claims that could have been raised in a first petition, failure to develop facts in state court, and failure to observe state procedural rules, including filing deadlines.

The miscarriage of justice exception, our decisions bear out, survived AEDPA's passage. These decisions "see[k] to balance the societal interests in finality, comity, and conservation of scarce judicial resources with the individual interest in justice that arises in the extraordinary case." Sensitivity to the injustice of incarcerating an innocent individual should not abate when the impediment is AEDPA's statute of limitations.

The State ties to §2244(d)'s text its insistence that AEDPA's statute of limitations precludes courts from considering late-filed actual-innocence gateway claims. "Section 2244(d)(1)(D)," the State contends, "forecloses any argument that a habeas petitioner has unlimited time to present new evidence in support of a constitutional claim." That is so, the State maintains, because AEDPA prescribes a comprehensive system for determining when its one-year limitations period begins to run.

The State's argument in this regard bears blinders. AEDPA's time limitations apply to the typical case in which no allegation of actual innocence is made. The miscarriage of justice exception, we underscore, applies to a severely confined category: cases in which new evidence shows "it is more likely than not that no reasonable juror would have convicted [the petitioner]." Section 2244(d)(1)(D) is both modestly more stringent (because it requires diligence) and dramatically less stringent (because it requires no showing of innocence). Many petitions that could not pass through the actual-innocence gateway will be timely or not measured by §2244(d)(1)(D)'s triggering provision. That provision, in short, will hardly be rendered superfluous by recognition of the miscarriage of justice exception.

Our reading of the statute is supported by the Court's opinion in *Holland*. "[E]quitable principles have traditionally governed the substantive law of habeas corpus," *Holland* reminded, and affirmed that "we will not construe a statute to displace courts' traditional equitable authority absent the clearest command." The text of §2244(d)(1) contains no clear command countering the courts' equitable authority to invoke the miscarriage of justice exception to overcome expiration of the statute of limitations governing a first federal habeas petition.

III

While we reject the State's argument that habeas petitioners who assert convincing actual-innocence claims must prove diligence to cross a federal court's threshold, we hold that the Sixth Circuit erred to the extent that it eliminated timing as a factor relevant in evaluating the reliability of a petitioner's proof of innocence. To invoke the miscarriage of justice exception to AEDPA's statute of limitations, we repeat, a petitioner "must show that it is more likely than not that no reasonable juror would have convicted him in the light of the new evidence." Unexplained delay in presenting new evidence bears on the determination whether the petitioner has made the requisite showing. Perkins so acknowledges.

As we stated in *Schlup*, "[a] court may consider how the timing of the submission and the likely credibility of [a petitioner's] affiants bear on the probable reliability of . . . evidence [of actual innocence]."

We stress once again that the *Schlup* standard is demanding. The gateway should open only when a petition presents "evidence of innocence so strong that a court cannot have confidence in the outcome of the trial unless the court is also satisfied that the trial was free of nonharmless constitutional error."

Justice SCALIA, with whom THE CHIEF JUSTICE and Justice THOMAS join, and with whom Justice ALITO joins as to Parts I, II, and III, dissenting.

The Antiterrorism and Effective Death Penalty Act of 1996 (AEDPA) provides that a "1-year period of limitation shall apply" to a state prisoner's application for a writ of habeas corpus in federal court. 28 U.S.C. §2244(d)(1). The gaping hole in today's opinion for the Court is its failure to answer the crucial question upon which all else depends: What is the source of the Court's power to fashion what it concedes is an "exception" to this clear statutory command?

That question is unanswered because there is no answer. This Court has no such power, and not one of the cases cited by the opinion says otherwise. The Constitution vests legislative power only in Congress, which never enacted the exception the Court creates today. That inconvenient truth resolves this case.

I

"Actual innocence" has, until today, been an exception only to judge-made, prudential barriers to habeas relief, or as a means of channeling judges' statutorily conferred discretion not to apply a procedural bar. Never before have we applied the exception to circumvent a categorical *statutory* bar to relief. We have not done so because we have no power to do so. Where Congress has erected a constitutionally valid barrier to habeas relief, a court *cannot* decline to give it effect.

Because we have no "equitable" power to discard statutory barriers to habeas relief, we cannot simply extend judge-made exceptions to judge-made barriers into the statutory realm. The Court's insupportable leap from judge-made procedural bars to *all* procedural bars, including *statutory* bars, does all the work in its opinion—and there is not a whit of precedential support for it.

The opinion for the Court also trots out post-AEDPA cases to prove the irrelevant point that "[t]he miscarriage of justice exception . . . survived AEDPA's passage." What it ignores, yet again, is that after AEDPA's passage, as before, the exception applied only to *nonstatutory* obstacles to relief.

There are many statutory bars to relief other than statutes of limitations, and we had never (and before today, have never) created an actual-innocence exception to *any* of them. The reason why is obvious: Judicially amending a validly enacted statute in this way is a flagrant breach of the separation of powers.

II

The Court has no qualms about transgressing such a basic principle. It does not even attempt to cloak its act of judicial legislation in the pretense that it is merely construing the statute; indeed, it freely admits that its opinion recognizes an "exception" that the statute does not contain. And it dismisses, with a series of transparent non sequiturs, Michigan's overwhelming textual argument that the statute provides no such exception and envisions none.

The key textual point is that two provisions of §2244, working in tandem, provide a comprehensive path to relief for an innocent prisoner who has newly discovered evidence that supports his constitutional claim. Section 2244(d)(1)(D) gives him a fresh year in which to file, starting on "the date on which the factual predicate of the claim or claims presented could have been discovered through the exercise of due diligence," while §2244(b)(2)(B) lifts the bar on second or successive petitions. Congress clearly anticipated the scenario of a habeas petitioner with a credible innocence claim and addressed it by crafting an exception (and an exception, by the way, more restrictive than the one that pleases the Court today). One cannot assume that Congress left room for other, judge-made applications of the actual-innocence exception, any more than one would add another gear to a Swiss watch on the theory that the watchmaker surely would have included it if he had thought of it. In both cases, the intricate craftsmanship tells us that the designer arranged things just as he wanted them.

The Court's feeble rejoinder is that its (judicially invented) version of the "actual innocence" exception applies only to a "severely confined category" of cases. Since cases qualifying for the actual-innocence exception will be rare, it explains, the statutory path for innocent petitioners will not "be rendered super-fluous." That is no answer at all. That the Court's exception would not *entirely* frustrate Congress's design does not weaken the force of the State's argument that Congress addressed the issue comprehensively and chose to exclude dilatory prisoners like respondent. By the Court's logic, a statute banning littering could simply be deemed to contain an exception for cigarette butts; after all, the statute as thus amended would still cover *something*. That is not how a court respectful of the separation of powers should interpret statutes.

III

Three years ago, in *Holland v. Florida* (2010), we held that AEDPA's statute of limitations is subject to equitable tolling. That holding offers no support for importing a novel actual-innocence exception. Equitable tolling—extending the deadline for a filing because of an event or circumstance that deprives the filer, through no fault of his own, of the full period accorded by the statute—seeks to vindicate what might be considered the genuine intent of the statute. By contrast, suspending the statute because of a separate policy that the court believes should trump it ("actual innocence") is a blatant overruling. Moreover, the doctrine of equitable tolling is centuries old, and dates from a time when the separation of the legislative and judicial powers was incomplete.

Here, by contrast, the Court has ambushed Congress with an utterly unprecedented (and thus unforeseeable) maneuver. Congressional silence, "while permitting an inference that Congress intended to apply *ordinary* background" principles, "cannot show that it intended to apply an unusual modification of those rules." Because there is no plausible basis for inferring that Congress intended or could have anticipated this exception, its adoption here amounts to a pure judicial override of the statute Congress enacted. "It is wrong for us to reshape" AEDPA "on the very lathe of judge-made habeas jurisprudence it was designed to repair."

* * *

"It would be marvellously inspiring to be able to boast that we have a criminal-justice system in which a claim of 'actual innocence' will always be heard, no matter how late it is brought forward, and no matter how much the failure to bring it forward at the proper time is the defendant's own fault." I suspect it is this vision of perfect justice through abundant procedure that impels the Court today. Of course, "we do not have such a system, and no society unwilling to devote unlimited resources to repetitive criminal litigation ever could." Until today, a district court could dismiss an untimely petition without delving into the underlying facts. From now on, each time an untimely petitioner claims innocence—and how many prisoners asking to be let out of jail do not?—the district court will be obligated to expend limited judicial resources wading into the murky merits of the petitioner's innocence claim. The Court notes "that tenable actual-innocence gateway pleas are rare." That discouraging reality, intended as reassurance, is in truth "the condemnation of the procedure which has encouraged frivolous cases."

It has now been 60 years since *Brown v. Allen*, in which we struck the Faustian bargain that traded the simple elegance of the common-law writ of habeas corpus for federal-court power to probe the substantive merits of state-court convictions. Even after AEDPA's pass through the Augean stables, no one in a position to observe the functioning of our byzantine federal-habeas system can believe it an efficient device for separating the truly deserving from the multitude of prisoners pressing false claims. "[F]loods of stale, frivolous and repetitious petitions inundate the docket of the lower courts and swell our own. . . . It must prejudice the occasional meritorious applicant to be buried in a flood of worthless ones."

The "inundation" that Justice Jackson lamented in 1953 "consisted of 541" federal habeas petitions filed by state prisoners. By 1969, that number had grown to 7,359. In the year ending on September 30, 2012, 15,929 such petitions were filed. Today's decision piles yet more dead weight onto a postconviction habeas system already creaking at its rusted joints.

FEDERAL RULES OF CRIMINAL PROCEDURE

Rule 4. Arrest Warrant or Summons on a Complaint

(a) Issuance.

If the complaint or one or more affidavits filed with the complaint establish probable cause to believe that an offense has been committed and that the defendant committed it, the judge must issue an arrest warrant to an officer authorized to execute it. At the request of an attorney for the government, the judge must issue a summons, instead of a warrant, to a person authorized to serve it. A judge may issue more than one warrant or summons on the same complaint. If a defendant fails to appear in response to a summons, a judge may, and upon request of an attorney for the government must, issue a warrant. If an organizational defendant fails to appear in response to a summons, a judge may take any action authorized by United States law.

(b) Form.

(1) Warrant.

A warrant must:

(A) contain the defendant's name or, if it is unknown, a name or description by which the defendant can be identified with reasonable certainty;

(B) describe the offense charged in the complaint;

(C) command that the defendant be arrested and brought without unnecessary delay before a magistrate judge or, if none is reasonably available, before a state or local judicial officer; and

(D) be signed by a judge.

(2) Summons.

A summons must be in the same form as a warrant except that it must require the defendant to appear before a magistrate judge at a stated time and place.

(c)   Execution or Service, and Return.

(1)   By Whom.

Only a marshal or other authorized officer may execute a warrant. Any person authorized to serve a summons in a federal civil action may serve a summons.

(2)   Location.

A warrant may be executed, or a summons served, within the jurisdiction of the United States or anywhere else a federal statute authorizes an arrest. A summons to an organization under Rule 4(c)(3)(D) may also be served at a place not within a judicial district of the United Statess.

(3)   Manner.

(A) A warrant is executed by arresting the defendant. Upon arrest, an officer possessing the original or a duplicate original warrant must show it to the defendant. If the officer does not possess the warrant, the officer must inform the defendant of the warrant's existence and of the offense charged and, at the defendant's request, must show the original or a duplicate original warrant to the defendant as soon as possible.

(B) A summons is served on an individual defendant:

(i) by delivering a copy to the defendant personally; or

(ii) by leaving a copy at the defendant's residence or usual place of abode with a person of suitable age and discretion residing at that location and by mailing a copy to the defendant's last known address.

(C) A summons is served on an organization by delivering a copy to an officer, to a managing or general agent, or to another agent appointed or legally authorized to receive service of process. If the agent is one authorized by statute and the statute so requires, a copy must also be mailed to the organization.

* * *

(4)   Return.

(A) After executing a warrant, the officer must return it to the judge before whom the defendant is brought in accordance with Rule 5. The officer may do so by reliable electronic means. At the request of an attorney for the government, an unexecuted warrant must be brought back to and canceled by a magistrate judge or, if none is reasonably available, by a state or local judicial officer.

(B) The person to whom a summons was delivered for service must return it on or before the return day.

(C) At the request of an attorney for the government, a judge may deliver an unexecuted warrant, an unserved summons, or a copy of the warrant or summons to the marshal or other authorized person for execution or service.

(D) Warrant by Telephone or Other Reliable Electronic Means. In accordance with Rule 4.1, a magistrate judge may issue a warrant or summons based on information communicated by telephone or other reliable electronic means.

Rule 5.   Initial Appearance

(a)   In General.

(1)   Appearance Upon an Arrest.

(A) A person making an arrest within the United States must take the defendant without unnecessary delay before a magistrate judge, or before a state or local judicial officer as Rule 5(c) provides, unless a statute provides otherwise.

(B) A person making an arrest outside the United States must take the defendant without unnecessary delay before a magistrate judge, unless a statute provides otherwise.

(2)   Exceptions.

(A) An officer making an arrest under a warrant issued upon a complaint charging solely a violation of 18 U.S.C. §1073 need not comply with this rule if:

(i) the person arrested is transferred without unnecessary delay to the custody of appropriate state or local authorities in the district of arrest; and

(ii) an attorney for the government moves promptly, in the district where the warrant was issued, to dismiss the complaint.

(B) If a defendant is arrested for violating probation or supervised release, Rule 32.1 applies.

(C) If a defendant is arrested for failing to appear in another district, Rule 40 applies.

(3)   Appearance Upon a Summons.

When a defendant appears in response to a summons under Rule 4, a magistrate judge must proceed under Rule 5(d) or (e), as applicable.

(b)   Arrest Without a Warrant.

If a defendant is arrested without a warrant, a complaint meeting Rule 4(a)'s requirement of probable cause must be promptly filed in the district where the offense was allegedly committed.

(c)   Place of Initial Appearance; Transfer to Another District.

(1)   Arrest in the District Where the Offense Was Allegedly Committed.

If the defendant is arrested in the district where the offense was allegedly committed:

(A) the initial appearance must be in that district; and

(B) if a magistrate judge is not reasonably available, the initial appearance may be before a state or local judicial officer.

(2)   Arrest in a District Other Than Where the Offense Was Allegedly Committed.

If the defendant was arrested in a district other than where the offense was allegedly committed, the initial appearance must be:

(A) in the district of arrest; or

(B) in an adjacent district if:

(i) the appearance can occur more promptly there; or

(ii) the offense was allegedly committed there and the initial appearance will occur on the day of arrest.

(d) *Procedure in a Felony Case.*

(1) Advice.

If the defendant is charged with a felony, the judge must inform the defendant of the following:

(A) the complaint against the defendant, and any affidavit filed with it;

(B) the defendant's right to retain counsel or to request that counsel be appointed if the defendant cannot obtain counsel;

(C) the circumstances, if any, under which the defendant may secure pretrial release;

(D) any right to a preliminary hearing; and

(E) the defendant's right not to make a statement, and that any statement made may be used against the defendant.

(F) that a defendant who is not a United States citizen may request that an attorney for the government or a federal law enforcement official notify a consular officer from the defendant's country of nationality that the defendant has been arrested – but that even without defendant's request, a treat or other international agreement may require consular notification.

(2) Consulting with Counsel.

The judge must allow the defendant reasonable opportunity to consult with counsel.

(3) Detention or Release.

The judge must detain or release the defendant as provided by statute or these rules.

(4) Plea.

A defendant may be asked to plead only under Rule 10.

(e) Procedure in a Misdemeanor Case.

If the defendant is charged with a misdemeanor only, the judge must inform the defendant in accordance with Rule 58(b)(2).

(f) Video Teleconferencing.

Video teleconferencing may be used to conduct an appearance under this rule if the defendant consents.

Rule 5.1. Preliminary Hearing

(a) In General.

If a defendant is charged with an offense other than a petty offense, a magistrate judge must conduct a preliminary hearing unless:

(1) the defendant waives the hearing;

(2) the defendant is indicted;

(3) the government files an information under Rule 7(b) charging the defendant with a felony;

(4) the government files an information charging the defendant with a misdemeanor; or

(5) the defendant is charged with a misdemeanor and consents to trial before a magistrate judge.

(b) Selecting a District.

A defendant arrested in a district other than where the offense was allegedly committed may elect to have the preliminary hearing conducted in the district where the prosecution is pending.

(c) Scheduling.

The magistrate judge must hold the preliminary hearing within a reasonable time, but no later than 14 days after the initial appearance if the defendant is in custody and no later than 21 days if not in custody.

(d) Extending the Time.

With the defendant's consent and upon a showing of good cause—taking into account the public interest in the prompt disposition of criminal cases—a magistrate judge may extend the time limits in Rule 5.1(c) one or more times. If the defendant does not consent, the magistrate judge may extend the time limits only on a showing that extraordinary circumstances exist and justice requires the delay.

(e) Hearing and Finding.

At the preliminary hearing, the defendant may cross-examine adverse witnesses and may introduce evidence but may not object to evidence on the ground that it was unlawfully acquired. If the magistrate judge finds probable cause to believe an offense has been committed and the defendant committed it, the magistrate judge must promptly require the defendant to appear for further proceedings.

(f) Discharging the Defendant.

If the magistrate judge finds no probable cause to believe an offense has been committed or the defendant committed it, the magistrate judge must dismiss the complaint and discharge the defendant. A discharge does not preclude the government from later prosecuting the defendant for the same offense.

(g) Recording the Proceedings.

The preliminary hearing must be recorded by a court reporter or by a suitable recording device. A recording of the proceeding may be made available to any party upon request. A copy of the recording and a transcript may be provided to any party upon request and upon any payment required by applicable Judicial Conference regulations.

(h) Producing a Statement.

(1) In General.

Rule 26.2(a)-(d) and (f) applies at any hearing under this rule, unless the magistrate judge for good cause rules otherwise in a particular case.

(2)   Sanctions for Not Producing a Statement.

If a party disobeys a Rule 26.2 order to deliver a statement to the moving party, the magistrate judge must not consider the testimony of a witness whose statement is withheld.

Rule 6.   The Grand Jury

(a)   *Summoning a Grand Jury.*

(1)   In General.

When the public interest so requires, the court must order that one or more grand juries be summoned. A grand jury must have 16 to 23 members, and the court must order that enough legally qualified persons be summoned to meet this requirement.

(2)   Alternate Jurors.

When a grand jury is selected, the court may also select alternate jurors. Alternate jurors must have the same qualifications and be selected in the same manner as any other juror. Alternate jurors replace jurors in the same sequence in which the alternates were selected. An alternate juror who replaces a juror is subject to the same challenges, takes the same oath, and has the same authority as the other jurors.

(b)   *Objection to the Grand Jury or to a Grand Juror.*

(1)   Challenges.

Either the government or a defendant may challenge the grand jury on the ground that it was not lawfully drawn, summoned, or selected, and may challenge an individual juror on the ground that the juror is not legally qualified.

(2)   Motion to Dismiss an Indictment.

A party may move to dismiss the indictment based on an objection to the grand jury or on an individual juror's lack of legal qualification, unless the court has previously ruled on the same objection under Rule 6(b)(1). The motion to dismiss is governed by 28 U.S.C. §1867(e). The court must not dismiss the indictment on the ground that a grand juror was not legally qualified if the record shows that at least 12 qualified jurors concurred in the indictment.

(c) *Foreperson and Deputy Foreperson.*

The court will appoint one juror as the foreperson and another as the deputy foreperson. In the foreperson's absence, the deputy foreperson will act as the foreperson. The foreperson may administer oaths and affirmations and will sign all indictments. The foreperson—or another juror designated by the foreperson—will record the number of jurors concurring in every indictment and will file the record with the clerk, but the record may not be made public unless the court so orders.

(d) *Who May Be Present.*

(1) While the Grand Jury Is in Session.

The following persons may be present while the grand jury is in session: attorneys for the government, the witness being questioned, interpreters when needed, and a court reporter or an operator of a recording device.

(2) During Deliberations and Voting.

No person other than the jurors, and any interpreter needed to assist a hearing-impaired or speech-impaired juror, may be present while the grand jury is deliberating or voting.

(e) *Recording and Disclosing the Proceedings.*

(1) Recording the Proceedings.

Except while the grand jury is deliberating or voting, all proceedings must be recorded by a court reporter or by a suitable recording device. But the validity of a prosecution is not affected by the unintentional failure to make a recording. Unless the court orders otherwise, an attorney for the government will retain control of the recording, the reporter's notes, and any transcript prepared from those notes.

(2) Secrecy.

(A) No obligation of secrecy may be imposed on any person except in accordance with Rule 6(e)(2)(B).

(B) Unless these rules provide otherwise, the following persons must not disclose a matter occurring before the grand jury:

(i) a grand juror;

(ii) an interpreter;

(iii) a court reporter;

(iv) an operator of a recording device;

(v) a person who transcribes recorded testimony;

(vi) an attorney for the government; or

(vii) a person to whom disclosure is made under Rule 6(e)(3)(A)(ii) or (iii).

(3)   Exceptions.

(A) Disclosure of a grand-jury matter—other than the grand jury's deliberations or any grand juror's vote—may be made to:

(i) an attorney for the government for use in performing that attorney's duty;

(ii) any government personnel—including those of a state, state subdivision, Indian tribe, or foreign government—that an attorney for the government considers necessary to assist in performing that attorney's duty to enforce federal criminal law; or

(iii) a person authorized by 18 U.S.C. §3322.

(B) A person to whom information is disclosed under Rule 6(e)(3)(A)(ii) may use that information only to assist an attorney for the government in performing that attorney's duty to enforce federal criminal law. An attorney for the government must promptly provide the court that impaneled the grand jury with the names of all persons to whom a disclosure has been made, and must certify that the attorney has advised those persons of their obligation of secrecy under this rule.

(C) An attorney for the government may disclose any grand-jury matter to another federal grand jury.

(D) An attorney for the government may disclose any grand-jury matter involving foreign intelligence, counterintelligence (as defined in 50 U.S.C.

§3003), or foreign intelligence information (as defined in Rule 6(e)(3)(D)(iii)) to any federal law enforcement, intelligence, protective, immigration, national defense, or national security official to assist the official receiving the information in the performance of that official's duties. An attorney for the government may also disclose any grand-jury matter involving, within the United States or elsewhere, a threat of attack or other grave hostile acts of a foreign power or its agent, a threat of domestic or international sabotage or terrorism, or clandestine intelligence gathering activities by an intelligence service or network of a foreign power or by its agent, to any appropriate federal, state, state subdivision, Indian tribal, or foreign government official, for the purpose of preventing or responding to such threat or activities.

    (i) Any official who receives information under Rule 6(e)(3)(D) may use the information only as necessary in the conduct of that person's official duties subject to any limitations on the unauthorized disclosure of such information. Any state, state subdivision, Indian tribal, or foreign government official who receives information under Rule 6(e)(3)(D) may use the information only in a manner consistent with any guidelines issued by the Attorney General and the Director of National Intelligence.

    (ii) Within a reasonable time after disclosure is made under Rule 6(e)(3)(D), an attorney for the government must file, under seal, a notice with the court in the district where the grand jury convened stating that such information was disclosed and the departments, agencies, or entities to which the disclosure was made.

    (iii) As used in Rule 6(e)(3)(D), the term "foreign intelligence information" means:

        (a) information, whether or not it concerns a United States person, that relates to the ability of the United States to protect against—

- actual or potential attack or other grave hostile acts of a foreign power or its agent;
- sabotage or international terrorism by a foreign power or its agent; or
- clandestine intelligence activities by an intelligence service or network of a foreign power or by its agent; or

        (b) information, whether or not it concerns a United States person, with respect to a foreign power or foreign territory that relates to—

- the national defense or the security of the United States; or
- the conduct of the foreign affairs of the United States.

(E) The court may authorize disclosure—at a time, in a manner, and subject to any other conditions that it directs—of a grand-jury matter:

(i) preliminarily to or in connection with a judicial proceeding;

(ii) at the request of a defendant who shows that a ground may exist to dismiss the indictment because of a matter that occurred before the grand jury;

(iii) at the request of the government, when sought by a foreign court or prosecutor for use in an official criminal investigation;

(iv) at the request of the government if it shows that the matter may disclose a violation of State, Indian tribal, or foreign criminal law, as long as the disclosure is to an appropriate state, state-subdivision, Indian tribal, or foreign government official for the purpose of enforcing that law; or

(v) at the request of the government if it shows that the matter may disclose a violation of military criminal law under the Uniform Code of Military Justice, as long as the disclosure is to an appropriate military official for the purpose of enforcing that law.

(F) A petition to disclose a grand-jury matter under Rule 6(e)(3)(E)(i) must be filed in the district where the grand jury convened. Unless the hearing is ex parte—as it may be when the government is the petitioner—the petitioner must serve the petition on, and the court must afford a reasonable opportunity to appear and be heard to:

(i) an attorney for the government;

(ii) the parties to the judicial proceeding; and

(iii) any other person whom the court may designate.

(G) If the petition to disclose arises out of a judicial proceeding in another district, the petitioned court must transfer the petition to the other court unless the petitioned court can reasonably determine whether disclosure is proper. If the petitioned court decides to transfer, it must send to the transferee court the material sought to be disclosed, if feasible, and a written evaluation of the need for continued grand-jury secrecy. The transferee court must afford those persons identified in Rule 6(e)(3)(F) a reasonable opportunity to appear and be heard.

(4)   Sealed Indictment.

The magistrate judge to whom an indictment is returned may direct that the indictment be kept secret until the defendant is in custody or has been released pending trial. The clerk must then seal the indictment, and no person may disclose the indictment's existence except as necessary to issue or execute a warrant or summons.

(5) Closed Hearing.

Subject to any right to an open hearing in a contempt proceeding, the court must close any hearing to the extent necessary to prevent disclosure of a matter occurring before a grand jury.

(6) Sealed Records.

Records, orders, and subpoenas relating to grand-jury proceedings must be kept under seal to the extent and as long as necessary to prevent the unauthorized disclosure of a matter occurring before a grand jury.

(7) Contempt.

A knowing violation of Rule 6, or of any guidelines jointly issued by the Attorney General and the Director of National Intelligence under Rule 6, may be punished as a contempt of court.

(f) Indictment and Return.

A grand jury may indict only if at least 12 jurors concur. The grand jury—or its foreperson or deputy foreperson—must return the indictment to a magistrate judge in open court. To avoid unnecessary cost or delay, the magistrate may take the return by video conference from the court where the grand jury sits. If a complaint or information is pending against the defendant and 12 jurors do not concur in the indictment, the foreperson must promptly and in writing report the lack of concurrence to the magistrate judge.

(g) Discharging the Grand Jury.

A grand jury must serve until the court discharges it, but it may serve more than 18 months only if the court, having determined that an extension is in the public interest, extends the grand jury's service. An extension may be granted for no more than 6 months, except as otherwise provided by statute.

(h)   Excusing a Juror.

At any time, for good cause, the court may excuse a juror either temporarily or permanently, and if permanently, the court may impanel an alternate juror in place of the excused juror.

(i)   "Indian Tribe" Defined.

"Indian tribe" means an Indian tribe recognized by the Secretary of the Interior on a list published in the Federal Register under 25 U.S.C. §479a-1.

Rule 7.   The Indictment and the Information

(a)   When Used.

(1)   Felony.

An offense (other than criminal contempt) must be prosecuted by an indictment if it is punishable:

(A) by death; or

(B) by imprisonment for more than one year.

(2)   Misdemeanor.

An offense punishable by imprisonment for one year or less may be prosecuted in accordance with Rule 58(b)(1).

(b)   Waiving Indictment.

An offense punishable by imprisonment for more than one year may be prosecuted by information if the defendant—in open court and after being advised of the nature of the charge and of the defendant's rights—waives prosecution by indictment.

(c)   Nature and Contents.

(1)   In General.

The indictment or information must be a plain, concise, and definite written statement of the essential facts constituting the offense charged and must be signed by an attorney for the government. It need not contain a formal introduction or conclusion. A count may incorporate by reference an allegation made in another count. A count may allege that the means by which the defendant committed the offense are unknown or that the defendant committed it by one or more specified means. For each count, the indictment or information must give the official or customary citation of the statute, rule, regulation, or other provision of law that the defendant is alleged to have violated. For purposes of an indictment referred to in section 3282 of title 18, United States Code, for which the identity of the defendant is unknown, it shall be sufficient for the indictment to describe the defendant as an individual whose name is unknown, but who has a particular DNA profile, as that term is defined in that section 3282.

(2) Citation Error.

Unless the defendant was misled and thereby prejudiced, neither an error in a citation nor a citation's omission is a ground to dismiss the indictment or information or to reverse a conviction.

(d) Surplusage.

Upon the defendant's motion, the court may strike surplusage from the indictment or information.

(e) Amending an Information.

Unless an additional or different offense is charged or a substantial right of the defendant is prejudiced, the court may permit an information to be amended at any time before the verdict or finding.

(f) Bill of Particulars.

The court may direct the government to file a bill of particulars. The defendant may move for a bill of particulars before or within 14 days after arraignment or at a later time if the court permits. The government may amend a bill of particulars subject to such conditions as justice requires.

Rule 8.   Joinder of Offenses or Defendants

(a)   Joinder of Offenses.

The indictment or information may charge a defendant in separate counts with 2 or more offenses if the offenses charged—whether felonies or misdemeanors or both—are of the same or similar character, or are based on the same act or transaction, or are connected with or constitute parts of a common scheme or plan.

(b)   Joinder of Defendants.

The indictment or information may charge 2 or more defendants if they are alleged to have participated in the same act or transaction, or in the same series of acts or transactions, constituting an offense or offenses. The defendants may be charged in one or more counts together or separately. All defendants need not be charged in each count.

Rule 11.   Pleas

(a)   Entering a Plea.

(1)   In General.

A defendant may plead not guilty, guilty, or (with the court's consent) nolo contendere.

(2)   Conditional Plea.

With the consent of the court and the government, a defendant may enter a conditional plea of guilty or nolo contendere, reserving in writing the right to have an appellate court review an adverse determination of a specified pretrial motion. A defendant who prevails on appeal may then withdraw the plea.

(3)   Nolo Contendere Plea.

Before accepting a plea of nolo contendere, the court must consider the parties' views and the public interest in the effective administration of justice.

(4)   Failure to Enter a Plea.

If a defendant refuses to enter a plea or if a defendant organization fails to appear, the court must enter a plea of not guilty.

(b)   Considering and Accepting a Guilty or Nolo Contendere Plea.

(1)   Advising and Questioning the Defendant.

Before the court accepts a plea of guilty or nolo contendere, the defendant may be placed under oath, and the court must address the defendant personally in open court. During this address, the court must inform the defendant of, and determine that the defendant understands, the following:

(A) the government's right, in a prosecution for perjury or false statement, to use against the defendant any statement that the defendant gives under oath;

(B) the right to plead not guilty, or having already so pleaded, to persist in that plea;

(C) the right to a jury trial;

(D) the right to be represented by counsel—and if necessary have the court appoint counsel—at trial and at every other stage of the proceeding;

(E) the right at trial to confront and cross-examine adverse witnesses, to be protected from compelled self-incrimination, to testify and present evidence, and to compel the attendance of witnesses;

(F) the defendant's waiver of these trial rights if the court accepts a plea of guilty or nolo contendere;

(G) the nature of each charge to which the defendant is pleading;

(H) any maximum possible penalty, including imprisonment, fine, and term of supervised release;

(I) any mandatory minimum penalty;

(J) any applicable forfeiture;

(K) the court's authority to order restitution;

(**L**) the court's obligation to impose a special assessment;

(**M**) in determining a sentence, the court's obligation to calculate the applicable sentencing-guideline range and to consider that range, possible departures under the Sentencing Guidelines, and other sentencing factors under 18 U.S.C. §3553(a);

(**N**) the terms of any plea-agreement provision waiving the right to appeal or to collaterally attack the sentence.

(**O**) that, if convicted, a defendant who is not a United States citizen may be removed from the United States, denied citizenship, and denied admission to the United States in the future.[1]

(2)   Ensuring That a Plea Is Voluntary.

Before accepting a plea of guilty or nolo contendere, the court must address the defendant personally in open court and determine that the plea is voluntary and did not result from force, threats, or promises (other than promises in a plea agreement).

(3)   Determining the Factual Basis for a Plea.

Before entering judgment on a guilty plea, the court must determine that there is a factual basis for the plea.

(c)   *Plea Agreement Procedure.*

(1)   In General.

An attorney for the government and the defendant's attorney, or the defendant when proceeding pro se, may discuss and reach a plea agreement. The court must not participate in these discussions. If the defendant pleads guilty or nolo contendere to either a charged offense or a lesser or related offense, the plea agreement may specify that an attorney for the government will:

(**A**) not bring, or will move to dismiss, other charges;

(**B**) recommend, or agree not to oppose the defendant's request, that a particular sentence or sentencing range is appropriate or that a particular provision

---

[1] Effective Dec. 1, 2013.

of the Sentencing Guidelines, or policy statement, or sentencing factor does or does not apply (such a recommendation or request does not bind the court); or

(C) agree that a specific sentence or sentencing range is the appropriate disposition of the case, or that a particular provision of the Sentencing Guidelines, or policy statement, or sentencing factor does or does not apply (such a recommendation or request binds the court once the court accepts the plea agreement).

(2)   Disclosing a Plea Agreement.

The parties must disclose the plea agreement in open court when the plea is offered, unless the court for good cause allows the parties to disclose the plea agreement in camera.

(3)   Judicial Consideration of a Plea Agreement.

(A) To the extent the plea agreement is of the type specified in Rule 11(c)(1)(A) or (C), the court may accept the agreement, reject it, or defer a decision until the court has reviewed the presentence report.

(B) To the extent the plea agreement is of the type specified in Rule 11(c)(1)(B), the court must advise the defendant that the defendant has no right to withdraw the plea if the court does not follow the recommendation or request.

(4)   Accepting a Plea Agreement.

If the court accepts the plea agreement, it must inform the defendant that to the extent the plea agreement is of the type specified in Rule 11(c)(1)(A) or (C), the agreed disposition will be included in the judgment.

(5)   Rejecting a Plea Agreement.

If the court rejects a plea agreement containing provisions of the type specified in Rule 11(c)(1)(A) or (C), the court must do the following on the record and in open court (or, for good cause, in camera):

(A) inform the parties that the court rejects the plea agreement;

(B) advise the defendant personally that the court is not required to follow the plea agreement and give the defendant an opportunity to withdraw the plea; and

(C) advise the defendant personally that if the plea is not withdrawn, the court may dispose of the case less favorably toward the defendant than the plea agreement contemplated.

(d)   Withdrawing a Guilty or Nolo Contendere Plea.

A defendant may withdraw a plea of guilty or nolo contendere:
   (1) before the court accepts the plea, for any reason or no reason; or

   (2) after the court accepts the plea, but before it imposes sentence if:

(A) the court rejects a plea agreement under Rule 11(c)(5); or

(B) the defendant can show a fair and just reason for requesting the withdrawal.

(e)   Finality of a Guilty or Nolo Contendere Plea.

After the court imposes sentence, the defendant may not withdraw a plea of guilty or nolo contendere, and the plea may be set aside only on direct appeal or collateral attack.

(f)   Admissibility or Inadmissibility of a Plea, Plea Discussions, and Related Statements.

The admissibility or inadmissibility of a plea, a plea discussion, and any related statement is governed by Federal Rule of Evidence 410.

(g)   Recording the Proceedings.

The proceedings during which the defendant enters a plea must be recorded by a court reporter or by a suitable recording device. If there is a guilty plea or a nolo contendere plea, the record must include the inquiries and advice to the defendant required under Rule 11(b) and (c).

(h)   Harmless Error.

A variance from the requirements of this rule is harmless error if it does not affect substantial rights.

Rule 14.   Relief from Prejudicial Joinder

(a)   Relief.

If the joinder of offenses or defendants in an indictment, an information, or a consolidation for trial appears to prejudice a defendant or the government, the court may order separate trials of counts, sever the defendants' trials, or provide any other relief that justice requires.

(b)   Defendant's Statements.

Before ruling on a defendant's motion to sever, the court may order an attorney for the government to deliver to the court for in camera inspection any defendant's statement that the government intends to use as evidence.

Rule 16.   Discovery and Inspection

(a)   Government's Disclosure.

(1)   Information Subject to Disclosure.

(A) Defendant's Oral Statement. Upon a defendant's request, the government must disclose to the defendant the substance of any relevant oral statement made by the defendant, before or after arrest, in response to interrogation by a person the defendant knew was a government agent if the government intends to use the statement at trial.

(B) Defendant's Written or Recorded Statement. Upon a defendant's request, the government must disclose to the defendant, and make available for inspection, copying, or photographing, all of the following:

(i) any relevant written or recorded statement by the defendant if:

- the statement is within the government's possession, custody, or control; and
- the attorney for the government knows—or through due diligence could know—that the statement exists;

(ii) the portion of any written record containing the substance of any relevant oral statement made before or after arrest if the defendant made the statement in response to interrogation by a person the defendant knew was a government agent; and

(iii) the defendant's recorded testimony before a grand jury relating to the charged offense.

(C) **Organizational Defendant.** Upon a defendant's request, if the defendant is an organization, the government must disclose to the defendant any statement described in Rule 16(a)(1)(A) and (B) if the government contends that the person making the statement:

(i) was legally able to bind the defendant regarding the subject of the statement because of that person's position as the defendant's director, officer, employee, or agent; or

(ii) was personally involved in the alleged conduct constituting the offense and was legally able to bind the defendant regarding that conduct because of that person's position as the defendant's director, officer, employee, or agent.

(D) **Defendant's Prior Record.** Upon a defendant's request, the government must furnish the defendant with a copy of the defendant's prior criminal record that is within the government's possession, custody, or control if the attorney for the government knows—or through due diligence could know—that the record exists.

(E) **Documents and Objects.** Upon a defendant's request, the government must permit the defendant to inspect and to copy or photograph books, papers, documents, data, photographs, tangible objects, buildings or places, or copies or portions of any of these items, if the item is within the government's possession, custody, or control and:

(i) the item is material to preparing the defense;

(ii) the government intends to use the item in its case-in-chief at trial; or

(iii) the item was obtained from or belongs to the defendant.

(F) **Reports of Examinations and Tests.** Upon a defendant's request, the government must permit a defendant to inspect and to copy or photograph the results or reports of any physical or mental examination and of any scientific test or experiment if:

(i) the item is within the government's possession, custody, or control;

(ii) the attorney for the government knows—or through due diligence could know—that the item exists; and

(iii) the item is material to preparing the defense or the government intends to use the item in its case-in-chief at trial.

(G) **Expert witnesses.** At the defendant's request, the government must give to the defendant a written summary of any testimony that the government intends to use under Rules 702, 703, or 705 of the Federal Rules of Evidence during its case-in-chief at trial. If the government requests discovery under subdivision (b)(1)(C)(ii) and the defendant complies, the government must, at the defendant's request, give to the defendant a written summary of testimony that the government intends to use under Rules 702, 703, or 705 of the Federal Rules of Evidence as evidence at trial on the issue of the defendant's mental condition. The summary provided under this subparagraph must describe the witness's opinions, the bases and reasons for those opinions, and the witness's qualifications.

(2)   Information Not Subject to Disclosure.

Except as permitted by Rule 16(a)(1)(A)-(D), (F), and (G), this rule does not authorize the discovery or inspection of reports, memoranda, or other internal government documents made by an attorney for the government or other government agent in connection with investigating or prosecuting the case. Nor does this rule authorize the discovery or inspection of statements made by prospective government witnesses except as provided in 18 U.S.C. §3500.

(3)   Grand Jury Transcripts.

This rule does not apply to the discovery or inspection of a grand jury's recorded proceedings, except as provided in Rules 6, 12(h), 16(a)(1), and 26.2.

(b)   Defendant's Disclosure.

(1)   Information Subject to Disclosure.

(A) **Documents and Objects.** If a defendant requests disclosure under Rule 16(a)(1)(E) and the government complies, then the defendant must permit the government, upon request, to inspect and to copy or photograph books, papers, documents, data, photographs, tangible objects, buildings or places, or copies or portions of any of these items if:

(i) the item is within the defendant's possession, custody, or control; and

(ii) the defendant intends to use the item in the defendant's case-in-chief at trial.

(B) Reports of Examinations and Tests. If a defendant requests disclosure under Rule 16(a)(1)(F) and the government complies, the defendant must permit the government, upon request, to inspect and to copy or photograph the results or reports of any physical or mental examination and of any scientific test or experiment if:

(i) the item is within the defendant's possession, custody, or control; and

(ii) the defendant intends to use the item in the defendant's case-in-chief at trial, or intends to call the witness who prepared the report and the report relates to the witness's testimony.

(C) Expert Witnesses. — The defendant must, at the government's request, give to the government a written summary of any testimony that the defendant intends to use under Rules 702, 703, or 705 of the Federal Rules of Evidence as evidence at trial, if—

(i) the defendant requests disclosure under subdivision (a)(1)(G) and the government complies; or

(ii) the defendant has given notice under Rule 12.2(b) of an intent to present expert testimony on the defendant's mental condition.

This summary must describe the witness's opinions, the bases and reasons for those opinions, and the witness's qualifications.

(2)   Information Not Subject to Disclosure.

Except for scientific or medical reports, Rule 16(b)(1) does not authorize discovery or inspection of:

(A) reports, memoranda, or other documents made by the defendant, or the defendant's attorney or agent, during the case's investigation or defense; or

(B) a statement made to the defendant, or the defendant's attorney or agent, by:

(i) the defendant;

(ii) a government or defense witness; or

(iii) a prospective government or defense witness.

(c) Continuing Duty to Disclose.

A party who discovers additional evidence or material before or during trial must promptly disclose its existence to the other party or the court if:

(1) the evidence or material is subject to discovery or inspection under this rule; and

(2) the other party previously requested, or the court ordered, its production.

(d) Regulating Discovery.

(1) Protective and Modifying Orders.

At any time the court may, for good cause, deny, restrict, or defer discovery or inspection, or grant other appropriate relief. The court may permit a party to show good cause by a written statement that the court will inspect ex parte. If relief is granted, the court must preserve the entire text of the party's statement under seal.

(2) Failure to Comply.

If a party fails to comply with this rule, the court may:

(A) order that party to permit the discovery or inspection; specify its time, place, and manner; and prescribe other just terms and conditions;

(B) grant a continuance;

(C) prohibit that party from introducing the undisclosed evidence; or

(D) enter any other order that is just under the circumstances.

Rule 23. Jury or Nonjury Trial

(a) Jury Trial.

If the defendant is entitled to a jury trial, the trial must be by jury unless:

(1) the defendant waives a jury trial in writing;

(2) the government consents; and

(3) the court approves.

(b) *Jury Size.*

(1) In General.

A jury consists of 12 persons unless this rule provides otherwise.

(2) Stipulation for a Smaller Jury.

At any time before the verdict, the parties may, with the court's approval, stipulate in writing that:

(A) the jury may consist of fewer than 12 persons; or

(B) a jury of fewer than 12 persons may return a verdict if the court finds it necessary to excuse a juror for good cause after the trial begins.

(3) Court Order for a Jury of 11.

After the jury has retired to deliberate, the court may permit a jury of 11 persons to return a verdict, even without a stipulation by the parties, if the court finds good cause to excuse a juror.

(c) *Nonjury Trial.*

In a case tried without a jury, the court must find the defendant guilty or not guilty. If a party requests before the finding of guilty or not guilty, the court must state its specific findings of fact in open court or in a written decision or opinion.

Rule 26.2. Producing a Witness's Statement

(a) *Motion to Produce.*

After a witness other than the defendant has testified on direct examination, the court, on motion of a party who did not call the witness, must order an attorney for the government or the defendant and the defendant's attorney to produce, for the examination and use of the moving party, any statement of the witness that is in their possession and that relates to the subject matter of the witness's testimony.

Rule 41.   Search and Seizure

(a)   Scope and Definitions.

(1)   Scope.

This rule does not modify any statute regulating search or seizure, or the issuance and execution of a search warrant in special circumstances.

(2)   Definitions.

The following definitions apply under this rule:

(**A**) "Property" includes documents, books, papers, any other tangible objects, and information.

(**B**) "Daytime" means the hours between 6:00 a.m. and 10:00 p.m. according to local time.

(**C**) "Federal law enforcement officer" means a government agent (other than an attorney for the government) who is engaged in enforcing the criminal laws and is within any category of officers authorized by the Attorney General to request a search warrant.

(**D**) "Domestic terrorism" and "international terrorism" have the meanings set out in 18 U.S.C. §2331.

(**E**) "Tracking device" has the meaning set out in 18 U.S.C. §3117(b).

(b)   Venue for a Warrant Application

At the request of a federal law enforcement officer or an attorney for the government:

(1) a magistrate judge with authority in the district—or if none is reasonably available, a judge of a state court of record in the district—has authority to issue a warrant to search for and seize a person or property located within the district;

(2) a magistrate judge with authority in the district has authority to issue a warrant for a person or property outside the district if the person or property is located within the district when the warrant is issued but might move or be moved outside the district before the warrant is executed;

(3) a magistrate judge—in an investigation of domestic terrorism or international terrorism—with authority in any district in which activities related to the terrorism may have occurred has authority to issue a warrant for a person or property within or outside that district; and

(4) a magistrate judge with authority in the district has authority to issue a warrant to install within the district a tracking device; the warrant may authorize use of the device to track the movement of a person or property located within the district, outside the district, or both; and

(5) a magistrate judge having authority in any district where activities related to the crime may have occurred, or in the District of Columbia, may issue a warrant for property that is located outside the jurisdiction of any state or district, but within any of the following:

(A) a United States territory, possession, or commonwealth;

(B) the premises—no matter who owns them—of a United States diplomatic or consular mission in a foreign state, including any appurtenant building, part of a building, or land used for the mission's purposes; or

(C) a residence and any appurtenant land owned or leased by the United States and used by United States personnel assigned to a United States diplomatic or consular mission in a foreign state.

(6) a magistrate with authority in any district where activities related to a crime may have occurred has authority to issue a warrant to use remote access to search electronic storage media and to seize or copy electronically stored information located within or outside that district if:

(A) the district where the media or information is located has been concealed through technological means; or

(B) in an investigation of a violation of 18 U.S.C. §1030(a)(5), the media are protected computers that have been damaged without authorization and are located in five or more districts.

(c) Persons or Property Subject to Search or Seizure.

A warrant may be issued for any of the following:

(1) evidence of a crime;

(2) contraband, fruits of crime, or other items illegally possessed;

(3) property designed for use, intended for use, or used in committing a crime; or

(4) a person to be arrested or a person who is unlawfully restrained.

(d) Obtaining a Warrant.

(1) In General.

After receiving an affidavit or other information, a magistrate judge—or if authorized by Rule 41(b), a judge of a state court of record—must issue the warrant if there is probable cause to search for and seize a person or property or to install and use a tracking device.

(2) Requesting a Warrant in the Presence of a Judge.

(A) In General. A magistrate judge may issue a warrant based on information communicated by telephone or other reliable electronic means.

(B) Recording Testimony. Upon learning that an applicant is requesting a warrant under Rule 41(d)(3)(A), a magistrate judge must:

(i) place under oath the applicant and any person on whose testimony the application is based; and

(ii) make a verbatim record of the conversation with a suitable recording device, if available, or by a court reporter, or in writing.

(C) Recording Testimony. Testimony taken in support of a warrant must be recorded by a court reporter or by a suitable recording device, and the judge must file the transcript or recording with the clerk, along with any affidavit.

(3) Requesting a Warrant by Telephonic or Other Means.

(A) In General. A magistrate judge may issue a warrant based on information communicated by telephone or other appropriate means, including facsimile transmission.

(B) Recording Testimony. Upon learning that an applicant is requesting a warrant, a magistrate judge must:

(i) place under oath the applicant and any person on whose testimony the application is based; and

(ii) make a verbatim record of the conversation with a suitable recording device, if available, or by a court reporter, or in writing.

(C) Certifying Testimony. The magistrate judge must have any recording or court reporter's notes transcribed, certify the transcription's accuracy, and file a copy of the record and the transcription with the clerk. Any written verbatim record must be signed by the magistrate judge and filed with the clerk.

(D) Suppression Limited. Absent a finding of bad faith, evidence obtained from a warrant issued under Rule 41(d)(3)(A) is not subject to suppression on the ground that issuing the warrant in that manner was unreasonable under the circumstances.

(e)   Issuing the Warrant.

(1)   In General.

The magistrate judge or a judge of a state court of record must issue the warrant to an officer authorized to execute it.

(2)   Contents of the Warrant.

(A) Warrant to Search for and Seize a Person or Property. Except for a tracking-device warrant, the warrant must identify the person or property to be searched, identify any person or property to be seized, and designate the magistrate judge to whom it must be returned. The warrant must command the officer to:

(i) execute the warrant within a specified time no longer than 14 days;

(ii) execute the warrant during the daytime, unless the judge for good cause expressly authorizes execution at another time; and

(iii) return the warrant to the magistrate judge designated in the warrant.

(B) Warrant Seeking Electronically Stored Information. A warrant under Rule 41(e)(2)(A) may authorize the seizure of electronic storage media or the seizure or copying of electronically stored information. Unless otherwise specified, the warrant authorizes a later review of the media or information consistent with the warrant. The time for executing the warrant in Rule 4(e)(2)(A) and (f)(1)(A) refers to the seizure or on-site copying of the media or information, and not to any later off-site copying or review.

(C) Warrant for a Tracking Device. A tracking-device warrant must identify the person or property to be tracked, designate the magistrate judge to whom it must be returned, and specify a reasonable length of time that the device may be used. The time must not exceed 45 days from the date the warrant was issued. The court may, for good cause, grant one or more extensions for a reasonable period not to exceed 45 days each. The warrant must command the officer to:

(i) complete any installation authorized by the warrant within a specified time no longer than 10 calendar days;

(ii) perform any installation authorized by the warrant during the daytime, unless the judge for good cause expressly authorizes installation at another time; and

(iii) return the warrant to the judge designated in the warrant.

(D) Return the warrant to the magistrate judge designated in the warrant.

(3)   Warrant by Telephonic or Other Means.

If a magistrate judge decides to proceed under Rule 41(d)(3)(A), the following additional procedures apply:

(A) Preparing a Proposed Duplicate Original Warrant. The applicant must prepare a "proposed duplicate original warrant" and must read or otherwise transmit the contents of that document verbatim to the magistrate judge.

(B) Preparing an Original Warrant. If the applicant reads the contents of the proposed duplicate original warrant, the magistrate judge must enter those contents into an original warrant. If the applicant transmits the contents by reliable electronic means, that transmission may serve as the original warrant.

(C) Modification. The magistrate judge may modify the original warrant. The judge must transmit any modified warrant to the applicant by reliable electronic means under Rule 41(e)(3)(D) or direct the applicant to modify the proposed duplicate original warrant accordingly.

(D) Signing the Warrant. Upon determining to issue the warrant, the magistrate judge must immediately sign the original warrant, enter on its face the exact date and time it is issued, and transmit it by reliable electronic means to the applicant or direct the applicant to sign the judge's name on the duplicate original warrant.

(f)   Executing and Returning the Warrant.

(1)   Warrant to Search for and Seize a Person or Property.

(A) Noting the Time. The officer executing the warrant must enter on it the exact date and time it was executed.

(B) Inventory. An officer present during the execution of the warrant must prepare and verify an inventory of any property seized. The officer must do so in the presence of another officer and the person from whom, or from whose premises, the property was taken. If either one is not present, the officer must prepare and verify the inventory in the presence of at least one other credible person. In a case involving the seizure of electronic storage media or the seizure or copying of electronically stored information, the inventory may be limited to describing the physical storage media that were seized or copied. The officer may retain a copy of the electronically stored information that was seized or copied.

(C) Receipt. The officer executing the warrant must give a copy of the warrant and a receipt for the property taken to the person from whom, or from whose premises, the property was taken or leave a copy of the warrant and receipt at the place where the officer took the property.

For a warrant to use remote access to search electronic storage media and seize or copy electronically stored information, the officer must make reasonable efforts to serve a copy of the warrant and receipt on the person whose property was searched or who possessed the information that was seized or copied. Service may be accomplished by any means, including electronic means, reasonably calculated to reach that person.

(D) Return. The officer executing the warrant must promptly return it—together with a copy of the inventory—to the magistrate judge designated on the warrant. The judge must, on request, give a copy of the inventory to the person from whom, or from whose premises, the property was taken and to the applicant for the warrant.

(2)   Warrant for a Tracking Device.

(A) Noting the Time. The officer executing a tracking-device warrant must enter on it the exact date and time the device was installed and the period during which it was used.

(B) Return. Within 10 calendar days after the use of the tracking device has ended, the officer executing the warrant must return it to the judge designated in the warrant.

   (C) Service. Within 10 calendar days after the use of the tracking device has ended, the officer executing a tracking-device warrant must serve a copy of the warrant on the person who was tracked or whose property was tracked. Service may be accomplished by delivering a copy to the person who, or whose property, was tracked; or by leaving a copy at the person's residence or usual place of abode with an individual of suitable age and discretion who resides at that location and by mailing a copy to the person's last known address. Upon request of the government, the judge may delay notice as provided in Rule 41(f)(3).

   (3)   Delayed Notice.

   Upon the government's request, a magistrate judge—or if authorized by Rule 41(b), a judge of a state court of record—may delay any notice required by this rule if the delay is authorized by statute.

   (4)   Return.

   The officer executing the warrant must promptly return it—together with a copy of the inventory—to the magistrate judge designated on the warrant. The judge must, on request, give a copy of the inventory to the person from whom, or from whose premises, the property was taken and to the applicant for the warrant.

   (g)   Motion to Return Property.

   A person aggrieved by an unlawful search and seizure of property or by the deprivation of property may move for the property's return. The motion must be filed in the district where the property was seized. The court must receive evidence on any factual issue necessary to decide the motion. If it grants the motion, the court must return the property to the movant, but may impose reasonable conditions to protect access to the property and its use in later proceedings.

   (h)   Motion to Suppress.

   A defendant may move to suppress evidence in the court where the trial will occur, as Rule 12 provides.

   (i)   Forwarding Papers to the Clerk.

   The magistrate judge to whom the warrant is returned must attach to the warrant a copy of the return, of the inventory, and of all other related papers and must deliver them to the clerk in the district where the property was seized.

Excerpted Statutes

18 U.S.C.

§3142.   RELEASE OR DETENTION OF A DEFENDANT PENDING TRIAL

(a) **In general.**—Upon the appearance before a judicial officer of a person charged with an offense, the judicial officer shall issue an order that, pending trial, the person be—

(1) released on personal recognizance or upon execution of an unsecured appearance bond, under subsection (b) of this section;

(2) released on a condition or combination of conditions under subsection (c) of this section;

(3) temporarily detained to permit revocation of conditional release, deportation, or exclusion under subsection (d) of this section; or

(4) detained under subsection (e) of this section.

(b) **Release on personal recognizance or unsecured appearance bond.**—The judicial officer shall order the pretrial release of the person on personal recognizance, or upon execution of an unsecured appearance bond in an amount specified by the court, subject to the condition that the person not commit a Federal, State, or local crime during the period of release and subject to the condition that the person cooperate in the collection of a DNA sample from the person if the collection of such a sample is authorized pursuant to section 3 of the DNA Analysis Backlog Elimination Act of 2000 (42 U.S.C. §14135a), unless the judicial officer determines that such release will not reasonably assure the appearance of the person as required or will endanger the safety of any other person or the community.

(c) **Release on conditions.**—(1) If the judicial officer determines that the release described in subsection (b) of this section will not reasonably assure the appearance of the person as required or will endanger the safety of any other person or the community, such judicial officer shall order the pretrial release of the person—

(A) subject to the condition that the person not commit a Federal, State, or local crime during the period of release and subject to the condition that the person cooperate in the collection of a DNA sample from the person if the collection of such a sample is authorized pursuant to section 3 of the DNA Analysis Backlog Elimination Act of 2000 (42 U.S.C. §14135a); and

(B) subject to the least restrictive further condition, or combination of conditions, that such judicial officer determines will reasonably assure the appearance of the person as required and the safety of any other person and the community, which may include the condition that the person—

(i) remain in the custody of a designated person, who agrees to assume supervision and to report any violation of a release condition to the court, if the designated person is able reasonably to assure the judicial officer that the person will appear as required and will not pose a danger to the safety of any other person or the community;

(ii) maintain employment, or, if unemployed, actively seek employment;

(iii) maintain or commence an educational program;

(iv) abide by specified restrictions on personal associations, place of abode, or travel;

(v) avoid all contact with an alleged victim of the crime and with a potential witness who may testify concerning the offense;

(vi) report on a regular basis to a designated law enforcement agency, pretrial services agency, or other agency;

(vii) comply with a specified curfew;

(viii) refrain from possessing a firearm, destructive device, or other dangerous weapon;

(ix) refrain from excessive use of alcohol, or any use of a narcotic drug or other controlled substance, as defined in section 102 of the Controlled Substances Act (21 U.S.C. §802), without a prescription by a licensed medical practitioner;

(x) undergo available medical, psychological, or psychiatric treatment, including treatment for drug or alcohol dependency, and remain in a specified institution if required for that purpose;

(xi) execute an agreement to forfeit upon failing to appear as required, property of a sufficient unencumbered value, including money, as is reasonably necessary to assure the appearance of the person as required, and shall provide the court with proof of ownership and the value of the property along with information regarding existing encumbrances as the judicial office may require;

(xii) execute a bail bond with solvent sureties; who will execute an agreement to forfeit in such amount as is reasonably necessary to assure appearance of the person as required and shall provide the court with information regarding the value of the assets and liabilities of the surety if other than an approved surety and the nature and extent of encumbrances against the surety's property; such surety shall have a net worth which shall have sufficient unencumbered value to pay the amount of the bail bond;

(xiii) return to custody for specified hours following release for employment, schooling, or other limited purposes; and

(xiv) satisfy any other condition that is reasonably necessary to assure the appearance of the person as required and to assure the safety of any other person and the community.

In any case that involves a minor victim under section 1201, 1591, 2241, 2242, 2244(a)(1), 2245, 2251, 2251A, 2252(a)(1), 2252(a)(2), 2252(a)(3), 2252A(a)(1), 2252A(a)(2), 2252A(a)(3), 2252A(a)(4), 2260, 2421, 2422, 2423, or 2425 of this title, or a failure to register offense under section 2250 of this title, any release order shall contain, at a minimum, a condition of electronic monitoring and each of the conditions specified at subparagraphs (iv), (v), (vi), (vii), and (viii).

(2) The judicial officer may not impose a financial condition that results in the pretrial detention of the person.

(3) The judicial officer may at any time amend the order to impose additional or different conditions of release.

(d) **Temporary detention to permit revocation of conditional release, deportation, or exclusion.**—If the judicial officer determines that—

(1) such person—

(A) is, and was at the time the offense was committed, on—

(i) release pending trial for a felony under Federal, State, or local law;

(ii) release pending imposition or execution of sentence, appeal of sentence or conviction, or completion of sentence, for any offense under Federal, State, or local law; or

(iii) probation or parole for any offense under Federal, State, or local law; or

(B) is not a citizen of the United States or lawfully admitted for permanent residence, as defined in section 101(a)(20) of the Immigration and Nationality Act (8 U.S.C. §1101(a)(20)); and

(2) such person may flee or pose a danger to any other person or the community; such judicial officer shall order the detention of such person, for a period of not more than ten days, excluding Saturdays, Sundays, and holidays, and direct the attorney for the Government to notify the appropriate court, probation or parole official, or State or local law enforcement official, or the appropriate official of the Immigration and Naturalization Service. If the official fails or declines to take such person into custody during that period, such person shall be treated in accordance with the other provisions of this section, notwithstanding the applicability of other provisions of law governing release pending trial or deportation or exclusion proceedings. If temporary detention is sought under paragraph (1)(B) of this subsection, such person has the burden of proving to the court such person's United States citizenship or lawful admission for permanent residence.

(e) **Detention.**—(1) If, after a hearing pursuant to the provisions of subsection (f) of this section, the judicial officer finds that no condition or combination of conditions will reasonably assure the appearance of the person as required and the safety of any other person and the community, such judicial officer shall order the detention of the person before trial.

(2) In a case described in subsection (f)(1) of this section, a rebuttable presumption arises that no condition or combination of conditions will reasonably assure the safety of any other person and the community if such judicial officer finds that—

(A) the person has been convicted of a Federal offense that is described in subsection (f)(1) of this section, or of a State or local offense that would have been an offense described in subsection (f)(1) of this section if a circumstance giving rise to Federal jurisdiction had existed;

(B) the offense described in subparagraph (A) was committed while the person was on release pending trial for a Federal, State, or local offense; and

(C) a period of not more than five years has elapsed since the date of conviction, or the release of the person from imprisonment, for the offense described in subparagraph (A), whichever is later.

(3) Subject to rebuttal by the person, it shall be presumed that no condition or combination of conditions will reasonably assure the appearance of the person as required and the safety of the community if the judicial officer finds that there is probable cause to believe that the person committed—

(A) an offense for which a maximum term of imprisonment of ten years or more is prescribed in the Controlled Substances Act (21 U.S.C. §801 et seq.), the Controlled Substances Import and Export Act (21 U.S.C. §951 et seq.), or chapter 705 of title 46;

(B) an offense under section 924(c), 956(a), or 2332b of this title;

(C) an offense listed in section 2332b(g)(5)(B) of title 18, United States Code, for which a maximum term of imprisonment of 10 years or more is prescribed;

(D) an offense under chapter 77 of this title for which a maximum term of imprisonment of 20 years or more is prescribed; or

(E) an offense involving a minor victim under section 1201, 1591, 2241, 2242, 2244(a)(1), 2245, 2251, 2251A, 2252(a)(1), 2252(a)(2), 2252(a)(3), 2252A(a)(1), 2252A(a)(2), 2252A(a)(3), 2252A(a)(4), 2260, 2421, 2422, 2423, or 2425 of this title.

(f) **Detention hearing.**—The judicial officer shall hold a hearing to determine whether any condition or combination of conditions set forth in subsection (c) of this section will reasonably assure the appearance of such person as required and the safety of any other person and the community—

(1) upon motion of the attorney for the Government, in a case that involves—

(A) a crime of violence, a violation of section 1591, or an offense listed in section 2332b(g)(5)(B) for which a maximum term of imprisonment of 10 years or more is prescribed;

(B) an offense for which the maximum sentence is life imprisonment or death;

(C) an offense for which a maximum term of imprisonment of ten years or more is prescribed in the Controlled Substances Act (21 U.S.C. §801 et seq.), the Controlled Substances Import and Export Act (21 U.S.C. §951 et seq.), or chapter 705 of title 46;

(D) any felony if such person has been convicted of two or more offenses described in subparagraphs (A) through (C) of this paragraph, or two or more State or local offenses that would have been offenses described in subparagraphs (A) through (C) of this paragraph if a circumstance giving rise to Federal jurisdiction had existed, or a combination of such offenses; or

(E) any felony that is not otherwise a crime of violence that involves a minor victim or that involves the possession or use of a firearm or destructive device (as those terms are defined in section 921), or any other dangerous weapon, or involves a failure to register under section 2250 of title 18, United States Code; or

(2) Upon motion of the attorney for the Government or upon the judicial officer's own motion, in a case that involves—

(A) a serious risk that such person will flee; or

(B) a serious risk that such person will obstruct or attempt to obstruct justice, or threaten, injure, or intimidate, or attempt to threaten, injure, or intimidate, a prospective witness or juror.

The hearing shall be held immediately upon the person's first appearance before the judicial officer unless that person, or the attorney for the Government, seeks a continuance. Except for good cause, a continuance on motion of such person may not exceed five days (not including any intermediate Saturday, Sunday, or legal holiday), and a continuance on motion of the attorney for the Government may not exceed three days (not including any intermediate Saturday, Sunday, or legal holiday). During a continuance, such person shall be detained, and the judicial officer, on motion of the attorney for the Government or sua sponte, may order that, while in custody, a person who appears to be a narcotics addict receive a medical examination to determine whether such person is an addict. At the hearing, such person has the right to be represented by counsel, and, if financially unable to obtain adequate representation, to have counsel appointed. The person shall be afforded an opportunity to testify, to present witnesses, to cross-examine witnesses who appear at the hearing, and to present information by proffer or otherwise. The rules concerning admissibility of evidence in criminal trials do not apply to the presentation and consideration of information at the hearing. The facts the judicial officer uses to support a finding pursuant to subsection (e) that no condition or combination of conditions will reasonably assure the safety of any other person and the community shall be supported by clear and convincing evidence. The person may be detained pending completion of the hearing. The hearing may be reopened, before or after a determination by the judicial officer, at any time before trial if the judicial officer finds that information exists that was not known to the movant at the time of the hearing and that has a material bearing on the issue whether there are conditions of release that will reasonably assure the appearance of such person as required and the safety of any other person and the community.

(g) **Factors to be considered.**—The judicial officer shall, in determining whether there are conditions of release that will reasonably assure the appearance of the person as required and the safety of any other person and the community, take into account the available information concerning—

(1) the nature and circumstances of the offense charged, including whether the offense is a crime of violence, a violation of section 1591, a Federal crime of terrorism, or involves a minor victim or a controlled substance, firearm, explosive, or destructive device;

(2) the weight of the evidence against the person;

(3) the history and characteristics of the person, including—

(A) the person's character, physical and mental condition, family ties, employment, financial resources, length of residence in the community, community ties, past conduct, history relating to drug or alcohol abuse, criminal history, and record concerning appearance at court proceedings; and

(B) whether, at the time of the current offense or arrest, the person was on probation, on parole, or on other release pending trial, sentencing, appeal, or completion of sentence for an offense under Federal, State, or local law; and

(4) the nature and seriousness of the danger to any person or the community that would be posed by the person's release. In considering the conditions of release described in subsection (c)(1)(B)(xi) or (c)(1)(B)(xii) of this section, the judicial officer may upon his own motion, or shall upon the motion of the Government, conduct an inquiry into the source of the property to be designated for potential forfeiture or offered as collateral to secure a bond, and shall decline to accept the designation, or the use as collateral, of property that, because of its source, will not reasonably assure the appearance of the person as required.

(h) **Contents of release order.**—In a release order issued under subsection (b) or (c) of this section, the judicial officer shall—

(1) include a written statement that sets forth all the conditions to which the release is subject, in a manner sufficiently clear and specific to serve as a guide for the person's conduct; and

(2) advise the person of—

(A) the penalties for violating a condition of release, including the penalties for committing an offense while on pretrial release;

(B) the consequences of violating a condition of release, including the immediate issuance of a warrant for the person's arrest; and

(C) sections 1503 of this title (relating to intimidation of witnesses, jurors, and officers of the court), 1510 (relating to obstruction of criminal investigations), 1512 (tampering with a witness, victim, or an informant), and 1513 (retaliating against a witness, victim, or an informant).

(i) **Contents of detention order.**—In a detention order issued under subsection (e) of this section, the judicial officer shall—

(1) include written findings of fact and a written statement of the reasons for the detention;

(2) direct that the person be committed to the custody of the Attorney General for confinement in a corrections facility separate, to the extent practicable, from persons awaiting or serving sentences or being held in custody pending appeal;

(3) direct that the person be afforded reasonable opportunity for private consultation with counsel; and

(4) direct that, on order of a court of the United States or on request of an attorney for the Government, the person in charge of the corrections facility in which the person is confined deliver the person to a United States marshal for the purpose of an appearance in connection with a court proceeding.

The judicial officer may, by subsequent order, permit the temporary release of the person, in the custody of a United States marshal or another appropriate person, to the extent that the judicial officer determines such release to be necessary for preparation of the person's defense or for another compelling reason.

(j) **Presumption of innocence.**—Nothing in this section shall be construed as modifying or limiting the presumption of innocence.

§3144.   Release or Detention of a Material Witness

If it appears from an affidavit filed by a party that the testimony of a person is material in a criminal proceeding, and if it is shown that it may become impracticable to secure the presence of the person by subpoena, a judicial officer may order the arrest of the person and treat the person in accordance with the provisions of section 3142 of this title. No material witness may be detained because of inability to comply with any condition of release if the testimony of such witness can adequately be secured by deposition, and if further detention is not necessary to prevent a failure of justice. Release of a material witness may be delayed for a reasonable period of time until the deposition of the witness can be taken pursuant to the Federal Rules of Criminal Procedure.

§3161.   Time Limits and Exclusions

(a) In any case involving a defendant charged with an offense, the appropriate judicial officer, at the earliest practicable time, shall, after consultation with the counsel for the defendant and the attorney for the Government, set the case for trial on a day certain, or list it for trial on a weekly or other short-term trial calendar at a place within the judicial district, so as to assure a speedy trial.

(b) Any information or indictment charging an individual with the commission of an offense shall be filed within thirty days from the date on which such individual was arrested or served with a summons in connection with such charges. If an individual has been charged with a felony in a district in which no grand jury has been in session during such thirty-day period, the period of time for filing of the indictment shall be extended an additional thirty days.

(c)(1) In any case in which a plea of not guilty is entered, the trial of a defendant charged in an information or indictment with the commission of an offense shall commence within seventy days from the filing date (and making public) of the information or indictment, or from the date the defendant has appeared before a judicial officer of the court in which such charge is pending, whichever date last occurs. If a defendant consents in writing to be tried before a magistrate judge on a complaint, the trial shall commence within seventy days from the date of such consent.

(2) Unless the defendant consents in writing to the contrary, the trial shall not commence less than thirty days from the date on which the defendant first appears through counsel or expressly waives counsel and elects to proceed pro se.

(d)(1) If any indictment or information is dismissed upon motion of the defendant, or any charge contained in a complaint filed against an individual is dismissed or otherwise dropped, and thereafter a complaint is filed against such defendant or individual charging him with the same offense or an offense based on the same conduct or arising from the same criminal episode, or an information or indictment is filed charging such defendant with the same offense or an offense based on the same conduct or arising from the same criminal episode, the provisions of subsections (b) and (c) of this section shall be applicable with respect to such subsequent complaint, indictment, or information, as the case may be.

(2) If the defendant is to be tried upon an indictment or information dismissed by a trial court and reinstated following an appeal, the trial shall commence within seventy days from the date the action occasioning the trial becomes final, except that the court retrying the case may extend the period for trial not to exceed one hundred and eighty days from the date the action occasioning the trial becomes final if the unavailability of witnesses or other factors resulting from the passage of time shall make trial within seventy days impractical. The periods of delay enumerated in section 3161(h) are excluded in computing the time limitations specified in this section. The sanctions of section 3162 apply to this subsection.

(e) If the defendant is to be tried again following a declaration by the trial judge of a mistrial or following an order of such judge for a new trial, the trial shall commence within seventy days from the date the action occasioning the retrial becomes final. If the defendant is to be tried again following an appeal or a collateral attack, the trial shall commence within seventy days from the date the action occasioning the retrial becomes final, except that the court retrying the case may extend the period for retrial not to exceed one hundred and eighty days from the date the action occasioning the retrial becomes final

213

if unavailability of witnesses or other factors resulting from passage of time shall make trial within seventy days impractical. The periods of delay enumerated in section 3161(h) are excluded in computing the time limitations specified in this section. The sanctions of section 3162 apply to this subsection.

(f) Notwithstanding the provisions of subsection (b) of this section, for the first twelve-calendar-month period following the effective date of this section as set forth in section 3163(a) of this chapter the time limit imposed with respect to the period between arrest and indictment by subsection (b) of this section shall be sixty days, for the second such twelve-month period such time limit shall be forty-five days and for the third such period such time limit shall be thirty-five days.

(g) Notwithstanding the provisions of subsection (c) of this section, for the first twelve-calendar-month period following the effective date of this section as set forth in section 3163(b) of this chapter, the time limit with respect to the period between arraignment and trial imposed by subsection (c) of this section shall be one hundred and eighty days, for the second such twelve-month period such time limit shall be one hundred and twenty days, and for the third such period such time limit with respect to the period between arraignment and trial shall be eighty days.

(h) The following periods of delay shall be excluded in computing the time within which an information or an indictment must be filed, or in computing the time within which the trial of any such offense must commence:

(1) Any period of delay resulting from other proceedings concerning the defendant, including but not limited to—

(A) delay resulting from any proceeding, including any examinations, to determine the mental competency or physical capacity of the defendant;

(B) delay resulting from trial with respect to other charges against the defendant;

(C) delay resulting from any interlocutory appeal;

(D) delay resulting from any pretrial motion, from the filing of the motion through the conclusion of the hearing on, or other prompt disposition of, such motion;

(E) delay resulting from any proceeding relating to the transfer of a case or the removal of any defendant from another district under the Federal Rules of Criminal Procedure;

(F) delay resulting from transportation of any defendant from another district, or to and from places of examination or hospitalization, except that any time consumed in excess of ten days from the date an order of removal or an order directing such transportation, and the defendant's arrival at the destination shall be presumed to be unreasonable;

(G) delay resulting from consideration by the court of a proposed plea agreement to be entered into by the defendant and the attorney for the Government; and

(H) delay reasonably attributable to any period, not to exceed thirty days, during which any proceeding concerning the defendant is actually under advisement by the court.

(2) Any period of delay during which prosecution is deferred by the attorney for the Government pursuant to written agreement with the defendant, with the approval of the court, for the purpose of allowing the defendant to demonstrate his good conduct.

(3)(A) Any period of delay resulting from the absence or unavailability of the defendant or an essential witness.

(B) For purposes of subparagraph (A) of this paragraph, a defendant or an essential witness shall be considered absent when his whereabouts are unknown and, in addition, he is attempting to avoid apprehension or prosecution or his whereabouts cannot be determined by due diligence. For purposes of such subparagraph, a defendant or an essential witness shall be considered unavailable whenever his whereabouts are known but his presence for trial cannot be obtained by due diligence or he resists appearing at or being returned for trial.

(4) Any period of delay resulting from the fact that the defendant is mentally incompetent or physically unable to stand trial.

(5) If the information or indictment is dismissed upon motion of the attorney for the Government and thereafter a charge is filed against the defendant for the same offense, or any offense required to be joined with that offense, any period of delay from the date the charge was dismissed to the date the time limitation would commence to run as to the subsequent charge had there been no previous charge.

(6) A reasonable period of delay when the defendant is joined for trial with a codefendant as to whom the time for trial has not run and no motion for severance has been granted.

(7)(A) Any period of delay resulting from a continuance granted by any judge on his own motion or at the request of the defendant or his counsel or at the request of the attorney for the Government, if the judge granted such continuance on the basis of his findings that the ends of justice served by taking such action outweigh the best interest of the public and the defendant in a speedy trial. No such period of delay resulting from a continuance granted by the court in accordance with this paragraph shall be excludable under this subsection unless the court sets forth, in the record of the case, either orally or in writing, its reasons for finding that the ends of justice served by the granting of such continuance outweigh the best interests of the public and the defendant in a speedy trial.

(B) The factors, among others, which a judge shall consider in determining whether to grant a continuance under subparagraph (A) of this paragraph in any case are as follows:

(i) Whether the failure to grant such a continuance in the proceeding would be likely to make a continuation of such proceeding impossible, or result in a miscarriage of justice.

(ii) Whether the case is so unusual or so complex, due to the number of defendants, the nature of the prosecution, or the existence of novel questions of fact or law, that it is unreasonable to expect adequate preparation for pretrial proceedings or for the trial itself within the time limits established by this section.

(iii) Whether, in a case in which arrest precedes indictment, delay in the filing of the indictment is caused because the arrest occurs at a time such that it is unreasonable to expect return and filing of the indictment within the period specified in section 3161(b), or because the facts upon which the grand jury must base its determination are unusual or complex.

(iv) Whether the failure to grant such a continuance in a case which, taken as a whole, is not so unusual or so complex as to fall within clause (ii), would deny the defendant reasonable time to obtain counsel, would unreasonably deny the defendant or the Government continuity of counsel, or would deny counsel for the defendant or the attorney for the Government the reasonable time necessary for effective preparation, taking into account the exercise of due diligence.

(C) No continuance under subparagraph (A) of this paragraph shall be granted because of general congestion of the court's calendar, or lack of diligent preparation or failure to obtain available witnesses on the part of the attorney for the Government.

(8) Any period of delay, not to exceed one year, ordered by a district court upon an application of a party and a finding by a preponderance of the evidence that an official request, as defined in section 3292 of this title, has been made for evidence of any such offense and that it reasonably appears, or reasonably appeared at the time the request was made, that such evidence is, or was, in such foreign country.

(i) If trial did not commence within the time limitation specified in section 3161 because the defendant had entered a plea of guilty or nolo contendere subsequently withdrawn to any or all charges in an indictment or information, the defendant shall be deemed indicted with respect to all charges therein contained within the meaning of section 3161, on the day the order permitting withdrawal of the plea becomes final.

(j)(1) If the attorney for the Government knows that a person charged with an offense is serving a term of imprisonment in any penal institution, he shall promptly—

(A) undertake to obtain the presence of the prisoner for trial; or

(B) cause a detainer to be filed with the person having custody of the prisoner and request him to so advise the prisoner and to advise the prisoner of his right to demand trial.

(2) If the person having custody of such prisoner receives a detainer, he shall promptly advise the prisoner of the charge and of the prisoner's right to demand trial. If at any time thereafter the prisoner informs the person having custody that he does demand trial, such person shall cause notice to that effect to be sent promptly to the attorney for the Government who caused the detainer to be filed.

(3) Upon receipt of such notice, the attorney for the Government shall promptly seek to obtain the presence of the prisoner for trial.

(4) When the person having custody of the prisoner receives from the attorney for the Government a properly supported request for temporary custody of such prisoner for trial, the prisoner shall be made available to that attorney for the Government (subject, in cases of interjurisdictional transfer, to any right of the prisoner to contest the legality of his delivery).

(k)(1) If the defendant is absent (as defined by subsection (h)(3)) on the day set for trial, and the defendant's subsequent appearance before the court on a bench warrant or other process or surrender to the court occurs more than 21 days after the day set for trial, the defendant shall be deemed to have first appeared before a judicial officer of the court in which the information or indictment is pending within the meaning of subsection (c) on the date of the defendant's subsequent appearance before the court.

(2) If the defendant is absent (as defined by subsection (h)(3)) on the day set for trial, and the defendant's subsequent appearance before the court on a bench warrant or other process or surrender to the court occurs not more than 21 days after the day set for trial, the time limit required by subsection (c), as extended by subsection (h), shall be further extended by 21 days.

28 U.S.C.

§2241.   POWER TO GRANT WRIT

(a) Writs of habeas corpus may be granted by the Supreme Court, any justice thereof, the district courts and any circuit judge within their respective jurisdictions. The order of a circuit judge shall be entered in the records of the district court of the district wherein the restraint complained of is had.

(b) The Supreme Court, any justice thereof and any circuit judge may decline to entertain an application for a writ of habeas corpus and may transfer the application for hearing and determination to the district court having jurisdiction to entertain it.

(c) The writ of habeas corpus shall not extend to a prisoner unless

(1) He is in custody under or by color of the authority of the United States or is committed for trial before some court there of; or

(2) He is in custody for an act done or omitted in pursuance of an Act of Congress, or an order, process, judgment or decree of a court or judge of the United States; or

(3) He is in custody in violation of the constitution or laws or treaties of the United States; or

(4) He, being a citizen of a foreign state and domiciled therein is in custody for an act done or omitted under any alleged right, title, authority, privilege, protection, or exemption claimed under the commission, order or sanction of any foreign state, or under color thereof, the validity and effect of which depend upon the law of nations; or

(5) It is necessary to bring him into court to testify or for trial.

(d) Where an application for a writ of habeas corpus is made by a person in custody under the judgment and sentence of a court of a State which contains two or more Federal judicial districts, the application may be filed in the district court for the district wherein such person is in custody or in the district court for the district within which the State court was held which convicted and sentenced him and each of such district courts shall have concurrent jurisdiction to entertain the application. The district court for the district wherein such an application is filed in the exercise of its discretion and in furtherance of justice may transfer the application to the other district court for hearing and determination.

(e)(1) No court, justice, or judge shall have jurisdiction to hear or consider an application for a writ of habeas corpus filed by or on behalf of an alien detained by the United States who has been determined by the United States to have been properly detained as an enemy combatant or is awaiting such determination.

(2) Except as provided in paragraphs (2) and (3) of section 1005(e) of the Detainee Treatment Act of 2005 (10 U.S.C. §801 note), no court, justice, or judge shall have jurisdiction to hear or consider any other action against the United States or its agents relating to any aspect of the detention, transfer, treatment, trial, or conditions of confinement of an alien who is or was detained by the United States and has been determined by the United States to have been properly detained as an enemy combatant or is awaiting such determination.

§2242. APPLICATION

Application for a writ of habeas corpus shall be in writing signed and verified by the person for whose relief it is intended or by someone acting in his behalf.

It shall allege the facts concerning the applicant's commitment or detention, the name of the person who has custody over him and by virtue of what claim or authority, if known.

It may be amended or supplemented as provided in the rules of procedure applicable to civil actions.

If addressed to the Supreme Court, a justice thereof or a circuit judge it shall state the reasons for not making application to the district court of the district in which the applicant is held.

§2243. ISSUANCE OF WRIT; RETURN; HEARING; DECISION

A court, justice or judge entertaining an application for a writ of habeas corpus shall forthwith award the writ or issue an order directing the respondent to show cause why the writ should not be granted, unless it appears from the application that the applicant or person detained is not entitled thereto.

The writ, or order to show cause shall be directed to the person having custody of the person detained. It shall be returned within three days unless for good cause additional time, not exceeding twenty days, is allowed.

The person to whom the writ or order is directed shall make a return certifying the true cause of the detention.

When the writ or order is returned a day shall be set for hearing, not more than five days after the return unless for good cause additional time is allowed.

Unless the application for the writ and the return present only issues of law the person to whom the writ is directed shall be required to produce at the hearing the body of the person detained.

The applicant or the person detained may, under oath, deny any of the facts set forth in the return or allege any other material facts.

The return and all suggestions made against it may be amended, by leave of court, before or after being filed.

The court shall summarily hear and determine the facts, and dispose of the matter as law and justice require.

§2244. FINALITY OF DETERMINATION

(a) No circuit or district judge shall be required to entertain an application for a writ of habeas corpus to inquire into the detention of a person pursuant to a judgment of a court of the United States if it appears that the legality of such detention has been determined by a judge or court of the United States on a prior application for a writ of habeas corpus except as provided in section 2255.

(b)(1) A claim presented in a second or successive habeas corpus application under section 2254 that was presented in a prior application shall be dismissed.

(2) A claim presented in a second or successive habeas corpus application under section 2254 that was not presented in a prior application shall be dismissed unless—

(A) the applicant shows that the claim relies on a new rule of constitutional law, made retroactive to cases on collateral review by the Supreme Court, that was previously unavailable; or

(B)(i) the factual predicate for the claim could not have been discovered previously through the exercise of due diligence; and

(ii) the facts underlying the claim, if proven and viewed in light of the evidence as a whole, would be sufficient to establish by clear and convincing evidence that, but for constitutional error, no reasonable factfinder would have found the applicant guilty of the underlying offense.

(3)(A) Before a second or successive application permitted by this section is filed in the district court, the applicant shall move in the appropriate court of appeals for an order authorizing the district court to consider the application.

(B) A motion in the court of appeals for an order authorizing the district court to consider a second or successive application shall be determined by a three-judge panel of the court of appeals.

(C) The court of appeals may authorize the filing of a second or successive application only if it determines that the application makes a prima facie showing that the application satisfies the requirements of this subsection.

(D) The court of appeals shall grant or deny the authorization to file a second or successive application not later than 30 days after the filing of the motion.

(E) The grant or denial of an authorization by a court of appeals to file a second or successive application shall not be appealable and shall not be the subject of a petition for rehearing or for a writ of certiorari.

(4) A district court shall dismiss any claim presented in a second or successive application that the court of appeals has authorized to be filed unless the applicant shows that the claim satisfies the requirements of this section.

(c) In a habeas corpus proceeding brought in behalf of a person in custody pursuant to the judgment of a State court, a prior judgment of the Supreme Court of the United States on an appeal or review by a writ of certiorari at the instance of the prisoner of the decision of such State court, shall be conclusive as to all issues of fact or law with respect to an asserted denial of a Federal right which constitutes ground for discharge in a habeas corpus proceeding, actually adjudicated by the Supreme Court therein, unless the applicant for the writ of habeas corpus shall plead and the court shall find the existence of a material and controlling fact which did not appear in the record of the proceeding in the Supreme Court and the court shall further find that the applicant for the writ of habeas corpus could not have caused such fact to appear in such record by the exercise of reasonable diligence.

(d)(1) A 1-year period of limitation shall apply to an application for a writ of habeas corpus by a person in custody pursuant to the judgment of a State court. The limitation period shall run from the latest of—

(A) the date on which the judgment became final by the conclusion of direct review or the expiration of the time for seeking such review;

(B) the date on which the impediment to filing an application created by State action in violation of the Constitution or laws of the United States is removed, if the applicant was prevented from filing by such State action;

(C) the date on which the constitutional right asserted was initially recognized by the Supreme Court, if the right has been newly recognized by the Supreme Court and made retroactively applicable to cases on collateral review; or

(D) the date on which the factual predicate of the claim or claims presented could have been discovered through the exercise of due diligence.

(2) The time during which a properly filed application for State post-conviction or other collateral review with respect to the pertinent judgment or claim is pending shall not be counted toward any period of limitation under this subsection.

§2245. CERTIFICATE OF TRIAL JUDGE ADMISSIBLE IN EVIDENCE

On the hearing of an application for a writ of habeas corpus to inquire into the legality of the detention of a person pursuant to a judgment the certificate of the judge who presided at the trial resulting in the judgment, setting forth the facts occurring at the trial, shall be admissible in evidence. Copies of the certificate shall be filed with the court in which the application is pending and in the court in which the trial took place.

§2246. EVIDENCE; DEPOSITIONS; AFFIDAVITS

On application for a writ of habeas corpus, evidence may be taken orally or by deposition, or, in the discretion of the judge, by affidavit. If affidavits are admitted any party shall have the right to propound written interrogatories to the affiants, or to file answering affidavits.

§2247. DOCUMENTARY EVIDENCE

On application for a writ of habeas corpus documentary evidence, transcripts of proceedings upon arraignment, plea and sentence and a transcript of the oral testimony introduced on any previous similar application by or in behalf of the same petitioner, shall be admissible in evidence.

§2248. RETURN OR ANSWER; CONCLUSIVENESS

The allegations of a return to the writ of habeas corpus or of an answer to an order to show cause in a habeas corpus proceeding, if not traversed, shall be accepted as true except to the extent that the judge finds from the evidence that they are not true.

§2249. CERTIFIED COPIES OF INDICTMENT, PLEA AND JUDGMENT; DUTY OF RESPONDENT

On application for a writ of habeas corpus to inquire into the detention of any person pursuant to a judgment of a court of the United States, the respondent shall promptly file with the court certified copies of the indictment, plea of petitioner and the judgment, or such of them as may be material to the questions raised, if the petitioner fails to attach them to his petition, and same shall be attached to the return to the writ, or to the answer to the order to show cause.

§2250.   INDIGENT PETITIONER ENTITLED TO DOCUMENTS WITHOUT COST

If on any application for a writ of habeas corpus an order has been made permitting the petitioner to prosecute the application in forma pauperis, the clerk of any court of the United States shall furnish to the petitioner without cost certified copies of such documents or parts of the record on file in his office as may be required by order of the judge before whom the application is pending.

§2251.   STAY OF STATE COURT PROCEEDINGS

A justice or judge of the United States before whom a habeas corpus proceeding is pending, may, before final judgment or after final judgment of discharge, or pending appeal, stay any proceeding against the person detained in any State court or by or under the authority of any State for any matter involved in the habeas corpus proceeding.

After the granting of such a stay, any such proceeding in any State court or by or under the authority of any State shall be void. If no stay is granted, any such proceeding shall be as valid as if no habeas corpus proceedings or appeal were pending.

§2252.   NOTICE

Prior to the hearing of a habeas corpus proceeding in behalf of a person in custody of State officers or by virtue of State laws notice shall be served on the attorney general or other appropriate officer of such State as the justice or judge at the time of issuing the writ shall direct.

§2253.   APPEAL

(a) In a habeas corpus proceeding or a proceeding under section 2255 before a district judge, the final order shall be subject to review, on appeal, by the court of appeals for the circuit in which the proceeding is held.

(b) There shall be no right of appeal from a final order in a proceeding to test the validity of a warrant to remove to another district or place for commitment or trial a person charged with a criminal offense against the United States, or to test the validity of such person's detention pending removal proceedings.

(c)(1) Unless a circuit justice or judge issues a certificate of appealability, an appeal may not be taken to the court of appeals from—

(A) the final order in a habeas corpus proceeding in which the detention complained of arises out of process issued by a State court; or

(B) the final order in a proceeding under section 2255.

(2) A certificate of appealability may issue under paragraph (1) only if the applicant has made a substantial showing of the denial of a constitutional right.

(3) The certificate of appealability under paragraph (1) shall indicate which specific issue or issues satisfy the showing required by paragraph (2).

§2254.   STATE CUSTODY; REMEDIES IN STATE COURTS

(a) The Supreme Court, a Justice thereof, a circuit judge, or a district court shall entertain an application for a writ of habeas corpus in behalf of a person in custody pursuant to the judgment of a State court only on the ground that he is in custody in violation of the Constitution or laws or treaties of the United States.

(b)(1) An application for a writ of habeas corpus on behalf of a person in custody pursuant to the judgment of a State court shall not be granted unless it appears that—

(A) the applicant has exhausted the remedies available in the courts of the State; or

(B)(i) there is an absence of available State corrective process; or

(ii) circumstances exist that render such process ineffective to protect the rights of the applicant.

(2) An application for a writ of habeas corpus may be denied on the merits, notwithstanding the failure of the applicant to exhaust the remedies available in the courts of the State.

(3) A State shall not be deemed to have waived the exhaustion requirement or be estopped from reliance upon the requirement unless the State, through counsel, expressly waives the requirement.

(c) An applicant shall not be deemed to have exhausted the remedies available in the courts of the State, within the meaning of this section, if he has the right under the law of the State to raise, by any available procedure, the question presented.

(d) An application for a writ of habeas corpus on behalf of a person in custody pursuant to the judgment of a State court shall not be granted with respect to any claim that was adjudicated on the merits in State court proceedings unless the adjudication of the claim—

(1) resulted in a decision that was contrary to, or involved an unreasonable application of, clearly established Federal law, as determined by the Supreme Court of the United States; or

(2) resulted in a decision that was based on an unreasonable determination of the facts in light of the evidence presented in the State court proceeding.

(e)(1) In a proceeding instituted by an application for a writ of habeas corpus by a person in custody pursuant to the judgment of a State court, a determination of a factual issue made by a State court shall be presumed to be correct. The applicant shall have the burden of rebutting the presumption of correctness by clear and convincing evidence.

(2) If the applicant has failed to develop the factual basis of a claim in State court proceedings, the court shall not hold an evidentiary hearing on the claim unless the applicant shows that—

(A) the claim relies on—

(i) a new rule of constitutional law, made retroactive to cases on collateral review by the Supreme Court, that was previously unavailable; or

(ii) a factual predicate that could not have been previously discovered through the exercise of due diligence; and

(B) the facts underlying the claim would be sufficient to establish by clear and convincing evidence that but for constitutional error, no reasonable factfinder would have found the applicant guilty of the underlying offense.

(f) If the applicant challenges the sufficiency of the evidence adduced in such State court proceeding to support the State court's determination of a factual issue made therein, the applicant, if able, shall produce that part of the record pertinent to a determination of the sufficiency of the evidence to support such determination. If the applicant, because of indigency or other reason is unable to produce such part of the record, then the State shall produce such part of the record and the Federal court shall direct the State to do so by order directed to an appropriate State official. If the State cannot provide such pertinent part of the record, then the court shall determine under the existing facts and circumstances what weight shall be given to the State court's factual determination.

(g) A copy of the official records of the State court, duly certified by the clerk of such court to be a true and correct copy of a finding, judicial opinion, or other reliable written indicia showing such a factual determination by the State court shall be admissible in the Federal court proceeding.

(h) Except as provided in section 408 of the Controlled Substances Act, in all proceedings brought under this section, and any subsequent proceedings on review, the court may appoint counsel for an applicant who is or becomes financially unable to afford counsel, except as provided by a rule promulgated by the Supreme Court pursuant to statutory authority. Appointment of counsel under this section shall be governed by section 3006A of title 18.

(i) The ineffectiveness or incompetence of counsel during Federal or State collateral post-conviction proceedings shall not be a ground for relief in a proceeding arising under section 2254.

§2255.   FEDERAL CUSTODY; REMEDIES ON MOTION ATTACKING SENTENCE

(a) A prisoner in custody under sentence of a court established by Act of Congress claiming the right to be released upon the ground that the sentence was imposed in violation of the Constitution or laws of the United States, or that the court was without jurisdiction to impose such sentence, or that the sentence was in excess of the maximum authorized by law, or is otherwise subject to collateral attack, may move the court which imposed the sentence to vacate, set aside or correct the sentence.

(b) Unless the motion and the files and records of the case conclusively show that the prisoner is entitled to no relief, the court shall cause notice thereof to be served upon the United States attorney, grant a prompt hearing thereon, determine the issues and make findings of fact and conclusions of law with respect thereto. If the court finds that the judgment was rendered without jurisdiction, or that the sentence imposed was not authorized by law or otherwise open to collateral attack, or that there has been such a denial or infringement of the constitutional rights of the prisoner as to render the judgment vulnerable to collateral attack, the court shall vacate and set the judgment aside and shall discharge the prisoner or resentence him or grant a new trial or correct the sentence as may appear appropriate.

(c) A court may entertain and determine such motion without requiring the production of the prisoner at the hearing.

(d) An appeal may be taken to the court of appeals from the order entered on the motion as from a final judgment on application for a writ of habeas corpus.

(e) An application for a writ of habeas corpus in behalf of a prisoner who is authorized to apply for relief by motion pursuant to this section, shall not be entertained if it appears that the applicant has failed to apply for relief, by motion, to the court which sentenced him, or that such court has denied him relief, unless it also appears that the remedy by motion is inadequate or ineffective to test the legality of his detention.

(f) A 1-year period of limitation shall apply to a motion under this section. The limitation period shall run from the latest of—

(1) the date on which the judgment of conviction becomes final;

(2) the date on which the impediment to making a motion created by governmental action in violation of the Constitution or laws of the United States is removed, if the movant was prevented from making a motion by such governmental action;

(3) the date on which the right asserted was initially recognized by the Supreme Court, if that right has been newly recognized by the Supreme Court and made retroactively applicable to cases on collateral review; or

(4) the date on which the facts supporting the claim or claims presented could have been discovered through the exercise of due diligence.

(g) Except as provided in section 408 of the Controlled Substances Act, in all proceedings brought under this section, and any subsequent proceedings on review, the court may appoint counsel, except as provided by a rule promulgated by the Supreme Court pursuant to statutory authority. Appointment of counsel under this section shall be governed by section 3006A of title 18.

(h) A second or successive motion must be certified as provided in section 2244 by a panel of the appropriate court of appeals to contain—

(1) newly discovered evidence that, if proven and viewed in light of the evidence as a whole, would be sufficient to establish by clear and convincing evidence that no reasonable factfinder would have found the movant guilty of the offense; or

(2) a new rule of constitutional law, made retroactive to cases on collateral review by the Supreme Court, that was previously unavailable.

§2261. PRISONERS IN STATE CUSTODY SUBJECT TO CAPITAL SENTENCE; APPOINTMENT OF COUNSEL; REQUIREMENT OF RULE OF COURT OR STATUTE; PROCEDURES FOR APPOINTMENT

(a) This chapter shall apply to cases arising under section 2254 brought by prisoners in State custody who are subject to a capital sentence. It shall apply only if the provisions of subsections (b) and (c) are satisfied.

(b) **Counsel.**—This chapter is applicable if—

(1) the Attorney General of the United States certifies that a State has established a mechanism for providing counsel in postconviction proceedings as provided in section 2265; and

(2) counsel was appointed pursuant to that mechanism, petitioner validly waived counsel, petitioner retained counsel, or petitioner was found not to be indigent.

(c) Any mechanism for the appointment, compensation, and reimbursement of counsel as provided in subsection (b) must offer counsel to all State prisoners under capital sentence and must provide for the entry of an order by a court of record—

(1) appointing one or more counsels to represent the prisoner upon a finding that the prisoner is indigent and accepted the offer or is unable competently to decide whether to accept or reject the offer;

(2) finding, after a hearing if necessary, that the prisoner rejected the offer of counsel and made the decision with an understanding of its legal consequences; or

(3) denying the appointment of counsel upon a finding that the prisoner is not indigent.

(d) No counsel appointed pursuant to subsections (b) and (c) to represent a State prisoner under capital sentence shall have previously represented the prisoner at trial in the case for which the appointment is made unless the prisoner and counsel expressly request continued representation.

(e) The ineffectiveness or incompetence of counsel during State or Federal post-conviction proceedings in a capital case shall not be a ground for relief in a proceeding arising under section 2254. This limitation shall not preclude the appointment of different counsel, on the court's own motion or at the request of the prisoner, at any phase of State or Federal post-conviction proceedings on the basis of the ineffectiveness or incompetence of counsel in such proceedings.

§2262.   MANDATORY STAY OF EXECUTION; DURATION; LIMITS ON STAYS OF EXECUTION; SUCCESSIVE PETITIONS

(a) Upon the entry in the appropriate State court of record of an order under section 2261(c), a warrant or order setting an execution date for a State prisoner shall be stayed upon application to any court that would have jurisdiction over any proceedings filed under section 2254. The application shall recite that the State has invoked the post-conviction review procedures of this chapter and that the scheduled execution is subject to stay.

(b) A stay of execution granted pursuant to subsection (a) shall expire if—

(1) a State prisoner fails to file a habeas corpus application under section 2254 within the time required in section 2263;

(2) before a court of competent jurisdiction, in the presence of counsel, unless the prisoner has competently and knowingly waived such counsel, and after having been advised of the consequences, a State prisoner under capital sentence waives the right to pursue habeas corpus review under section 2254; or

(3) a State prisoner files a habeas corpus petition under section 2254 within the time required by section 2263 and fails to make a substantial showing of the denial of a Federal right or is denied relief in the district court or at any subsequent stage of review.

(c) If one of the conditions in subsection (b) has occurred, no Federal court thereafter shall have the authority to enter a stay of execution in the case, unless the court of appeals approves the filing of a second or successive application under section 2244 (b).

§2263.   FILING OF HABEAS CORPUS APPLICATION; TIME REQUIREMENTS; TOLLING RULES

(a) Any application under this chapter for habeas corpus relief under section 2254 must be filed in the appropriate district court not later than 180 days after final State court affirmance of the conviction and sentence on direct review or the expiration of the time for seeking such review.

(b) The time requirements established by subsection (a) shall be tolled—

(1) from the date that a petition for certiorari is filed in the Supreme Court until the date of final disposition of the petition if a State prisoner files the petition to secure review by the Supreme Court of the affirmance of

a capital sentence on direct review by the court of last resort of the State or other final State court decision on direct review;

(2) from the date on which the first petition for post-conviction review or other collateral relief is filed until the final State court disposition of such petition; and

(3) during an additional period not to exceed 30 days, if—

(A) a motion for an extension of time is filed in the Federal district court that would have jurisdiction over the case upon the filing of a habeas corpus application under section 2254; and

(B) a showing of good cause is made for the failure to file the habeas corpus application within the time period established by this section.

§2264.   Scope of Federal Review; District Court Adjudications

(a) Whenever a State prisoner under capital sentence files a petition for habeas corpus relief to which this chapter applies, the district court shall only consider a claim or claims that have been raised and decided on the merits in the State courts, unless the failure to raise the claim properly is—

(1) the result of State action in violation of the Constitution or laws of the United States;

(2) the result of the Supreme Court's recognition of a new Federal right that is made retroactively applicable; or

(3) based on a factual predicate that could not have been discovered through the exercise of due diligence in time to present the claim for State or Federal post-conviction review.

(b) Following review subject to subsections (a), (d), and (e) of section 2254, the court shall rule on the claims properly before it.

§2265.   Certification and Judicial Review

(a) Certification.—

(1) In general.—If requested by an appropriate State official, the Attorney General of the United States shall determine—

(A) whether the State has established a mechanism for the appointment, compensation, and payment of reasonable litigation expenses of competent counsel in State postconviction proceedings brought by indigent prisoners who have been sentenced to death;

(B) the date on which the mechanism described in subparagraph (A) was established; and

(C) whether the State provides standards of competency for the appointment of counsel in proceedings described in subparagraph (A).

(2) Effective date.—The date the mechanism described in paragraph (1)(A) was established shall be the effective date of the certification under this subsection.

(3) **Only express requirements.**—There are no requirements for certification or for application of this chapter other than those expressly stated in this chapter.

(b) **Regulations.**—The Attorney General shall promulgate regulations to implement the certification procedure under subsection (a).

(c) **Review of certification.**—

(1) **In general.**—The determination by the Attorney General regarding whether to certify a State under this section is subject to review exclusively as provided under chapter 158 of this title.

(2) **Venue.**—The Court of Appeals for the District of Columbia Circuit shall have exclusive jurisdiction over matters under paragraph (1), subject to review by the Supreme Court under section 2350 of this title.

(3) **Standard of review.**—The determination by the Attorney General regarding whether to certify a State under this section shall be subject to de novo review.

§2266. Limitation Periods for Determining Applications and Motions

(a) The adjudication of any application under section 2254 that is subject to this chapter, and the adjudication of any motion under section 2255 by a person under sentence of death, shall be given priority by the district court and by the court of appeals over all noncapital matters.

(b)(1)(A) A district court shall render a final determination and enter a final judgment on any application for a writ of habeas corpus brought under this chapter in a capital case not later than 450 days after the date on which the application is filed, or 60 days after the date on which the case is submitted for decision, whichever is earlier.

(B) A district court shall afford the parties at least 120 days in which to complete all actions, including the preparation of all pleadings and briefs, and if necessary, a hearing, prior to the submission of the case for decision.

(C)(i) A district court may delay for not more than one additional 30-day period beyond the period specified in subparagraph (A), the rendering of a determination of an application for a writ of habeas corpus if the court issues a written order making a finding, and stating the reasons for the finding, that the ends of justice that would be served by allowing the delay outweigh the best interests of the public and the applicant in a speedy disposition of the application.

(ii) The factors, among others, that a court shall consider in determining whether a delay in the disposition of an application is warranted are as follows:

(I) Whether the failure to allow the delay would be likely to result in a miscarriage of justice.

(II) Whether the case is so unusual or so complex, due to the number of defendants, the nature of the prosecution, or the existence of novel questions of fact or law, that it is unreasonable to expect adequate briefing within the time limitations established by subparagraph (A).

(III) Whether the failure to allow a delay in a case that, taken as a whole, is not so unusual or so complex as described in subclause (II), but would otherwise deny the applicant reasonable time to obtain counsel, would unreasonably deny the applicant or the government continuity of counsel, or would deny counsel for the applicant or the government the reasonable time necessary for effective preparation, taking into account the exercise of due diligence.

(iii) No delay in disposition shall be permissible because of general congestion of the court's calendar.

(iv) The court shall transmit a copy of any order issued under clause (i) to the Director of the Administrative Office of the United States Courts for inclusion in the report under paragraph (5).

(2) The time limitations under paragraph (1) shall apply to—

(A) an initial application for a writ of habeas corpus;

(B) any second or successive application for a writ of habeas corpus; and

(C) any redetermination of an application for a writ of habeas corpus following a remand by the court of appeals or the Supreme Court for further proceedings, in which case the limitation period shall run from the date the remand is ordered.

(3)(A) The time limitations under this section shall not be construed to entitle an applicant to a stay of execution, to which the applicant would otherwise not be entitled, for the purpose of litigating any application or appeal.

(B) No amendment to an application for a writ of habeas corpus under this chapter shall be permitted after the filing of the answer to the application, except on the grounds specified in section 2244 (b).

(4)(A) The failure of a court to meet or comply with a time limitation under this section shall not be a ground for granting relief from a judgment of conviction or sentence.

(B) The State may enforce a time limitation under this section by petitioning for a writ of mandamus to the court of appeals. The court of appeals shall act on the petition for a writ of mandamus not later than 30 days after the filing of the petition.

(5)(A) The Administrative Office of the United States Courts shall submit to Congress an annual report on the compliance by the district courts with the time limitations under this section.

(B) The report described in subparagraph (A) shall include copies of the orders submitted by the district courts under paragraph (1)(B)(iv).

(c)(1)(A) A court of appeals shall hear and render a final determination of any appeal of an order granting or denying, in whole or in part, an application brought under this chapter in a capital case not later than 120 days after the date on which the reply brief is filed, or if no reply brief is filed, not later than 120 days after the date on which the answering brief is filed.

(B)(i) A court of appeals shall decide whether to grant a petition for rehearing or other request for rehearing en banc not later than 30 days after the date on which the petition for rehearing is filed unless a responsive pleading is required, in which case the court shall decide whether to grant the petition not later than 30 days after the date on which the responsive pleading is filed.

(ii) If a petition for rehearing or rehearing en banc is granted, the court of appeals shall hear and render a final determination of the appeal not later than 120 days after the date on which the order granting rehearing or rehearing en banc is entered.

(2) The time limitations under paragraph (1) shall apply to—

(A) an initial application for a writ of habeas corpus;

(B) any second or successive application for a writ of habeas corpus; and

(C) any redetermination of an application for a writ of habeas corpus or related appeal following a remand by the court of appeals en banc or the Supreme Court for further proceedings, in which case the limitation period shall run from the date the remand is ordered.

(3) The time limitations under this section shall not be construed to entitle an applicant to a stay of execution, to which the applicant would otherwise not be entitled, for the purpose of litigating any application or appeal.

(4)(A) The failure of a court to meet or comply with a time limitation under this section shall not be a ground for granting relief from a judgment of conviction or sentence.

(B) The State may enforce a time limitation under this section by applying for a writ of mandamus to the Supreme Court.

(5) The Administrative Office of the United States Courts shall submit to Congress an annual report on the compliance by the courts of appeals with the time limitations under this section.